Bank Notes

Series editor **David Palfreman**
Senior Lecturer
Central Manchester College

This series provides a structured revision programme for students taking their Institute of Bankers Stage 2 Banking Diploma examinations.

By answering a series of Short Answer Tests at the front of the book, students can decide on their revision priorities. Taking one topic at a time, they can refresh their knowledge of the topic using the Study Guide, and then test themselves using the Multiple Choice Questions. Most importantly, detailed notes on *all* answers to the Multiple Choice Questions are given, so that students can reinforce their learning by discovering why wrong answers *are* wrong.

Finally, by tackling the Post-tests for each topic, students can test the effectiveness of their revision.

There are eight titles in the series:

Law Relating to Banking
Monetary Economics
Accountancy
Investment
Nature of Management
Finance of International Trade
Practice of Banking 1
Practice of Banking 2

INSTITUTE OF BANKERS
STAGE 2 BANKING DIPLOMA

Practice of Banking 2

P FORD

 Van Nostrand Reinhold (UK) Co. Ltd

First published in 1987 by
Van Nostrand Reinhold (UK) Co. Ltd
Molly Millars Lane, Wokingham, Berkshire,
England

Typeset in Ehrhardt 10 on 11½ point by
Columns Ltd, Reading

Printed and bound in Great Britain by
Billing & Sons Ltd, Worcester

British Library Cataloguing in Publication Data
Ford, P. (Phillip)
    Practice of banking 2. — (Institute of
    Bankers stage 2 banking diploma). —
    (Bank notes).
    1. Banks and banking
    I. Title   II. Series   III. Series
    332.1   HG1601

ISBN 0–278–00002–9

Contents

Contents

Editor's Introduction

What's this book about?

This book will help you pass your Institute of Bankers examination.
Interested? Well, read on and you'll see how.

You're probably at the stage in your studies when you've got information coming out of your ears, a huge file of notes and the exam looming ever nearer! Quite possibly, you're beginning to get that familiar feeling of desperation: 'Where do I start?', 'I'll never learn all this.'

Help is at hand. If you use this book properly you'll discover where you should start and you'll learn more efficiently. Perhaps this will be the first time you'll have approached study in a methodical, effective fashion. By the way, we won't be throwing a whole lot of new information at you — you probably know quite enough already; there's nothing in this book which you shouldn't already know or, perhaps, knew once but have forgotten! Our aim is to help you understand, learn and use it.

So you want to pass the exam . . .

Well, your study should be: *positive, efficient* and *effective*. Remember two *key ideas*:
— *Organization*
— *Activity*

Organization

Let's explain whaat we mean. *How well organized are you?* Do you waste time looking for things, do you spend as long getting ready to do something as actually doing it? How many times have we seen students ploughing through a thoroughly disorganized file to find something? What a waste of time! The point is made, we think; so get yourself organized.

Time: When are you going to study? Only you know when you've the time and only you know when you work best. For example, are you a 'lark' or an 'owl'? Be realistic. It's no good trying to revise for a few minutes here and there, while the adverts are on, for example. You must commit a *realistic* amount of time to any one session — probably not less than one hour and not more than three.

Have you ever thought of formally timetabling your study? Look at the timetable shown. You could draw similar ones (one for each week) and mark in your revision times.

As you can see, the timetable caters for both 'larks' and 'owls', as well as for all tendencies in between. Clearly there'll be major blocks of time when you can't do any study — you have to go to work — but that still leaves a lot of available time. Make the best use of it. A word of warning, however: if you have long-standing or important domestic or leisure commitments, think twice about breaking them. At least try first to build them into your timetable.

Study Timetable

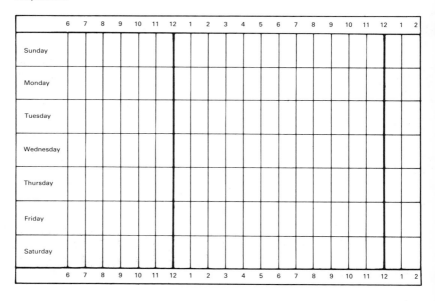

Place: The kitchen table or the sofa in front of the TV are *not* the ideal places to work. You need to be able to concentrate and this means finding somewhere *reasonably quiet* — don't try to revise with the Hi-Fi on! Equally important you need somewhere which is *comfortable*: a good chair, a desk or table, and good lighting. Ideally, you should be able to leave your work out, ready to come back to, so that you don't waste time at the start of your next session — one reason why the kitchen table isn't suitable.

Pace: Contrary to popular practice, it's *not* a good idea to leave revision to the last minute, particularly if you want to revise positively, efficiently and effectively.

Plan your revision: We've included some short answer tests which you should complete before reading the rest of the book. These exercises will help you identify your own strengths and weaknesses and so help you to determine how long you need to spend on each topic.

Use your study timetable to plan a revision campaign. Believe me, the more carefully you plan, the more you'll get done in any given time. Of course, you're bound to end up working like crazy for the few days immediately before the exam, so you might as well plan for this as well! What must not happen, and a planned revision campaign will prevent this, is finding that you haven't allocated your time properly and that there's just no way you're going to be able to study everything thoroughly in time.

Activity

How long can you concentrate on any one thing? If you're honest, not very long. And when it comes to revision, let's face it, it really takes the prize in the boredom stakes. No one likes to just sit there trying to learn something. But don't despair — there are ways to make it more bearable and effective. Read on.

What you should not do is sit there reading the same original notes over and over again. It's not only excrutiatingly boring, it's also very unproductive. After you've read your notes through once, you'll find you know much of what you're reading already and progressively more of your time will be wasted each time you repeat the exercise.

Bank notes: *Be active*, and this is where the *Bank Notes* series comes into its own. If you use each book properly (see *How to use this book* on p. xv) you'll find yourself very active in your study. In particular, you'll be interacting with the subject matter instead of being a passive, and not particularly absorbant, sponge.

Your aims: Remember, however, that this series is not a substitute for your own hard work; you'll still have to put in *time* and *effort*. Your study should have three aims:
— Complete *understanding of the topic.*
— *Retention* and *recall* of it.
— The ability to *explain* and *apply* what you have learnt.

Study activities: So, a few general suggestions for *study activities*, all tried and tested, to achieve these aims. You'll find further ideas and guidance in the Study Guides to the Topics.

Revision Notes: Your course notes and text books are not particularly suitable to revise from. Making revision notes is a good investment of your time. They can consist of just the headings in your notes/text book with, perhaps, a brief note about important principles or unusual points.

Do take care in the way you lay out your notes. Don't try to economize on paper; it's probably the lowest of your overheads anyway! Your notes should look 'attractive' and be easy to follow. Allow space to add other brief comments later. Try the following as a model:

MAIN HEADING
SUB-HEADING

....

Sub-sub-Heading

....

   1. Important point ....

....

   2. Important point ....

....

When you've made your revision notes, you can use them in the following way. Take each note in turn and try to recall and explain the subject matter. If you can, go on to the next; if you can't, look back to your notes/text book — perhaps noting a page number for future reference. By doing this, you'll revise, test your knowledge and generally spend your time productively by concentrating your revision on those aspects of the subject with which you're least familiar. In addition, you'll have an excellent last-minute revision aid.

Summary diagrams: These could be alternatives or additions to revision notes. Many people respond well to diagrammatic explanations and summaries; in particular, the visual association of the different aspects of a subject is useful.

We've two specific types of diagrams in mind: the 'family tree' type and the 'molecule' type, as you'll see below. Of course, if you've seen or can devise other types, use those as well.

Constructing diagrams is a particularly useful form of active study because you have to think how best to construct them and in so doing you'll find you better understand the subject. As with revision notes, don't include too much on each diagram and don't economise on paper. The impact and usefulness of a diagram depends very much on its visual simplicity.

You can use summary diagrams in much the same way as revision notes.

Useful definitions and explanations: Each subject has a handful of points that are almost certain to come up in at least one question in the exam. So, why not prepare for them? (The *Study Guides* will suggest what these could be.) In practical terms, you may save yourself two or three minutes

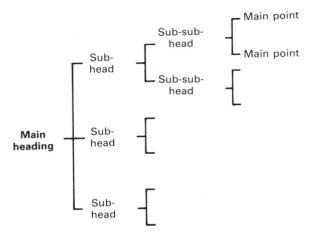

'Family tree' summary diagram (can be constructed vertically or horizontally, as here).

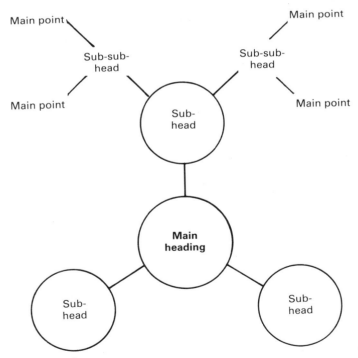

'Molecule' summary diagram.

on each question simply because you don't have to think about how to define or explain something which you probably know well but cannot easily put into words there and then. Multiplied five times, those two or three minutes represent a considerable time saving. We've all wished for another 10–15 minutes in the exam before now!

Plan answers to past questions: Plan them, don't answer them fully. Once you've planned an answer, the writing out is largely a mechanical exercise. If, however, you feel you need the practice, answer some fully.

Examination technique

At this stage in your studies, there's not much we can say to give you a better answering technique. However, there are a number of general points you should remember about actual exam technique.

— *Read the instructions carefully.* You get no extra marks for answering an extra question and you automatically lose a proportion of the possible marks by answering too few. Also, answer the right number of questions from each section. Basic points, perhaps, but you would not believe . . .

— Read all the questions through and provisionally select which questions to answer. Be careful in your choice; an apparently simple question may have a hidden twist — don't get caught. Similarly, in a multi-part question be sure you can answer all parts and not just the first.

— Everyone suffers from *exam nerves* and these will probably affect you for the first fifteen minutes or so. Consequently, it's often good practice to answer your 'best' question second or third. By that time you'll be thoroughly relaxed and working well.

— *Plan all your answers* — this is absolutely vital.

— *Divide your time more or less equally between questions.* There's no point spending an extra 15 minutes on your best question if it results in a very poor final question.

— *Check through your answers.* If you spend a few minutes doing this at the end of the exam, you can eliminate minor errors and give a final 'polish' to your answers. When allocating your time, allow five minutes for this.

What do I do now?

You may have been fortunate in your studies and have been taught some or all of the techniques outlined above. If you were, you should now be doubly persuaded of their effectiveness. If you weren't, you've already invested your time well because you're virtually guaranteed to perform better in the exam through having used them than you would otherwise have done.

Back to *Bank Notes*, and where they fit in. We've talked about being 'organized' and 'active' and we've given you a sound set of general ideas as a start. *Bank Notes* go further; not only do they provide an organized and active structure for study, thy are also your *personal revision tutor*. Now turn to *How to use this Book* on page xv and start your revision campaign.

How to use this book

At any time in your revision campaign is the simple answer, but the earlier the better. Because we've designed the book to identify any weak areas you may have, and suggest positive ideas to help you study and revise, you'll find this book the ideal basis on which to plan that revision campaign. However, it's equally useful just before the exam when some self-assessment and new revision activities may well revive the flagging spirit!

The different sections

You'll find that this book has *five* sections:

— *Editor's Introduction*: a short but very important section which gives you tried and tested advice on how to revise positively, efficiently and effectively. If you haven't read it, go back and read it now and *only then continue with this section*.

— *How to use this Book*: the section you're reading now.

— *Short Answer Tests*: designed to help you identify your strengths and weaknesses in this subject.

— Ten *Topic Sections*: broadly following the order of the Institute's syllabus and containing:
   An overview of and advice on how best to revise each of the topics,
   Multiple choice questions and full explanatory answers designed both to test and to teach.

— *Post-tests*: designed to help you asses the effectiveness of your revision and identify any remaining weaknesses.

The short answer tests

You start with these; there's one test for each main section of the syllabus. Complete them all before you go on to the *Topic Sections*. Each test is scored out of 20 and we've allocated marks to the questions — usually two marks to each — and explained in the answers how to score. These tests will quickly give you a good idea of how much you know. By filling in the *Score Grid* — you'll find it inside the back cover — you'll be able to compare your knowledge and understanding on the different parts of the syllabus and identify your revision priorities.

Remember what we said about the value of organization? The *Score Grid* provides an effective chart on which not only to identify and order your revision priorities but also to plot the progress of your revision campaign and assess its efficiency. Look at the *Score Grid* now, and then turn back to here.

The topic sections

When you've completed all ten *Short Answer Tests*, filled in the *Score Grid* and determined the order of your revision, you can turn to the *Topic Sections*.

Study Guides: These, if you like, are your personal revision tutor. Each gives you an overview of the topic and a study framework. We indicate the points you really must know and be able to explain and use, and we point out common student mistakes and give advice on how best to tackle each topic. Some sections already contain revision notes and summary diagrams — remember the *Editor's Introduction* — and you can use these as guides for your further work. For example, if you're given a diagram which summarizes the entire topic, you could take each of the sub-sub-headings in that diagram, use them as main headings and produce more detailed diagrams on those particular parts of the topic.

You can also combine these introductions with the more general advice on study we've already given you. So, you should find that the *Study Guides* form the bases for very thorough revision campaigns on the topics.

Multiple-Choice Questions: You've probably answered 'MCQ' tests before. Such questions are an excellent way of testing knowledge and understanding but the feedback from the tutor is usually minimal, often non-existent. You don't usually know why your answer was right or wrong. Here's where the *Bank Notes* series is different.

It's through the MCQs that the books start to *work with you* to remedy your weaknesses in the different topics and reinforce the knowledge and understanding you already have.

For each question we've given you four possible answers; all are plausible and, indeed, all may be partially correct but only one is totally correct. After each question there's a space to put your answer — **a**, **b**, **c** or **d**. You could also briefly write down the reason you chose that answer, just to stop yourself succumbing to the temptation of guessing!

When you've finished all the MCQs for a topic, turn to the answers

— they follow immediately — and mark your own answers.

You score two marks for each correct answer. (Keep a note of your score at the end of the test and enter it on the Score Grid.) We don't just tell you whether you're right or wrong in the answers — we give you a full explanation of why. You'll find these explanations very useful; quite probably the 'penny will drop' where it didn't before.

References to other books: We think you will find all of the following books useful on this subject, although the first is very strongly recommended:

Practice of Banking 1, Kelly, Pitman.

Law of Banking, 3rd edition, Palfreman, Pitman.

Practice of Banking 2, D.G. Wild and J.R. Marsh. Macdonald & Evans.

Balance Sheets and the Lending Banker, J.H. Clemens and L.S. Dyer. Europa.

Management Accounting for the Lending Banker, M.A. Pitcher. Institute of Bankers.

Lending Guides, F.E. Perry and D.W. Fiddes. Waterlow.

Service Banking, D.G. Hanson. Institute of Bankers.

The post-tests

The final section consists of 10 *post-tests*. These also use MCQs but this time you're just told which answer is correct.

You'll find that the post-tests largely retest what was covered in the main MCQs. This is deliberate. The purpose of the post-tests is to assess the progress you've made in your revision campaign.

You may wish to answer them all together — a kind of mock exam if you like — and record your scores — *two* marks for each correct answer — on the Score Grid. You can then compare your score with those on the corresponding Short Answer Test and Main MCQ Test. While the comparisons won't be 'scientific', you will get a good indication of the effectiveness of your revision.

What do I do when I've finished?

If you work through this book properly and revise conscientiously following our guidance, you should be well prepared for the exam. However, if the post-tests reveal that you still have some areas of weakness you'll have to go back and revise these again — at least you'll know which ones they are and how to go about it!

Finally, remember our general advice on exam technique. The best of luck; we're sure you'll do well.

David Palfreman *Editor*
Philip Ford *Author*

Short Answer Tests

Start your revision by attempting the short answer tests on pages 2–7.

Questions

Topic 1   Principles of lending

1   When vetting a loan application, what would be the single deciding factor in your conclusion?   *(2 marks)*
2   Why would you always wish to know the purpose to which the advance would be put?   *(2 marks)*
3   What portion of the funds required should be provided by the customer?   *(2 marks)*
4   Why is it particularly important to verify that a requested advance is sufficient for the customer's needs?   *(2 marks)*
5   For which type of advance would a Cash Flow Forecast be *most* appropriate as a check on the requested amount of the advance?   *(2 marks)*
6   Can funds anticipated under insurance claims be acceptable as proposed sources for repayment of personal advances?   *(2 marks)*
7   If the customer cannot afford to repay a proposed loan within the normal period, what would you do?   *(2 marks)*
8   What is the maximum period over which a bank will grant a Personal Loan for purchase of a car for private use?   *(2 marks)*
9   What decides the term over which a bank will grant an advance?   *(2 marks)*
10   Why is security taken for an advance?   *(2 marks)*

Answers on page 8

Topic 2   Personal lending

1   When is a *bridging loan* required?   *(2 marks)*
2   What is an *open bridge*?   *(2 marks)*
3   What is the maximum amount that a customer may usually borrow on a House Purchase Loan?   *(2 marks)*
4   Would a bank be prepared to lend a homeowner the deposit for the purchase of a new house, and if so where would repayment come from?   *(2 marks)*
5   What is the purpose of a *probate advance*?   *(2 marks)*
6   How is a probate advance repaid?   *(2 marks)*
7   What would be the usual term over which a *professional practice loan* should be rapaid?   *(1 mark)*
8   What particular dangers are there in lending to a customer to enable him to build his own house?   *(3 marks)*

9 What facilities could be suggested to a customer who needs to borrow to cover a temporary excess of expenditure over income? *(3 marks)*
10 What is the upper limit up to which loans to individuals are regulated under the Consumer Credit Act? *(1 mark)*

Answers on page 9

Topic 3   Balance sheet analysis

1 What is the 'Gone concern' approach to balance sheet analysis? *(2 marks)*
2 Why is a series of financial statements preferable to a single balance sheet? *(2 marks)*
3 How would you calculate the 'current ratio' and what does it reveal? *(3 marks)*
4 What does the 'acid test' (or quick) ratio tell you? *(1 mark)*
5 What is overtrading? *(2 marks)*
6 What rate of stock turnover would you expect to see in a healthy business? *(2 marks)*
7 What is the *net worth* of a business? *(2 marks)*
8 How would you calculate the periods of credit given and taken by a business? *(3 marks)*
9 What is the significance of the 'gross profit : turnover' ratio? *(2 marks)*
10 What does it matter if a company is 'highly geared'? *(1 mark)*

Answers on page 10

Topic 4   Business lending/1

1 If a business is intending to increase its annual turnover, is there likely to be any impact on its need to borrow? *(2 marks)*
2 How is depreciation treated in the construction of a cash flow forecast? *(1 mark)*
3 What are *management accounting figures*? How can they help in the assessment of a borrowing proposition? *(2 marks)*
4 What methods are there for the appraisal of capital expenditure? *(3 marks)*
5 Apart from loans and overdrafts, what other sources of finance are there for the financing of capital expenditure? *(2 marks)*
6 From an 'advances appraisal' viewpoint, is building a new factory fundamentally different from any other capital project? *(2 marks)*

3

7   Which is more important when financing a specific contract: the ability of the customer to complete the work or the ability of the contractor to pay? *(2 marks)*
8   What are 'retentions'? *(2 marks)*
9   Why is the assessment of the proprietor particularly important when lending to a new business venture? *(2 marks)*
10 What limitations are there on the amount that can be covered by a guarantee under the Small Firms Loans Guarantee Scheme? *(2 marks)*

Answers on page 14

Topic 5   Business lending/2

1   What limitation on directors' borrowing powers is contained in Table A of the Companies Act 1948? *(2 marks)*
2   Does a company automatically have the power to guarantee the borrowing of other companies in the same group? *(2 marks)*
3   What specific checks would you make into the stock to be acquired as part of the purchase of retail business? *(2 marks)*
4   What impact would the availability of trade credit from suppliers have on a shopkeeper's requirement for working capital finance? *(2 marks)*
5   How is an arable farmer's requirement for working capital finance likely to differ from that of a dairy farmer? *(2 marks)*
6   What formula do banks generally use to set the limit for advances for speculative estate development? *(2 marks)*
7   What is the simplest way to keep to a minimum the borrowing requirement associated with a speculative housing development? *(2 marks)*
8   Is a cargo of canned goods acceptable as security for a produce advance? Explain your answer briefly. *(2 marks)*
9   Are accommodation bills acceptable as the basis of a discounted bill facility? *(2 marks)*
10 Can a franchised retail outlet be a suitable subject for a bank advance? *(2 marks)*

Answers on page 15

Topic 6   Marketing and selling

1   How would you describe the members of socio-economic group D? *(2 marks)*

2 What is a market segment? *(2 marks)*
3 Is marketing the same thing as selling? *(2 marks)*
4 What is a 'trigger point'? *(2 marks)*
5 What is a SWOT analysis and when is it used? *(2 marks)*
6 What is the difference between the attributes and the benefits of a service? *(3 marks)*
7 Is 'customer care' important? *(1 mark)*
8 Which types of organization are a bank's major competitors in the field of funds transfer? *(2 marks)*
9 Is it correct to state that market research is concerned primarily with finding out what the public says that it wants? *(2 marks)*
10 What is probability sampling? *(2 marks)*

Answers on page 16

Topic 7   Personal services

1 Which type of customer is most likely to benefit from opening a 'money fund' type of interest-bearing current account? *(2 marks)*
2 At which class of customer are the banks' regular savings schemes targeted? *(2 marks)*
3 What are the banks' principal sources of competition for medium-term variable rate deposits? *(2 marks)*
4 How does a credit card differ from a charge card? *(2 marks)*
5 What are the principal differences between an endowment mortgage and a capital repayment mortgage? *(2 marks)*
6 When should a customer be advised to make a will? *(2 marks)*
7 Explain the difference between the benefits and the attributes of a personal service. *(2 marks)*
8 What do the initials EFTPOS stand for, and what is it? *(2 marks)*
9 What is a Unit Trust 'share exchange' scheme? *(2 marks)*
10 What is a 'discretionary trust'? *(2 marks)*

Answers on page 18

Topic 8   Business sercvices, financial

1 What is factor finance? *(2 marks)*
2 Is it possible to arrange factor finance in respect of export contracts? *(2 marks)*
3 What is finance leasing? *(2 marks)*
4 What is the purpose of an acceptance facility? *(2 marks)*

5 What is the minimum amount that can normally be dealt with on the money markets? *(1 mark)*

6 When is a placing undertaken? *(2 marks)*

7 What are the conditions that must be met for a loan to qualify for consideration under the Small Firm Loan Guarantee Scheme? *(3 marks)*

8 What is the USM used for? *(2 marks)*

9 What are the different financial vehicles that can be used to raise company finance on the Stock Market? *(2 marks)*

10 How do 'high interest' accounts differ from traditional deposit accounts? *(2 marks)*

Answers on page 19

Topic 9 Business services, administration

1 What type of customer might use the bank's registrar service? *(2 marks)*

2 What are the benefits to a company of using a computer bureau to run its sales ledger? *(2 marks)*

3 What are the benefits to an employee of payment of wages by bank transfer? *(3 marks)*

4 What benefits does the bank gain from offering the CHAPs service? *(2 marks)*

5 What is the minimum amount that can be remitted via the CHAPs system? *(1 mark)*

6 What are the functions of BACs? *(2 marks)*

7 At what types of customer are Personal Pension Plans targeted? *(2 marks)*

8 Why would a customer arrange a 'loanback' facility on a Personal Pension Plan? *(2 marks)*

9 What is 'keyman' insurance? *(2 marks)*

10 Why should a self-employed customer arrange permanent disability cover? *(2 marks)*

Answers on page 21

Topic 10 Foreign business

1 What are the advantages to an exporter of foreign currency loans? *(2 marks)*

2 What is the primary function of the ECGD? *(3 marks)*

3 What do you know about the ECGD (Bills & Notes) Loan account scheme? *(2 marks)*
4 Under what terms will a bank negotiate a foreign cheque? *(2 marks)*
5 What is SWIFT? *(2 marks)*
6 What are the advantages to exporters of the documentary credit? *(2 marks)*
7 Is it possible to obtain factoring finance on foreign sales? *(1 mark)*
8 What are the specific risks of invoicing abroad in foreign currencies? *(2 marks)*
9 What methods are available to overcome the risks of currency invoicing? *(3 marks)*
10 What is 'buyer credit'? *(1 mark)*

Answers on page 22

Answers

Topic 1   Principles of lending

1   There is no single deciding factor; the decision depends on weighing up all the pro's and con's.   /2

2   To assess the level of risk and to ensure that the purpose is acceptable from both the legal and moral viewpoints. Score 1 mark for each of the above two points.   /2

3   It varies according to the proposition; the customer should always provide some of the finance but the level varies. Score 2 marks for knowing this.   /2

4   If the original amount is insufficient the loan may need to be increased later; score 1 mark. Score your second mark for mentioning that the bank may need to agree the increase even if it goes beyond the level which it considers as 'safe'.   /2

5   It is most appropriate when dealing with overdrafts requested to allow customers to overcome temporary excesses of expenditure over income.   /2

6   Yes, but only when it is certain that the claim will succeed and that the funds will be received. Score 2 marks for knowing *all* of this.   /2

7   Decline the advance unless it can be restructured in such a way as to permit repayment within a reasonable period. Score only 1 mark if you just said 'decline'.   /2

8   Normally 3 years.   /2

9   The nature of the loan and the purpose for which funds are utilized. Score 1 mark for each point.   /2

10 To protect the bank against loss if unforeseen circumstances prevent repayment by the proposed method. Award yourself 2 marks only if you clearly indicated that the problems must be 'unforseen'.   /2

➡ *your total score for this Topic* . . . . /20

Topic 2   Personal lending

1   A bridging loan is required when a homeowner who is moving house has to pay for the new house before receiving payment for the old one.

/2

2   An 'open-bridge' is a bridging loan arranged for a customer who does not yet have a firm contract for the sale of his existing home. Score 1 mark for knowing this. Score another mark for knowing that it is much harder to pursuade a bank to enter into this type of arrangement.

/2

3   The advance is generally limited to a sum equal to $2\frac{1}{2}$ times the borrower's gross annual income. Score 1 mark. Score a second mark if you also noted that when borrowing is in joint names the limit may be increased by the gross amount of the second salary (counted once only).

/2

4   Yes: score 1 mark. Repayment would come from the final settlement of the sale of the existing house. The customer would have to convince the bank that — including any increase in mortgage facilities — enough cash will be released to accomplish this. Score another mark.

/2

5   A probate advance is granted to enable personal representatives to pay the tax on the estate. Score 1 mark. For your second mark you should note that until the tax has been paid, probate will not be granted, and assets cannot be realized.

/2

6   The advance is repaid out of the realization of assets: 1 mark. In general it is important to ensure that there are sufficient liquid assets to enable this to be accomplished: another mark.

/2

7   The normal term would be 10–15 years.

/1

8   The particular dangers are:
    ● inadequate costing of the project
    ● inadequate standard of building
    ● failure of the building contractor part way through the work
    Score 1 mark for each point.

/3

9 The most appropriate facilities would be:
  • Overdraft on current A/c
  • Budget A/c
  • Credit card
  Score 1 mark for each point.

Your score /3

10 £15,000.

/1

➤ *your total score for this Topic* . . . . /20

Topic 3 Balance sheet analysis

1 The gone concern approach represents an attempt to work out how much would be left over (or would be short!) if a business was to be liquidated. In order to produce it you would have to place a realistic valuation on all the assets — this may bear little relationship to their book values as shown in the balance sheet! Score 1 mark for this.

   The gone concern approach is much less important than the going concern approach, which concerns itself with the health of a business and whether it can trade profitably rather than with what would happen if it were to cease trading. Score a second mark for knowing this.

/2

2 A series of financial statements is more than preferable — it is vital if you are going to be able to establish the trends in the way a business is going: whether trade is improving or deteriorating and whether profitability is rising or falling. Score one mark.

   For another mark, you should have mentioned that a single balance sheet can be very misleading. A profit of £1 million from a turnover of £10 million might look very encouraging in isolation, but what if you discovered that it had been £1.5 million last year and £2 million the year before that . . . ?

/2

3 The current ratio is calculated by dividing the amount of the current assets by the amount of the current liabilities. The result is expressed as a ratio ($x : 1$). If there is a liquid surplus the ratio will be

better than 1 : 1. If there is a deficiency the ratio will be worse than 1 : 1. Score 1 mark.

It is a measure of the liquidity of the business, indicating whether there are likely to be any problems in meeting day-to-day outgoings. Generally, you would expect a successful business to have a liquid surplus and for its current ratio to be somewhere in the region of $1\frac{1}{2} : 1$ to $2 : 1$. Greater liquidity would probably represent unprofitable use of liquid resources, while lower liquidity is usually a danger signal. However, you must never look just at one ratio in isolation — it is the overall pattern that counts. Some businesses are by their nature illiquid, while others may be holding high levels of unsaleable stocks which make their liquidity levels look very good. Score a mark for mentioning 'liquidity' and a further one for mentioning the practical consider-ations.

/3

4 The 'acid test' ratio is a development of the current ratio which compares the truly liquid assets of the business with the current liabilities. It tells you more exactly than the current ratio whether the concern is likely to have any difficulty in the day-to-day settlement of outstanding bills. Give yourself one mark for knowing this. Its importance can be judged from the banker's 'rule of thumb' that more businesses collapse from illiquidity than cease trading as a result of insolvency. It is no use having massive assets if there is no cash to pay the electricity bill!

/1

5 Overtrading is the term given to the situation in which a firm takes on more business than can safely be supported by the available capital. The symptoms of overtrading soon manifest themselves as liquidity problems — the firm takes on a 'hand to mouth' existence where debts can only be settled as and when money due in is received. One mark for these points.

The great danger of overtrading is that any interruption in the cycle of receipts and payments can bring the business down — it has inadequate resources to 'tide over' the delay.

Tell-tale signs are a low (and worsening) *current ratio* and a high *trading ratio* (turnover : net worth). You get a second mark if you covered these points.

/2

6 This question is impossible to answer directly — sorry!

There is no 'ideal' rate of turnover because each type of business operates under different conditions and therefore will turn over its stock differently. A newspaper seller or a fishmonger should have a fairly rapid rate of turnover (especially the latter, or I for one would not want to go too near his shop), but an antique dealer would expect to hold stock a lot longer. Award yourself 2 marks if you knew all of this.

As with many 'Accounts' questions, therefore, there is no absolute answer. Too often students want to apply simple rules of thumb 'across the board'. You can't — you have to use your judgement, experience, and plain common sense to adjust your thinking to the circumstances of the particular business you are being asked to consider.

/2

7 The *net worth* of a business — often also referred to as the 'proprietors' stake! — represents what (in theory at least) would be left over to go to the proprietors if the business was to be liquidated and the assets sold off at their balance sheet values. Score 1 mark.

Score a second mark if you have noted that it is calculated basically by deducting the total liabilities (other than those to the proprietors) from the total assets. In calculating the total assets, however, it is normal to leave out intangible and fictitious assets (such as goodwill and trademarks) since these will probably not have any real value in a break-up situation.

/2

8 You would calculate the periods of credit given and taken by comparing the figures given in the balance sheet for debtors and creditors with the annual turnover. Thus the formula (Debtors × 52/Turnover) tells you on average how many weeks any one debt remains outstanding before collection. It is more accurate to compare the creditors figure with

Your score

the amount of annual purchases if this can be established, giving the formula (Creditors × 52/ Purchases) = the number of weeks, on average, any one debt remains unpaid by the business.

Give yourself 1 mark for each calculation correctly stated.

Usually the purchases figure isn't available to you, in which case the turnover figure can be used with reasonable accuracy — at the very least it will be consistent in giving results from year to year so that you can establish the *trend*. Score an extra mark if you made this point.

/3

9   The gross profit : turnover ratio tells you what rate of return a business is generating from its annual sales. The formula (Gross profit × 100/Turnover) gives us the figure as a percentage. The result can be compared first with the business's own results for previous years as a guide to whether it is improving its profitability; score 1 mark.

Secondly, it can be compared with rates of return on turnover in that sector of the economy in general. Is the concern doing better or worse than its competitors — and if there is a significant difference, why has it arisen? Don't forget that these rates of a return vary dramatically from sector to sector. A second mark for this part of the answer.

/2

10   Gearing is a term used to denote the relationship between the loan capital and the equity capital (proprietors' funds) used in the financing of a business. A business which has a high proportion of borrowed money is said to be 'highly geared' — a business with a low proportion of borrowed money is thus termed 'low geared'.

A highly geared company is very vulnerable to fluctuations in profits. The interest on loan capital has to be paid whether or not profits are being made, whereas dividends on equity capital can be reduced or suspended in poor years. Score your mark raising this point.

/1

your total score for this Topic . . . . /20

Topic 4   Business Lending/1

1   Yes, it may well create (or increase) the need to borrow; score 1 mark. Score a second mark if you have explained that this occurs because increasing turnover will almost certainly lead to a need for working capital to be increased.

/2

2   It is excluded from the forecast because it does not represent an atual flow of funds out of the business.

/1

3   'Management accounting' figures comprise both up-to-date statistics on the finances of a business and forecasts of anticipated performance. Score 1 mark for this point. All carefully considered advances decisions revolve around an assessment of what is likely to happen in the future, and you can do that much more accurately if you know where you are now. Score 1 mark for this.

/2

4   The three methods are:
   • The 'pay-back' method
   • The 'rate of return' method
   • Discounted cash flow.
   Score 1 mark for each one correctly identified.

/3

5   The principal alternatives are *leasing* and *hire purchase*. Score 1 mark for each.

/2

6   No, the lender's main concern in either case will be to establish that the project will ultimately generate sufficient income to repay the advance within reasonable timescales.

/2

7   Neither (score 1 mark). Award yourself a second mark if you explained that the bank would need to be satisfied on both points before it would feel safe to grant the advance. By and large, *all* advances require positive answers to a number of questions, no one of which is more important than the others.

/2

8   Many contracts will specify that payments for work completed will be reduced by a stated proportion (usually 10%) which will be 'retained' until the whole of the contract has been satisfactorily completed. Score 2 marks only if you explained all this.

/2

9 There are two related reasons:
- The business has no previous 'track record' which can be used to judge its future prospects.
- The proprietor's dynamism is largely what determines the extent to which a good idea can be converted into a thriving business.

Score 1 mark for each point.

/2

10 Guarantees under the Small Firms Loans Guarantee Scheme are available for advances up to £75,000: score 1 mark. For a second mark you need to have noted that the cover is limited to 70% of the amount advanced.

/2

your total score for this Topic . . . . /20

Topic 5   Business lending/2

1 Directors' borrowing powers are limited to an amount equivalent to the nominal amount of the issued share capital.

/2

2 No, it has the powre only if specifically conferred by the Memorandum: score 1 mark. Score a second mark if you noted that exercise of the power must be with 'commercial justification'.

/2

3 The two main points to check are whether the stock is all saleable and whether the valuation is a reasonable reflection of the market value. Score 1 mark for each point made.

/2

4 It would reduce the amount of bank borrowing by postponing the need to pay for a proportion of the stock supplied.

/2

5 An arable farmer's overdraft is likely to fluctuate on an annual cycle centred on harvest time. Score 1 mark for knowing this. Score your second mark for knowing that a dairy farmer's overdraft will fluctuate on a monthly basis around his receipts from the Milk Marketing Board.

/2

6 Advances are normally limited to an amount equal to:

1/2 the cost of the land plus
2/3 building costs.
Score 2 marks if you knew *both* components of t... equation.

/2

7 The simplest method is to restrict the building programme and complete the estate in phases. This enables funds realized from sales to finance later building.

/2

8 Yes, a cargo of canned goods should be acceptable. Score 1 mark. To be acceptable the 'produce' must be imperishable with a steady, ready market. Score a further mark for explaining this.

/2

9 No, they are not usually acceptable; the bank would wish to see a genuine underlying commercial transaction.

/2

10 Yes, it can: score 1 mark. If the franchisor is reputable, the business should have a better than average chance of succeeding. Score a second mark for knowing this.

/2

your total score for this Topic . . . . /20

Topic 6 Marketing and selling

1 The members of this group are usually termed 'working class'. Score one mark for knowing this. In occupational terms they will be semi-skilled or unskilled manual workers. Score a second mark for this point.

/2

2 A market segment consists of a group of customers and potential customers who have similar needs for (in our case) banking services.

/2

3 No, it isn't. Selling is only part of the overall marketing process which embraces the researching, designing and provision of services aimed at fulfilling customer needs. Score 2 marks if you explained this. Score 1 if you just said 'no', but don't give yourself any marks if you wre guessing. (Be honest!)

/2

4 A 'trigger point' is a request (whether explicit or implicit) for a particular service which should trigger

Your score

/2

off the offering of a range of further services which might be of use to the same customer. Score 2 marks if you knew all of this.

5 A SWOT analysis is used when preparing a branch (or other) business development plan: 1 mark. It is an analysis of current Strengths, Weaknesses, Opportunities, and Threats. Score a second mark for this.

/2

6 The attributes of a service are its operational details (how it works, what rates of interest apply, what the costs are, and so on). The benefits are what the customer gets out of it, and therefore why it is used (e.g. the benefit of Home Contents Insurance is peace of mind when you're away from home). Score 3 marks if you knew all of this; score 1 if you defined only one of the two elements accurately.

/3

7 Yes, looking after existing customers should not be forgotten in the search for new ones.

/1

8 Competition comes primarily from:
   • Other banks (including secondary banks, National Giro, and so on)
   • Post Office
   • Building societies (though not all)
   • Credit cards and charge cards.
   Score 1 mark for two correct; score 2 marks for all four.

/2

9 No, it isn't correct — for 1 mark, unless you were just guessing. For your second mark you should have explained that market research is more concerned with finding out what the public really wants than what it says it wants. The two things are not the same, though both are important.

/2

10 'Probability sampling' involves testing the reactions of a number of people selected at random from the market segment appropriate to the product/service which is being researched.

/2

your total score for this Topic . . . . /20

Topic 7 Personal services

1 These accounts are targeted principally at wealthier customers who require a measure of liquidity on some of their savings; the minimum balance requirement (around £1000) will deter the less well off. Score 2 marks if you mentioned all of this. Score just 1 if you only said 'wealthier customers'.

/2

2 Generally speaking, the principal market segment for this service comprises:
 • Wage earners
 • Usually younger (20s–40s)
 • Whose income exceeds expenditure
 • Who wish to amass a capital sum.
Score 1 mark for each *two* points made.

/2

3 Other 'homes' for such funds are principally:
 • Gilt edged securities
 • Finance houses
 • Local authorities
 • Building societies.
Score 1 mark for each *two* alternatives offered.

/2

4 The principal difference is that with a charge card, the whole of the balance shown on the monthly statement must be paid off straight away. With a credit card, the user may elect to pay off the whole or just a part of the outstanding balance, subject to the legal minimum of £5 or 5% of the total, whichever is the higher. Score 2 marks for getting all (or nearly all) of this.

/2

5 An endowment mortgage is repaid in one lump sum at term out of the proceeds of an endowment policy; interest is charged on the whole of the standing balance throughout the period of the loan. A capital repayment mortgage is reduced gradually to nil by regular payments throughout the period, to cover both interest and repayments of capital. A mortgage protection policy is required. Score 1 mark for describing fully the features of each type of arrangement.

/2

6 A will should be made at any time when there is an important change in the customer's circumstances

Your score

(e.g. marriage, birth of children, divorce, inheritance of a large sum, etc.) Score 1 mark. Score a second mark for knowing that this may mean making a *new* will if there is already one in existence; the provisions of existing wills should be reviewed regularly.

/2

7 The attributes of a service are the technical details of how it operates: what rate of interest applies, how much notice of withdrawal is required, and so on. The benefits of the service are the satisfactions of needs that the customer gets out of it — a safe home for his savings, the means to buy a new car, freedom from worry about balancing the household budget every week, and so on.
Score 2 marks if you got all of that; otherwise score zero.

/2

8 'Electronic Funds Transfer at Point Of Sale', for 1 mark. For your second, you must have explained that it is a system which enables a retailer to charge the customer's bank account *immediately* with the cost of goods or services supplied by means of a direct electronic entry to the bank's computer.

/2

9 A 'share exchange' scheme permits clients who already hold stocks and shares to exchange them for units in a unit trust: score 1 mark. It is beneficial in that it allows the customer to spread his investment risk more widely while avoiding (most of) the brokerage that would be incurred if he was to sell the shares directly in the market. Score a second mark for this point.

/2

10 A 'discretionary trust' is one in which — subject to any specific instructions in the trust instrument — the trustees have wide powers to manage the investments without reference to the beneficiaries or to anyone else.

/2

your total score for this Topic . . . . /20

Topic 8   Business services, financial

1 Factor finance is a way of raising finance under which the factor will immediately make advances

against invoices sent out. Score 1 mark. Score a second mark if you noted that finance is not usually available for 100% of the invoice value.

/2

2   Yes, factor finance is available for the export trade. It is most common in respect of trade with Europe and North America, but it can be available for other countries. Score 2 marks for the whole explanation; just 1 if you only said 'yes'.

/2

3   Finance leasing is an alternative to borrowing for a customer who wishes to acquire the use of a capital asset: score 1 mark. The leasing company purchases the asset in its own name but has no responsibility for maintaining or servicing it. Score your second mark for knowing this.

/2

4   An acceptance facility is a means of raising finance, for 1 mark. Score a second mark for explaining that bills of exchange accepted by the bank are then available for discount at competitive rates.

/2

5   Usually the minimum figure will be £500,000, although banks offer money market related facilities for considerably smaller amounts.

/1

6   A placing is a method of bringing a stock 'to the market': score 1 mark. It is used with the smaller issues which can be 'placed' with institutional investors, although an adequate proportion must be available to the public at large. Score a second mark for knowing this.

/2

7   Loans under the Small Firms Loan Guarantee Scheme must:
   - not exceed £75,000
   - have a term of 2–7 years
   - be secured by the applicant business wherever possible
   - appear to be viable propositions.

Score 1 mark if two points made, 2 marks if you got three right, 3 for the whole thing.

/3

8   The USM is the Unlisted Securities Market; it is part of the Stock Market and is therefore used to raise equity capital. Score 1 mark. The USM is specifically organized to promote trade in smaller

/2

companies whose capitalization is too small to allow them to obtain a Stock Exchange 'listing' on the main market. Score a second mark.

/2

9 The principal vehicles are:
  - Ordinary shares
  - Preference shares
  - Loan stocks and debentures.

Score 2 marks if you got all three; 1 mark if you got one or two right.

/2

10 These accounts differ from deposit accounts in two ways:
  - Withdrawals are available on demand and a full money transfer service is available (cheque books etc.).
  - Interest rates usually vary according to the level of the balance maintained. There will be a threshold below which interest is not paid.

Score 1 mark for each point.

/2

your total score for this Topic .... /20

Topic 9 Business services, administration

1 The registrar service is available to limited companies: score 1 mark. Its use is worthwhile for the larger concerns having significant numbers of shareholders. Score your second mark for knowing this.

/2

2 The principal benefits are:
  - Professional control of invoicing and related procedures
  - Release of staff time, and/or saving of staff costs

Possibility of improved cash flow by more accurate control.

Score 2 marks if you got all three; 1 mark for one or two.

/2

3 The employee benefits include:
  - Security from theft
  - Access to bank money transfer systems and other services
  - Enhanced capacity for regular budgeting

Score 1 mark for each valid point made.

/3

4 The CHAPs system reduces the cost and operational complexity of funds transfer by reducing the need to process paper. Score 1 mark. It is an improved service for customers and is an added factor in attracting/retaining accounts. Score a further mark for this point.

/2

5 The minimum amount is £10,000.

/1

6 BACs is set up to permit electronic funds transfer between participating organizations: score 1 mark. Score a second mark if you mentioned that it can be used to transmit both debits and credits between beneficiary and payer.

/2

7 Personal pension plans are targeted at self-employed people who have no pension arrangements available to them as part of any of their employment arrangements. Score 2 marks if you got all of this; score 1 if you just said 'self-employed'.

/2

8 The 'loanback' facility enables the customer to obtain a long-term tax effective loan which can be used for any purpose, but which is most appropriate for buying into a business. Score 2 marks only if you got *all* of this.

/2

9 'Keyman' policies are taken out to cover a business against financial loss resulting from the early death of a 'key' employee (including directors/partners).

10 Such cover is required to protect against the loss of income if disability was to prevent him from following his trade or profession; simple life assurance would cover only the death risk. Score 2 marks if you got all of this.

/2

your total score for this Topic .... /20

Topic 10   Foreign business

1 Currency loans can permit an exporter to invoice in foreign currency without exchange risks: score 1 mark. They can also have cost advantages since the interest rate applicable to the particular currency

may be lower than that for sterling. Score a second mark for this point.

/2

2   The ECGD exists primarily to provide credit insurance against the specific risks of exporting goods on credit: score 1 mark. The particular risks for which cover is provided are the *buyer risk* (insolvency), the *sovereign risk* (revolution, war, etc.), and the *reserve risk* (unavailability of foreign exchange). Score 2 marks if you knew all three of these; score 1 if you knew only two.

/3

3   The ECGD (Bills and Notes) loan guarantee shceme is no longer available, but most banks have brought in their own comparable schemes.

/2

4   The bank will negotiate foreign cheques only on a 'with recourse' basis so that it can reclaim the funds paid over if the cheque is returned unpaid. Score 1 mark. This facility will be made available only to customers who are 'good for the money'. Score your second mark for knowing this.

/2

5   SWIFT is the Society for Worldwide Interbank Financial Telecommunications. Score 1 mark. It is a computer-based system for passing messages between participating banks. Score another mark for knowing this.

/2

6   The Documentary Credit system provides the exporter with a degree of certainty of payment provided that he complies with the terms of the credit.

7   Yes, it is. Score 1 mark — provided that you weren't just guessing!

/1

8   The principal risk is the exchange risk: that the value of the currency will fluctuate downwards as against sterling before payment is received. Score 2 marks for the answer and the explanation.

/2

9   The risks can be overcome by:
    ● Forward contracts
    ● Currency loans
    ● Currency accounts (if the customer has both currency income and expenditure)
    ● Currency options.

Score 1 mark for each point made — up to a maximum of 3.

Your score /3

10 Buyer credit is a method of financing exports by advancing funds to the buyer so as to enable immediate payment to be made to the supplier. Score 1 mark.

/1

your total score for this Topic .... /20

When you have completed all the short answer tests, fill in your scores on the score grid (inside the back cover). You can now use your results in this section to rank your revision priorities, starting with your weakest topic first.

Topics

For each topic, start with the study guide and then try to answer the multiple choice questions which follow.

Topic 1   Principles of lending

Study guide

Introduction

Putting it in context

The Principles of Lending lie at the heart of the Section A questions for POB 2, but you should not expect to be tested on them *directly* — the examiner is not going to ask you to write out the Principles of Lending, or anything like it! You will, however, be expected to show *clearly* in your answers that you have an understanding of them and can apply them to practical lending situations. Now — you have probably heard all this before and are starting to think that you can do without all these tired old platitudes. Well, perhaps so, *but* you should consider that despite the fact that they probably could write a first class essay on the principles (if asked!), many students write answers to problems *as if they had never heard of them*. Why they do this is a mystery to all and a constant source of amazement to the examiner. The purpose of this section of the book is to prevent you from becoming part of that sad (and disappointingly large) crowd.

How to succeed (by really trying)

To gain really high marks in Section A you have chiefly to do just two things.

1 Get the answer right (to lend or not to lend, or sometimes to say why a decision can't be given), and
2 Show that you reached your conclusion by a reasoned and considered path.

In fact, 1 follows on from 2 — if you follow the right path, you should get the right answer — and to get the right answer you should consider each of the 'principles of lending' in turn and consider the extent to which the proposition under consideration matches up to sound banking practice. You also need to show the examiner what you have done, of course.

In practice, this means that it is a good idea to write your answer to lending questions as if the examiner *had* asked you to set out the principles, illustrating your answer by reference to the situation given in the question. Adopting a standard approach to all questions — looking at each of the principles in a set order — will help to ensure that no vital point is missed and will give a structure to your answers that will help the examiner to give you the marks you (probably) deserve.

Your tuition so far will probably have given you a 'mnemonic prompt' to help you remember the basic principles — we shall be using 'PARTS' but there are several others (CAMPARI, CALIPERS etc.) — whichever one you prefer, stick to it and *use it*.

Sometimes there may be nothing important to say about a particular principle, so don't say anything — the examiner does not set 'booby traps' designed specifically to make life difficult for you, although there may be marks available for saying that there is nothing to say.

Words of warning

Just a couple of points before you begin your studies proper.

Credit scoring. Personal lending propositions are, in 'the real world' these days, often evaluated by way of an arithmetical credit scoring system based on the particular bank's experience. These systems do not specifically follow the general 'principles of lending', but rather evaluate the borrower by drawing on the bank's overall experience of the types of people who are (or are not) 'good payers'. In the examination it is quite possible that you will be asked to decide about a personal loan type of proposal — but you will be expected to reach your decision from first principles. You may not shelter behind the lack of credit scoring tables (or take any into the exam with you).

Character of borrower. The discrepancy between reality and the exam which we have just mentioned should not disturb you too much. It comes about because in personal lending situations the banks have found that the principal consideration with such borrowers is their *character*. Some people will make very effort to repay you however difficult it may be for them and others will stop repaying at the first slight difficulty. Furthermore, the good ones will not, in the first place, enter into any commitments which they cannot see their way to fulfilling.

Your first question about any lending proposition should therefore be, 'Can I trust the information and the promises that this person is giving me?'. Only if the answer is 'yes' should you proceed to look at the extent to which the proposition matches up to the principles of good lending. In other words there are two basic questions:

- *Will/won't* the customer repay?
- *Can/can't* the customer repay?

The first of these is the more subjective but should be satisfactorily answered before the second is considered. Credit scoring provides an answer by measuring the *stability* of the customer: people with a stable background and home life are much less likely to leave you in the lurch. In a written exam, it is difficult to test you on your ability to judge character, and it is unusual to see questions based on propositions put forward by out-and-out rogues. What *does* happen is that the examiner will often give you clues about the borrower's character: his reliability, judgement, experience (if in business) and so on. It is up to you to pick these up and respond to them.

Giving a decision. By and large, the lending questions will require you to come to a decision on whether to lend or not, and the question will contain adequate information to enable you to do so. If you try to hedge your bets, you will be detected and will lose marks!

Inexperienced lenders generally fall into one of two categories: the over-cautious and the over-indulgent, both of whom often voice a decision which goes against their better judgement, 'just in case'. Does this apply to you? Which type are you? The best advice we can give you is to say *no* if you think the loan is too risky. Don't be afraid to say *yes* if you think it is a good one. Know your own pre-dispositions and guard against them.

Read the question. Yes, we know that you've been told this until you are tired of it, but it is important. You *must* clarify in your own mind what the question requires you to do. Normally, as we have said, you will have to say 'yes' or 'no' to a loan proposition — but not always. If the question says 'Set out what further information you will require' or 'Prepare a report detailing the areas which require further investigation', the examiner is telling you that you do not have enough data on which to base a decision. You would be surprised how many students nevertheless persist in giving one.

Always look behind the words of the question for its *meaning.* Ask yourself what the examiner is wanting you to do — if you can do that, you are always well on the way to a pass mark.

The principles of lending

Do you have a mnemonic 'prompt' for the basic principles? If so, jot it down, now and ensure that you know what is important about each heading and why. If you haven't one yet, learn ours.

*P*urpose
*A*mount

PARTS

Repayment
Term
Security

The reason for looking at these five topics is to establish the *risk* element of the proposition.

Purpose

- Is it *acceptable*? Speculative and illegal purposes are not.
- Are there any specific *risks* to be considered?
- Will the customer use the funds for the *stated* purpose?

Amount

- Is the amount required *correctly calculated*?
  This frequently forms the basis of questions, especially those relating to:
  — Budget deficit finance (e.g. business working capital, household bills etc.).
  — Bridging loans
  — Financing of specific projects (e.g. building contracts, purchasing new machinery).
- Is the *customer's contribution* adequate? Much depends on the circumstances, but as a general rule:
  — Consumer borrowing — will expect at least 20% from customer
  — Business borrowing — 50% is ideal, but special schemes may lead to greater proportions advanced.
- Where has the customer's contribution *come from*?
  — Does this tell you anything about the ability to repay?

Repayment

Where is repayment to come from? How safe is it? What evidence is there?

- *Lump sums* — sale of assets (e.g. bridging loans), maturity of investments, legacies etc. Ensure that receipt of expected amount is adequately certain.
- *Income* — (individuals) is there an adequate margin between income and expenditure?
- *Profits* — (businesses) what have profits been in the past, and can projections for future be trusted/verified?
- *Cash flow* — if borrowing is to cover a temporary budgeting 'hiccup' (business 'stocking' loan etc.), can a forecast of cash flow

(in and out) be produced to demonstrate capacity to repay?
* *Funds flow* — being used with increasing frequency to reconcile profits and cash, and to demonstrate repayment capacity.

Term

How long is borrowing required over and is the period acceptable? Banks are no longer merely short-term lenders but the period of the advance must be appropriate to the purpose. Rules of thumb for maximum periods:

— Consumer finance	3/5 years
— House purchase	20/25 years
— House improvements	5/10 years
— Business expansion	5/10 years

Shorter term self liquidating loans (working capital, stocking loans etc.) will be granted for appropriate periods.

Security

You will not be questioned on *how to take* security in POB 2 — the examiner will take it for granted(!) that you know. You *will* be expected to comment on:

* the *need* for security
* what could be *available*
* the relative *merits* of such items.

Security should not be discussed as a deciding factor in whether a proposition is good or bad — it should be sought only when you have already concluded that you would like to lend. It is taken to protect the bank against something unforseen happening: make sure you let the examiner know you understand this.

Other factors

Remuneration. Will the loan be profitable for the bank? *NB* Do not let big profits (hopefully) lead you to accept an excessively risky proposal. Similarly, don't be led astray by the opportunity to sell other bank services.

Overall picture. Ensure you have a full understanding of the customer. We have already mentioned character, but don't forget the following pointers.

— Assets/liabilities overall

— Past record
— Experience (business loans).

Finally. Don't forget that no one is wholly good or bad (as a prospect for a loan, that is). All the questions will have some plus points and some minus points. Your task is to identify and evaluate them all and decide whether *on balance* the good outweigh the bad or vice versa.

Once you feel confident about your knowledge of this topic, try to answer the 10 multiple choice questions which follow.

Multiple choice questions

The following question is taken from the April 1985 POB 2 exam. Read it carefully and then answer the following questions.

Henry Cottboy works for a local printing company which banks with you. Twelve months ago, the directors requested the work force to transfer from weekly to monthly pay and Mr Cottboy opened an account with you. Over the year his monthly credit has averaged £480.

Six months ago Mr Cottboy purchased the house he was renting from the local authority. The house was valued at £17,000 but he was allowed a discount of 35%. A 25-year endowment mortgage of £11,000 was arranged through a building society.

At this time you opened a budget account for Mr Cottboy. This involved a monthly transfer of £200 and allowed a borrowing facility of £500; the balance is now standing at £400 debit. The account is used mainly for regular payments, including mortgage, life policy premiums, rates, gas, electricity, T.V. rental and clothing account, but other transactions have been made. Mr Cottboy calls to see you today. His car has failed its Ministry of Transport test and he has been offered another car costing £2,000 with an allowance of £300 for the old car. He also wishes to instal a new kitchen and double glazing at his home; this will cost £2,500.

You question Mr Cottboy and establish that he is married with two young children. His wife works part-time in the evenings earning £20 per week — with the state child benefit allowance, his contribution to his wife for the housekeeping can be restricted to £40 per week. From 1 May, he will be promoted and will receive an additional £500 p.a. A general pay increase of 5% is also expected in three months' time.

Mr Cottboy requests a loan of £3,600 towards the cost of the car and home improvements, repayable over four years. His wife has recently won £750 in a newspaper competition and is prepared to cover the balance.

How would you respond to the request?

1 What general impression do you have of this married couple:

   a they are excellent prospects for a loan; undoubted for repayment?
   b generally good prospects; the type of customer to be encouraged to borrow?
   c rather poor prospects; they are taking on too much at one time?
   d rogues who are out to defraud the bank?

 *answer*

2   What do you think about the wife's part-time earnings:

    a   they should be excluded from any calculation of ability to repay?

    b   they can be included in any calculation of ability to repay?

    c   they are a bad sign which indicates that the couple are in financial difficulties?

    d   they are a good sign which indicates that the couple take their responsibilities seriously?

 b   *answer*

3   What do you think about the purpose of the advance:

    a   it is unacceptable as it encompasses several purposes at once?

    b   it includes taking over borrowing from elsewhere which is unacceptable?

    c   the purposes are acceptable but a little risky, so caution is advisable?

    d   the differing purposes are nevertheless acceptable?

 d   *answer*

4   The customers' proposed contribution to the project is:

    a   too small; more than 20% should be provided.

    b   adequate and good evidence of thrift.

    c   adequate but not good evidence of the ability to save.

    d   too small since 1/3 comes from the sale of an existing vehicle.

 *answer*

5   Which of these statements is correct:

    a   the loan should not be granted since the term proposed is too long for a car loan?

    b   the loan should not be granted since the term is too long for a home improvement loan?

    c   two loans of different terms should be considered for the two purposes?

    d   the term of the loan is irrelevant provided that the customers can repay?

 *answer*

6   What do you think about the borrowing on the budget account:

   a   it should be paid off before any other loans are granted?
   b   it indicates clearly that the customers are already in financial difficulties?
   c   it is worrying, since it includes some items that should not have been applied to the account?
   d   it may indicate the need to increase the monthly payment.

answer

7   The husband says he is expecting his pay to increase. Which of the following is true:

   a   the statement should be ignored in case it does not come to fruition?
   b   the possibility of promotion should be ignored since it may not occur?
   c   the 'general increase' may be absorbed by rises in the cost of living?
   d   both elements of the increase will generate a real increase in the level of his income?

answer

8   What do you think about the couple's ability to repay the loan:

   a   they can not afford to repay within a reasonable length of time?
   b   they can afford to repay with ease?
   c   they should be able to repay with some care?
   d   there is no need to worry about the repayment since adequate security is available?

answer

9   If repayment of loans for both purposes appears to be a problem, what would you do:

   a   lend only if adequate security is provided?
   b   lend for the home improvements and suggest that borrowing for the car is taken by way of hire purchase finance?
   c   lend for the car and suggest that the building society be approached for the home improvement finance?

d decline to lend if both projects are to be pursued?

 *answer*

10 What security would you propose for the advance:

    a the question is irrelevant since the proposal is a 'non-starter'?
    b a second legal charge over the house?
    c guarantee by the husband?
    d the new car will be security for the car loan?

 answer

Answers follow on pages 36–42. Score 2 marks for each correct answer.

Answers

1 The correct answer is **c**.

It is not wise to prejudge any lending proposition — but even so, it is usually worthwhile to begin by clarifying your first impressions. In this case, we can start by disposing of the two extremes. There is nothing in the information given to suggest that the customers are in any way dishonest, so answer **d** should be eliminated. Likewise, answer **a** cannot be supported by the evidence and if you gave this as your response you must have an over-generous nature!

The balance of the evidence points to growing financial difficulties. The customers have not banked with us (or anywhere) long enough for a track record to be built up. They do not have any savings and any financial requirement has to be met by borrowing: the conversion to monthly pay necessitated a budget account, their house purchase required a 100% mortgage, now they cannot find any money to repair their car. The customer does not appear to have any qualms about taking on further commitments and probably expects us to help him — but bear in mind that we would not be helping him by putting him into a hole which he cannot get out of. 'Proceed with caution' appears to be the overall message.

2 The correct answer is **b**.

It would be presumptuous at this stage to draw any moral conclusions from the fact that the wife works part time, so we cannot know whether it is a good or bad sign. We do not know why she has a job — the motives might not be financial at all, so answer **c** can be ruled out. We also do not know how the wife views the money that she earns; her husband has indicated that it can be used to supplement his contribution to the housekeeping budget, but she might not agree! Answer **d** has to be ruled out on this basis. It is not what people earn that demonstrates their attitude to their responsibilities; it is how they spend it — and we do not know that yet.

For the purposes of estimating whether or not the loan can be repaid, however, it is reasonable to assume that the wife will be amenable to adding her wages to the family budget. Unless we have any reason to believe that her job might be insecure or that she might leave it, there is no reason why we should not include the whole of her wages into our calculation of the family budget.

3 The correct answer is **d**.

If you gave **a** as your answer, you have identified one of the difficulties of the proposition — but one that is not great enough for us to cause us to reject the whole proposal outright. Many of the questions which you will encounter will require you to come up with some way of restructuring the proposition so as to make it more acceptable. In this case, the simple thing to do is to separate the two purposes and consider them independently — possibly even looking at the possibility of two individual loans: the purposes are not interdependent.

The two 'purposes' are:

1 Purchase of a second hand car, and
2 Home improvements (kitchen and double glazing)

Both of these are quite acceptable as the basis of a borrowing proposition and in fact are among the *least* risky types of proposal (answer **c**). Most credit scoring schemes treat loans for second hand cars as slightly more uncertain than those for new cars, but the different is only marginal and need not perturb you.

If you gave **b** as your answer, you must have been reading a different question from the rest of us! There is no suggestion of taking over borrowing from elsewhere — indeed, the only external borrowing mentioned is the building society mortgage which is not in question. It is true that experience has shown us that taking over borrowing from elsewhere is fraught with danger. We are usually asked to do it only when the customer is in severe financial difficulties; unless we can work out a strategy which will stop the overspending *and* be certain that the customer will adhere to it, we would just be taking over someone else's problems.

4 The correct answer is **c**. Adding together the £300 allowance on the car and the £750 competition prize, the customers are providing some 20% of the total required. This is just about adequate for both of these purposes — we would not really be happy with anything less, but if you gave **a** as your answer you are really looking for too much.

In computing the adequacy of the customer's contribution, we do not really have to worry about the source, so answer **d** is wrong. In fact, the customer's contribution to the majority of car loans comes from the trade-in allowance on an existing vehicle. If we took the line suggested in **d**, very few car loans would be granted!

The source of such funds, however, can be a good clue to the customer's ability to repay the loan. If, for example, the 'deposit' has been saved up over a period by setting aside £50 per month in a deposit

A/c, this would be good evidence of the ability to find £50 per month, wouldn't it! The trade-in value of a car on its own doesn't really tell us much. Most car owners borrow to make the purchase, changing the car soon after the loan on it has been paid off. In such cases, the ability to repay the loan on the old car will tell us something about the ability to repay the new loan. Unfortunately, there is no suggestion that *these* customers had been paying into a car loan, so we are no further forward.

Nearly 3/4 of the money which these customers have contributed comes from the wife's competition prize. This of course tells us nothing about their ability repay — unless we have reason to believe that she will continue to win such prizes on a regular basis! Thus answer **b** is not a reflection of the truth. In fact, on balance it appears that these customers have been unable to build up any real savings which they could utilize towards these projects — not an encouraging sign at all.

5   The correct answer is **c**.

We have already said that it would be a good idea to consider the two proposals separately — if necessary arranging two separate loans. To do so would also help to reconcile the problems of differing appropriate *terms*.

The period over which funds are lent for car purchase should not exceed either the length of time that the customers might be expected to keep the vehicle or its useful life. Usually it is the first of these that is the deciding factor, and banks will lend over (up to) 3 years for new cars or 2 years for second hand ones. Answer **a** is correct therefore when it says that the term is too long for a car loan, but it is too sweeping to say that the loan should not be granted. It may be possible to grant the loan over a shorter term.

Home improvement loans are granted over longer periods — terms of 5–7 years are usually available, so answer **b** is certainly wrong. It would not be unreasonable to extend the period to 5 years in this case. Thus the borrowing requirements appear to be:

- Car loan £1500 over 2 years
- Home improvements £2100 over 5 years

It can never be right to say that the term of a loan is irrelevant, as in answer **d**. If nothing else, it is important to establish the period over which the bank requires the loan to be extinguished, so that the customers ability *to* repay can be established. Without a set term you will not know what level of repayments would be required.

6 The correct answer is **d**.

There is no need for the outstanding balance on the budget account to be paid off at this stage (answer **a**); provided that the bank is satisfied that the customers can meet all their commitments, there should be no problem.

The balance outstanding on the account does merit further investigation, though. The balance appears to have risen close to the limit quite rapidly and this may indicate that the customers are overspending. On the other hand, however, it may be explicable. Over any 12 month period, the family's commitments should be quite predictable, but *within* that period there may be bad months when many outgoings fall due and good months when few payments have to be made. It may be that these customers have just come to the end of such a 'bad' period and the debit balance of the account will now start to subside.

It is to cover such a situation that the banks have introduced 'budget' accounts, so it should not be too ready to criticize when customers make use of them. It is therefore not fair to say that there is *clear* evidence of financial difficulty as in answer **b**.

If the customers cannot show that the normal payments into the account will be adequate to reduce the balance, however, it will be necessary to increase the monthly contribution to it. This is important because any such increase will of course reduce the amount available to repay the proposed loan. On a practical point, it is worth noting that with most bank schemes increasing the monthly payment will also result in an increase in the credit limit available! This might be an added temptation to overspend if they are in difficulties, so the branch will have to beware.

There is nothing to worry about in the fact that 'non-regular' payments have been applied to the budget account — answer **c**. Modern 'budget account' facilities are designed to allow customers to make both regular payments and unexpected 'one-off' payments out of them. It is therefore important when setting them up to ensure that the monthly contributions amount to more than 1/12 of the estimated annual regular expenditure. If they don't, there will be no leeway for other payments to be made.

7 The correct answer is **c**.

As a general rule, statements that income will rise soon should be treated with some reserve. Many borrowers will be over-optimistic in their expectations which can cause some (financial) embarrassment when their hopes are not realized. However, that does not mean that their statement should just be ignored (**a**); it should be *tested*. If the customer can substantiate the prediction, then we can take the increase into account.

In this case, there are two sources of extra income: the promotion and the general rise. Looking at the promotion first, **b**, the customer should be asked whether this is a general hope (that he might get a job that he believes may become available) or whether he has definitely been informed that he has got it. If the latter, then we can allow for a real increase in his income. If the former then we should ignore it — but only if it *is* the former.

Likewise the general increase mentioned in **c** should be questioned: has it been agreed or is it merely a claim at this stage? A note of caution is appropriate here, however — any such settlement will be granted to counter rises in the cost of living and will therefore not result in a real increase in the long-term level of the customer's income, which is why answer **d** is not correct. There is no reason why we should not include the amount of the rise — if proved — in our calculations. Even so, we should bear in mind that over the forthcoming 3 months continued inflation may well erode the whole of the increase. If, therefore, the whole of it is needed to finance repayments, matters could become strained by this time next year.

While on the topic of 'customer optimism', it is worthwhile reflecting on the dangers of accepting at face value promises of lump-sum repayment from such sources as legacies, law suits, compensation or insurance claims and so on. Before agreeing to lend against them you should be entirely satisfied that the payments will certainly be made at the level anticipated within a reasonable period of time. Sad to say, many such hopes *do not* come to pass!

8   The correct answer is **a**.

At this point, you should be able to make some estimate of the customers' income and expenditure with a view to checking the ability to repay. If you have not done this yet, do so now. Don't forget to include in your calculations such items as increases in budget account payments and funds to be set aside for adequate car maintenance in future. The examiner's estimate goes something like this (if yours doesn't correspond *exactly*, don't worry provided that you have got it approximately correct):

Income	£
Present monthly income	480
Promotion increase	30
General increase	20
	530

Expenditure

Budget A/c (currently	200
Budget A/c (increase)	50
Housekeeping to wife	175
Car expenses (not inc. loan)	50
	475

Thus there is a surplus of about £55 *without* allowing for any personal expenditure at all. It is hard to imagine a family of four having *any* of this £55 left at the end of the month. The only conclusion that one can draw is that the family cannot afford to make repayments on any further loans — answer **a**. Not only that, but until the two pay rises are received they cannot make ends meet on their current level of commitments at all.

In such circumstances, the question of security should not arise — answer **c** — since the loan should not be granted in any case. Probably the only way that the bank could recover its money would be to realize the security, and while this may happen from time to time (!) we should never go into a situation knowing it to be the only way out.

9 The correct answer is **d**.

On balance, it seems that these customers cannot afford to borrow any more. It is just possible that they may be able to explain the balance on their budget account — remember question 6? — in which case the extra £50 per month which we have allowed for will not be needed, but would that be enough to finance the borrowing? Have you worked out the cost? Obviously, to an extent it depends on the prevailing rates of interest but we will not be far wrong if we assume that the monthly figures are:

- Car loan £75
- Home improvement loan £55

They may therefore be able (just about) to manage one of the loans *but not both*, and we must decline to lend if both projects are to be pursued.

If you gave **b** or **c** as your answers, you seem to have forgotten that wherever the funds are borrowed from, the same problem of repayment will be encountered. It helps no one to shift part of the (probable) problem elsewhere — and who is to say that if in difficulties the customer would not elect to pay the building society or finance company in preference to the bank?

We hope no one needs reminding why answer **a** is incorrect! (Anyone who does can refer back to question 8).

10   The correct answer is **a** — and we hope you got it right. Assuming that the loan *had* been one that would merit your support, would any of these items of security be of value?

A second legal charge, **b**, would have an equity value of £6000 plus, and has some attraction. Until recently, it was common practice for banks to take such security for home improvement loans. Now, however, this is much less common: the Consumer Credit Act has restricted the banks' abilities to realize such securities, and legal decisions (Brown and Boland cases etc.) have made it more difficult to take an effective security.

If you gave **c** as your answer, you have not read the question properly! The suggestion appears to be that the advance will be in the name of the husband — so he will hardly have to guarantee it! A guarantee from the wife might be possible, but a better suggestion would be to arrange the borrowing in joint names. Even so, this would not get us much further forward, since neither of these two appear to have any personal assets that would enable them to repay the loan on demand.

We hope you did not give **d** as your answer. The bank will have no direct rights over the car which has been purchased with the loan monies.

Score 2 marks for each correct answer. What was your score? Fill it in on the score grid.

If you scored 12 or less and are still a bit shaky on some points go back and look at the study guide again before proceeding any further.

If you are sure you really understand and are familiar with this topic now, try the 10 further questions which are on pages 222–4. Alternatively you can go on to your next topic and do all the post-tests together at the end.

Topic 2   Personal lending

Study guide

Introduction

Getting it into context

From a 'practical' (exam passing!) point of view there are two important observations that can be made about questions of *personal lending* in POB 2:

- You are not going to see a *lot* of them — there will usually be only one (if any) of the four dealing with personal borrowing.
- The ones that are set will draw on only a limited number of general situations. If you prepare properly, you are unlikely to be presented with a question dealing with *principles* that you have never come across.

It is, in fact, quite difficult for the examiner to set really testing questions about borrowing by personal customers — so you should be able to obtain good marks, even though the 'simplicity' of many of the questions mean that they are marked quite firmly.

Range of topics

What, then, are the choices open to the examiner when setting questions? He can really look to only two options as the basis of any question.

Principles of lending — the simplest thing for him to do is to ask a question which will require you simply to apply the principles of lending to an everyday situation. You will be given the background facts about a lending proposition — overdraft, car loan, or whatever — so that you can isolate the pro's and con's and make a recommendation.

As well as applying the principles as set out in Topic 1, you will need to know which method of lending is most appropriate to the customer's needs — overdraft, personal loan, etc. — and what considerations are particularly important in that type of lending. We shall be giving you some guidelines for this later.

Specific propositions

There are a few specific types of proposition which come up quite frequently in real life and which involve certain *technical* considerations which must be dealt with satisfactorily. The examiner can ask you a question about one of these topics in order to check your understanding of the technicalities; if you know what he is looking for, you can score highly in these questions — without having to 'think' too hard. We shall be looking at the construction of 'checklists' for these areas (which include such items as bridging loans and Inheritance Tax advances). You should commit these checklists to memory.

Types of advance

You should concentrate first on making sure that you are fully familiar with the various ways in which personal finance can be made available. Make sure that you know the particular features of the various types of facility — and the situations to which they are appropriate.
Particular points to bear in mind for the exam include the following:

Overdrafts

Useful to balance out *temporary* excesses of expenditure over income — the vital point is to ensure that the customer is not over-committed and *overall* income does exceed expenditure. Repayment should be possible over a period.

Budget accounts

Beware — there are two types:

- Traditional — purely to spread commitments over the year.
- Revolving credit — allow expenditure on (small) capital items too. Halfway between loans and overdrafts.

Note: Don't forget the use of credit cards and 'gold' cards in this area too.

Loan accounts

Granted for specific purposes with set repayments over a specified period. Most banks offer special variants, e.g.

Personal loans — for consumer spending. Repayable over up to 5 years. Interest charged at a flat rate — not directly linked to Base Rate and usually marginally higher than 'Base Linked' rates. Be familiar with usual contributions expected for customer e.g.

'New' cars (up to 3 years old)	20%
Older cars	33%
Consumer goods	10%

Home improvement loans — similar to personal loans but for longer periods (10 years) and for larger amounts (£5000+) incurred in undertaking home improvements.

Consumer Credit Act 1974

You are unlikely to be tested *in depth* on the provisions of the Consumer Credit Act 1974 — although it could turn up in POB 1. However, the examiner will expect you to be familiar with the general provisions. It would not be a bad idea to demonstrate this knowledge to him when appropriate. Be sure you know the following points (in a little more detail!) at least:

- *Regulated agreements* comprise borrowing of up to £15,000 by persons (private and business).
- *Written agreements* must be obtained for all loan accounts and structured loans if 'regulated'.
- Agreements signed *outside* the bank are *cancellable* within 5 days of receipt of the copy agreement.
- *Overdrafts* are excluded from the provisions.
- *Mortgages* over land are acceptable only if the advance is for the purposes of house purchase or bridging.

Type of proposal

There are a few specific types of proposal which you should study — the examiner likes to set questions on the *technical* aspects of these. What you need is a mental *checklist* of the major points to be considered, as you will often be able to pick up 'easy' marks by making reference to the appropriate points at the right stage in your analysis of the problem set. That doesn't mean that you can get away without thinking at all — your answer must consist of reasoned comment on the facts presented — but you don't need to make things harder for yourself by having to work out every answer from first principles!

Recommended reading for Section A includes the 'lending guides' written by Perry & Fiddes, and these are a useful aid to your studies (and revision!). The examiner has often commented on how many students do not appear to have studied them. It is not our intention to try to reproduce the guides here, but the following brief checklists are given as an aid to your revision.

Bridging loans

Usually for home owners when moving house if the new house has to be paid for before the old house is sold.

- *Closed bridge*: contracts are signed and exchanged on both sale and purchase, so customer knows exact amount and term of loan.
- *Open bridge*: no firm contract for *sale*. Much less certain and great care is required to ensure no residual debt is left.
- *Bridging mortgage moneys*: may be separate or part of a 'normal' bridge; required when building society mortgage is promised but not immediately available.
- *Bridging deposit*: usually 10% deposit is required when contracting to buy a house. The customer may need to borrow this as (part of) a bridge too!

In the exam, the *amount* and the *repayment* are usually the most important points to consider. The amount must reflect the fact that usually it is not possible to have two mortgages at one time. To keep bank borrowing to a minimum, if the mortgage on the new house is bigger (it usually is), the trick is to lend the customer enough to pay off the *old* mortgage — plus the balance required for the purchase. Memorise this equation:

Amount of loan required

	Cost of new house
plus	Existing mortgage
less	New mortgage
less	Deposit paid (if from own resources)
less	Any other contribution by the customer
=	£ Loan amount

Repayment will come from the sale of the old house — now not subject to a mortgage. The expected price must usually be sufficient to cover both the loan *and* the costs of moving. Make a list of these costs now and compare it with the list which will almost certainly appear in your textbook. Customers moving at their employer's behest will have an advantage since these costs will usually be paid for them.

Open bridges can have repayment problems:

— unsaleability of house (who valued it?)
— price reductions
— build up of interest if loan long-term.

At the very least an adequate *margin* is required.
Other 'technical' points that are usually worth a mention include:

— status enquiry on solicitors if not known
— solicitors' undertakings (to protect bank's position)
— introduction/reference for borrower
— 'Letter of Intent' re mortgage for Building Society (*NB* The bank could offer its own house loan services if appropriate)
— MIRAS may be available if the borrowing is taken on a separate loan A/c
— Security: is a charge required over new house/existing house?

House purchase loans

Make sure that you know the basic details of the different types of house purchase loan schemes which are available. What are the operating differences between an endowment mortgage and a capital repayment mortgage?
Term of these loans is usually 10–30 years — not extending beyond retirement age.
Amount: maximum available often decided by formula:

80/90% of valuation, and
2½ times gross annual salary *plus*
1 times spouse's gross annual salary.

Repayments should not normally exceed about 30% of gross income (including insurance policies and other long term commitments). Again, the formula indicates the slightly different approach to these loans.
Other technical points to mention include

— Charge over property as security
— Satisfactory surveys?
— Mortgage protection policies (if appropriate)
— Fire insurance
— MIRAS — Do you know the thresholds?

Self employed customers may be able to link repayment to a pension policy. Make sure you note down how such a scheme would work.

House building

Loans to enable a customer to build his own house can be granted, but carry some risk. Extra care is required concerning the following.

Amount: must be carefully checked:

— Are costings right?
— Fixed price contracts with builder?
— Is land included? Has customer a good title?
— What is customers contribution — is there a margin for bank if it has to sell?
— Stage payments required?

Repayment

— From sale of existing house? (Similar considerations to open bridge)
— From mortgage on new house?
  • Letter of intent
  • Is house mortgageable/well built?

Other technical points:

— Ability of builder
  • Status reports
  • What if business fails?
  • NHBC guarantee
— Planning permission
— Insurance cover as building proceeds

Probate advances

Granted on executors/administrators to pay off Inheritance Tax liability on the estate. The grant of representation will not be made until the Inland Revenue is satisfied in this respect!
Amount: the examiner will not expect you to know the current tax bands/rates in detail, but he will expect you to know the principles. Important points include:

— Tax on land and shares in unquoted companies may be paid over 10 years.

— Shares in unquoted companies qualify for 50% 'business relief'.

Repayment: generally from realizations of liquid assets. If these are insufficient, care is needed to ensure that repayment *is* possible. Take an undertaking from the executors to repay out of first realizations.

Other technical points:

— Usual formalities re Death Certificate, etc.
— Executors' mandate assumes joint and several liability for the advance.

Once you feel confident about your knowledge of this topic, try to answer the 10 multiple choice questions which follow.

Multiple choice questions

The first five questions are based around the following scenario which is taken from a question set in the POB2 exam in April 1986.

> Leslie Brown has maintained a satisfactory account with you for over five years. Salary credits, currently averaging £700, are seen each month. You have recorded an overdraft limit of £400 and this has never been abused. His account is today standing at £150 credit.
>
> Mr Brown calls to see you today. He explains that he is a supervisor at a local engineering company. He is married with two sons aged 10 and 8, and his wife works part-time, earning £35 per week. His elder son is due to start secondary school in September; there is a very good local secondary school but the Browns' home is outside the catchment area and they, therefore, wish to move house into the catchment area of that school.
>
> His existing house has been valued by a local estate agent at £36,000 and there is a mortgage outstanding to the building society of £23,000. Mr and Mrs Brown have seen a property they wish to purchase. The asking price is £43,000 and the building society has agreed in principle to a mortgage of £30,000.
>
> Mr Brown asks for your assistance with the transaction; the building society has indicated that he is allowed to have only one mortgage outstanding with them.
>
> How would you respond and why?

1   In the above question, what sort of facility does the customer appear to require:

    a   an open bridge?
    b   a closed bridge?
    c   a bridge for mortgage monies?
    d   house purchase loan?

answer

2   Leaving aside any consideration of a deposit or other contribution from the customers own resources, how much does he need to raise from the bank:

    a   £43,000?
    b   £36,000?
    c   £23,000?

d £13,000?

answer

3   If the advance is granted, for what term would you allow it to run:

a   it will be very short term — until the sale of the present house?
b   the term is unimportant since there is adequate security?
c   the term is indeterminate — the sale of the present house may take a long time?
d   long term — usually house purchase facilities run for 20/25 years.

answer

4   How will you arrange for the customer to repay the advance:

a   the proceeds of sale will be adequate to repay?
b   it is unlikely that the customer will be able to repay from the proceeds of sale alone, so the advance must be declined?
c   it is unlikely that the customer will be able to repay from the proceeds of sale alone, so there must be another source of funds to deal with any shortfall?
d   the whole amount of the advance should be repaid over a period out of income?

answer

5   On balance, what recommendation would you make on this proposition:

a   the loan should be granted without further question?
b   the loan should be declined and the customer advised to forget the project?
c   it may be possible to grant the loan on the basis of a closed bridge; otherwise decline?
d   the loan should be granted only if the customer also arranges his HPL with the bank?

answer

The next five problems relate to the facts detailed in the following question which was set in the April 1985 POB2 paper. Bearing that date in mind, read the question and then select your responses in the test.

Twenty years ago, Peter and Jane Harrison, then in their mid-twenties, found an engineering business, P J Engineering Ltd. Accounts for the company and their personal account were opened at your branch. The share capital of the company was split equally between Mr and Mrs Harrison. The balance sheet as at 31 March 1984 is shown opposite.

Over the years the bank has agreed various facilities for the company. Currently, there is a loan of £60,000 and an overdraft of £150,000 secured by a charge over the freehold factory, a debenture, giving a fixed and floating charge, and an unlimited guarantee of Peter and Jane Harrison. The balances on the accounts today are: current account £52,000 debit, loan account £55,000 debit. The balance sheet of the company as at 31 March 1984 is shown below.

In April 1984, Jane died. Peter was appointed executor and was sole beneficiary under her will. However, 6,000 shares each were transferred to their two sons, aged 20 and 18. The share valuation of £5 each has been accepted and no tax was payable.

One month ago, Peter was killed in a car accident.

Jeremy Forder and Albert Tiddler, one a well-known local solicitor and the other an accountant, have been appointed executors of Peter's will made two years ago. Under the terms of the will, following Jane's death, the two sons are joint beneficiaries.

Mr Tiddler calls to see you today and produces a provisional schedule of the assets of Peter's estate:

	£
Bank accounts	7,500
Building Society	12,500
Sundry quoted shares	15,000
Life policies	50,000
Freehold deeds (estimate)	80,000

From earlier discussions in connection with Jane's estate, Mr Tiddler expects the Inland Revenue to accept a valuation of £5 per share for P & J Engineering Ltd.

He requests an advance of £160,000 to settle the inheritance tax.

How would you respond?

P J ENGINEERING LTD
Balance Sheet as at 31 March, 1984

	£000	£000	£000
Freehold factory		240	
Other fixed assets		240	480
Debtors	270		
Stock/work-in-progress	125	395	

Tax	20	
Creditors	145	
Bank	110	
Hire Purchase	30	305

Net current assets	90
Net tangible assets	570

Financed by:

Share capital (£1 shares)	100
Capital reserve	150
Profit and loss account	320
	570

Sales	1200
Net profit	50

After charging Tax	20
Directors' remuneration	60
Depreciation	50

Rates for tax should be taken as follows:

DEATH SCALE

		(£'000)
First	64	Free
	64–85	30%
	85–116	35%
	116–148	40%
	148–185	45%
	185–232	50%
	232–285	55%
Above	285	60%

6 'Probate advances' are often requested by executors because probate will not be granted until:

a the estate's liability for Inheritance Tax has been wholly paid off.

b agreement has been reached with the Inland Revenue on a payment schedule for the estate's tax liability.

c all of the estate's creditors have been paid off.

d agreement has been reached with all of the estate's creditors on a schedule for payment of the debts.

b

answer

53

7 What is the extent of the liability of the estate for which borrowing will be required (to the nearest £1000 above):

   a £160,000?
   b £267,000?
   c £292,000?
   d £399,000?

 answer

8 What action needs to be taken in respect of the company:

   a the company should be liquidated, any surplus or deficiency being applied to the estate?
   b the executors should sell the shares as soon as possible and apply the funds to the estate?
   c the executors should make arrangements for the appointment of someone to manage the business until the sons can take it over?
   d the bank should call in the advance, in order to fix the estate's liability as guarantor?

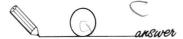 answer

9 If the advance requested is approved, how will repayment be effected?

   a realization of the liquid assets of the estate will be sufficient to clear the borrowing?
   b realization of the liquid assets will not be sufficient to clear the borrowing but if possible the excess should be repaid out of income?
   c realization of the liquid assets will not be sufficient to clear the borrowing, so the house will have to be sold to repay the remainder?
   d realization of the liquid assets will not be sufficient to clear the borrowing, so the advance should *not* be approved?

 answer

10 In order to ensure that the advance is properly repaid, would you look for:

a a guarantee from the executors?
b a guarantee from the beneficiaries?
c a charge over the assets of the estate?
d an undertaking from the executors that proceeds of liquid assets will be utilized in reduction of the debt?

 answer

Answers follow on pages 56–63. Score 2 marks for each correct answer.

Answers

1 The correct answer is **a**.

On the facts as stated, it appears that the customer is asking the bank to provide a *bridging loan* — to enable him to pay for the new house prior to receiving payment for the sale of his existing house. When the existing house is sold, the sale proceeds can be applied in reduction of the debt. If purchase and sale can be arranged to occur at the same time, no such requirement arises, of course — sale proceeds can be applied direct to the purchase of the new house (once any existing mortgage has been paid off).

There are two types of bridging loan — open (answer **a**) and closed (answer **b**) — the difference between them being the extent to which the sale of the existing house has been tied up. A closed bridge occurs only when there is a firm contract for this sale — i.e. when contracts have been exchanged on the deal. Once this situation has been reached, the purchaser cannot simply back out of the transaction and refuse to go through with the purchase. The borrower therefore knows exactly how much he expects to receive and when: this enables the bank to calculate with some accuracy how long the loan will be outstanding, how much it will cost the customer and whether he can afford it. It does *sometimes* happen that the purchaser will back out even after exchange of contracts but if he does so, he is legally responsible for any losses incurred by the seller, so the proposition should not be prejudiced by this eventuality.

In this particular case, there is no indication that the customer *has* arranged a firm sale for his house — or even that he has had any enquiries, which means that we are probably dealing with an *open bridge*. That means that there is a much greater degree of uncertainty about the deal. The customer does not really know whether he can sell at the price quoted, or how long it will take him, or even whether he can sell at all. This does not mean that the advance is completely out of the question, but it *does* mean that we must allow a greater margin for error. Somewhere in the proposition we have to find adequate resources to deal with such items as possible price reductions and interest accruals (which can be significant if the loan runs on for any long period of time).

Bridging of mortgage monies, **c**, is sometimes called for when a customer arranges a building society mortgage but has to wait some time for the funds to be made available. This can occur when the building society is experiencing a shortage of lendable funds (i.e. when it has lent up to its maximum available). It knows that before long funds will become available — owing to the repayment of existing loans and/or the deposit of 'new money' — so it agrees the mortgage, promising to let the customer draw down the funds in (perhaps) two months time. Provided that the customer can produce documentary evidence of the commitment, a bank will be quite willing to lend the required sum to 'bridge' the gap — unless it offers to take over the mortgage itself, of course. There is no evidence in this question, however, that the Building Society is not in a position to release the funds straight away.

The requirement for a bridge of mortgage monies will sometimes be combined with an ordinary bridge, which can make things a little more complicated. Although the examiner is unlikely to ask you about this possibility, it is as well to be prepared.

Just for the practice, see if you can work out what would happen if the customer in this question also had to wait three months for the new mortgage. (Here's a hint — the fact that he cannot have two mortgages at once is not *immediately* relevant in such a situation.)

Answer **d** is clearly wrong — the customer is not actually seeking a house purchase loan from the bank; he has already arranged one with his building society. Does that mean that you should not discuss the idea with him though? Certainly in real life it would be a shame to miss an opportunity for business development. In this case, though, I don't think the examiner is looking for you to consider this area.

2   The correct answer is **b**.

Let's start at the bottom of the list. If you gave **d** as your answer, you have assumed that all that the customer would need would be the difference between the *purchase price* of the new house and the *new mortgage* (£43,000 − £30,000 = £13,000). Unfortunately, that will not be enough — the question clearly tells you that he cannot have two mortgages at once, so the £30,000 is not yet available to him. It is normal practice for building societies to include such a proviso in their loan offers, so even if the question doesn't tell you that it applies, the examiner will expect you to mention it.

If you had worked out that the £30,000 new mortgage is not immediately available, you might have given **a** as your answer — the £13,000 already calculated plus £30,000, i.e. the full cost of the new house. Now — to lend that amount would certainly work, but it might not be to the customer's best advantage. The bank loan will almost certainly be at a higher rate of interest than the building society loan, so we ought to minimize the former and maximize the latter. Can we therefore find a way to release the new (larger) mortgage?

Yes we can — if we lend the customer enough to repay the existing mortgage — £23,000 — that will allow the building society to release the £30,000. However, if you gave £23,000 (c) as your answer, you're still wrong! You must have forgotten that even once he has secured the £30,000, the customer will not be able to buy the house — he is paying £43,000, so he'll need a further £13,000. Thus, the minimum that the bank could lend is £36,000 (£23,000 to lift the existing mortgage plus £13,000 shortfall on the new house).

3 The correct answer is c.

If the customer is borrowing £36,000, how will he repay? Clearly, this will be out of the proceeds of sale of the existing house — which by now is clear of the building society mortgage of course. Now — we have already established that there does not appear to be a firm contract for the sale of the house, so answer **a** cannot be right. The advance *may* be short-term if the seller is lucky; but sometimes it can be months before a buyer turns up, and to be on the safe side, this is the assumption that we should make.

Given that the advance might not be short-term, the bank may wish to take formal security — a first charge over the house to be sold is available of course, so why is answer **b** not right? For two reasons. Firstly the apparent value of the house is exactly the same as the apparent amount of the loan — £36,000. For security to be 'adequate' the bank would be looking for some margin of excess in the value. This is required to cover such possibilities as the need to reduce the price to secure a sale or the build up of interest if the loan is outstanding for any length of time.

That brings us to the second point. The bank is not just interested in the customer's capability to repay the loan; he must be able to service the borrowing while it is outstanding. The interest on £36,000 is going to come to a substantial sum each month (work it out) which the customer will have to meet on top of his commitments to his new mortgage of £30,000. His income of £700 per month will probably not be adequate to enable him to pay if off each month, so it will be added to the loan. The security will therefore become less and less 'adequate' as time goes by.

We hope you didn't give **d** as your answer, therefore. This is not the sort of proposition that we should be 'happy' to accept as a long-term loan. It would not be fair to the customer. The question that we have to resolve is whether we should accept the proposal at all, given the possibility that it may end up a long-term liability.

4 The correct answer is c.

We have just noted in the answer to question 3 that the amount of the advance appears to be the same as the expected sale price of the 'old' house — which does not leave a lot of leeway for things to go wrong! Answer **a** therefore appears to be a little optimistic and, as we have noted, a lot *could* go wrong. A reduction in price or interest over a prolonged period could well result in a significant shortfall. Furthermore, there will be considerable *costs* involved in the move which will have to be covered — legal fees, estate agents' commission, removal expenses and so on will consume (probably) well over £1000, possibly over £2000. People usually find this out of the sale proceeds, but in this case it all appears to be needed to repay the bridge.

It is starting to look as if answer **b** is correct, but let's not be too hasty or superficial in our judgements. We have not yet looked at whether the customer has any other sources of funds that could redress the balance. The information is not given in the question, so the examiner must be expecting you to discuss it. In this case it really comes down to asking whether he has any lump sum funds available and, if so, how much. It may be that he has already paid a deposit on the house to be purchased — usually 10% is required — and if so this will have to be taken into account.

It is not directly relevant to *this* question, but it is worth remembering how different the situation can be if the customer is being moved by his employers. Bank employees probably know better than anyone else how the expenses and gratuities that are usual in such situations can dramatically affect the arithmetic of the finances.

We should not dismiss out of hand the idea of the customer paying off at least *some* of the loan out of income. However, the amount available for this is likely to be small — remember that he will also have to pay his mortgage — so the amount of any shortfall that can be paid off in this way cannot be too large. Certainly it would be unreasonable to think of paying off the whole amount in this way — so answer **d** is wholly wrong.

5   The correct answer is **c**.

We have established that there is too much uncertainty *on the facts given* to grant the loan without further question — **a**. In particular, it is clear that unless the customer has substantial funds of his own to put into the project or can arrange a firm contract for the sale, there is a risk that there will be significant residual borrowing. And his level of commitments appears to be such that he will find it difficult to deal with such a balance out of income. Even if the customer can arrange to 'close' the bridge, the proposal is still 'tight' and we would need to be convinced that he could deal with the other expenses of moving — including the bank's own arrangement fee and interest of course! But answer **c** does say '*may* be possible'.

It would certainly be unfair to the customer to tell him to 'forget the project' — **b** — *without* making these checks. But if he *cannot* satisfy us that the project is viable, is that the end of it? Perhaps not. It may be that the customer could arrange an increased mortgage over the new house — provided that he can afford it — which would release adequate funds to cover the other expenses. We could even consider — if appropriate — offering HPL facilities to him ourselves. That is not the same, however, as the suggestion in **d** that the bridge should be made *conditional* on him taking up such an offer. Even so, any such proposal *must* be dependent on the bridge being 'closed' — it is just too risky otherwise.

If the bridge cannot be closed, then the customer *should* be advised to forget the project — at least in respect of this particular house. (Let's hope that he hasn't yet entered into a binding contract to buy it!) To soften the blow, there is one final practical suggestion that could be made (and the examiner likes practical suggestions). The customer wants to move into a different area — he does not particularly want *this* house. There would probably be several houses on the market at any time which would be suitable for him. Why not put his own house up for sale first? Then when he has a firm sale arranged he can go out and take his pick of the available houses that fall within his price range and catchment area.

6   The correct answer is **b**.

If you gave **a** as your answer, you are thinking along the right lines, but you have been a little too 'definite' in your opinion. It is certainly true that the *general principle* is that probate will not be granted until the tax liability has been sorted out. This causes a problem since until probate has been granted, the executors cannot realize any of the estate's assets — and until they have realized some of the assets, they will not be able to pay the tax! A bank advance can be used to break this vicious circle, and it is quite a simple thing to arrange — provided that the bank has confidence that the realization of the estate's assets will suffice to pay off the loan.

It may not be necessary, however, to pay off the whole of the tax in one go. There is a facility whereby tax on certain assets — including land and shares in unquoted companies — may be paid by 10 equal *annual* instalments. Provided that the agreement of the Revenue is obtained to their proposals, therefore, the executors may be able to secure the grant of probate without paying off the entire tax liability at once.

If you gave **d** as your answer you were probably thinking of the procedures to be followed where the executors wish to carry on a business of which the deceased was the proprietor. In such cases all the creditors of the business should agree to the proposed arrangement if the bank is to have a prior claim over the assets of the estate. However, that does not apply in this case; remember that the business in question is a limited company which in law is quite separate from the shareholders.

We hope you did not give **c** as your answer. It would be just about impossible to deal with even the simplest estate if such a strict provision was to be incorporated into the law! It is only the Inland Revenue who are accorded such preferential treatment; everyone else has to wait until *after* probate has been granted.

7   The correct answer is **a.**

This isn't a trick question, although it may look like it at first! All we are saying is — the executors have asked for £160,000; are they right? Well, let's see what the liabilities *are* first of all. Clearly there is the tax to be paid, and we shall come back to the calculation of the amount later. Is there anything else? You might think tht the borrowing on the business accounts requires to be included — if you gave **b** or **d** as your answers you must have done so. In fact, however, it does not need to be included. There is no direct liability on the estate for this amount (£107,000) since the business is a limited company, the shareholders of which have no personal responsibility for debts.

Indirectly, the estate is liable for the amount via the unlimited guarantee which was executed by the deceased. However, it is very unlikely that the bank would be looking to this guarantee since the business is clearly healthy. The balance sheet shows that even if the company was to be liquidated there would be little difficulty in paying off the debt. In all probability, therefore, the bank will realease the estate from the guarantee liability, thus leaving just the tax to deal with.

So how much will it come to? Clearly, it will be based on the value of the assets. You will note that the examiner *does not* expect you to know all the tax bands and rates (thank heavens!) since he has quoted them for you. The total value of the estate os £605,000, valuing the shares at £5 each as agreed. Calculating tax on this total at the rates shown gives a figure of £292,000 — answer **b**. This answer is wrong, but you would not have been unduly penalized for having based your answer around it in the exam *provided* that you had mentioned the need to discuss with the executors — one of whom is an accountant — the discrepancy between this and the figure which they have quoted.

The reason for the discrepancy is that the shares in the company qualify for 50% *business relief* — this means that tax will be due on only £220,000 in this respect, rather than £440,000. This will reduce the tax bill by £132,000 — not an inconsiderable sum! As we've noted, the examiner wouldn't necessarily expect you to able to spot this, though!

8 The correct answer is **c**.

No one is expecting you to spend a long time analysing the balance sheet of the business, but even a brief glance should have told you that it appears to be prospering and should have no difficulty in paying off its debts. It follows therefore that liquidation — answer **a** — is not a possibility that should be given serious consideration at this time. If the estate's executors wished to realize the value of the shares, it would be a much better idea to sell them. The value of the business as a going concern is likely to be much higher than the 'break-up' value that would be realized in a liquidation.

But there is a better option even than selling the shares. If the executors can find someone to manage the business until the sons can take it over, there is every possibility that the value of their 'investment' can be increased while *at the same time* generating dividend income for them. This is certainly the course that they should seek to follow at first.

Calling in the advance — answer **d** — was dealt with in our answer to question 6. The bank is unlikely to do this provided that the executors come up with a sensible plan for keeping the business in operation.

9 The correct answer is **b**.

A major consideration with probate advances is how repayment will be effected. Clearly, the general intention will be to repay out of the realization of some of the assets once probate has been granted. That sounds easy enough, but if the assets are not items that can be easily sold a problem will be encountered. The bank will therefore usually wish to see adequate *liquid* assets to repay the advance in a short period. In this case the liquid assets are:

Bank deposits	7,500
Building society deposits	12,500
Life policies	50,000
Shares (quoted)	15,000
	85,000

Thus, if the whole of the tax liability is paid off at once — by way of a bank loan — there will be a shortfall of £75,000. Answer **a** is not correct then! However, it would be an over-reaction to jump to answer **d** and refuse to help at all. We should first look to see whether there is any way in which we can safely help the executors. An obvious solution would be to sell the house — answer **c** — which should raise £5000 more than would be required. That would be a rather drastic step though! It would leave the sons without anywhere to live — somewhat harsh at the present moment in any case — and would thus serve to complicate the planning for their futures.

Answer **b** offers a much better route. If the income from the shares is sufficient, it may well be possible to repay the excess over a period of years without any further realizations of capital. We shall have to explore this with the executors but it may well be that the sons have income from sources outside the estate — such as payments from the company's pension scheme if there is one.

Of course, as we have previously noted, the best course of all — not on offer as an option in question 9 — would be to negotiate with the Revenue to take an immediate part payment of the tax. The balance could be paid off out of income over 10 years as above without the bank being involved in the long term. One particular advantage of this course is that the Revenue would not charge interest on the amount as yet unpaid — the Bank *would* charge interest on any outstanding borrowing of course.

10 The correct answer is **d**.

As we have already seen, the chief 'security' for the repayment of a probate loan is the adequacy of the liquid assets. One would also look for executors of known (or verifiable) trustworthiness, of course, since we shall be relying on them to repay the loan out of realizations of assets. Well — you may say — why not increase the extent to which we can rely on them by taking their personal guarantees for the borrowing — answer **a**? It simply isn't necessary; the mandate on the executors' account will specify that they assume joint and several personal liability for any borrowing. A guarantee would not make them any more liable, would it?

A charge over the assets of the estate as in **c** might sound like a reasonable idea until you come to look at the practicalities of taking it. Such a charge could not be given by the executors until probate has been granted, which is long after the funds have been lent, so there will have been a period of time during which the borrowing was unsecured. By the time the charge *can* be executed, the executors will already be starting on the realizations, so it would be somewhat unnecessary — not to say excessive.

To ensure that the executors appreciate fully the requirement that early realizations of funds are paid into the bank, however, it would be usual practice to take their *undertaking* to this effect.

That leaves answer **b** to deal with. Presumably it would be possible to ask for such a guarantee but it is not usual practice to do so. If the executors cannot arrange matters satisfactorily with the bank, it is unlikely that the beneficiaries could improve on the situation.

Score 2 marks for each correct answer. What was your score? Fill it in on the score grid.

If you scored 12 or less and are still a bit shaky on some points go back and look at the study guide again before proceeding any further.

If you are sure you really understand and are familiar with this topic now, try the 10 further questions which are on pages 224–7. Alternatively you can go on to your next topic and do all the post-tests together at the end.

Topic 3   Balance sheet analysis

Study guide

Introduction

Getting it into context

There is no longer any specific question on Balance Sheet Analysis in the Practice of Banking 2 paper, but there will be at least one (usually more than one) question in the lending section that will require an understanding of the principles and an *ability to apply them*.

That brings us immediately to the first point that you should have in mind when doing your revision — you must be able actually to do the analysis: it is not enough just to know how to do it. There is a world of difference between knowing the formula for calculating (say) the 'trading ratio' of a business and being able to do it. Your watchword here is *practice*, and more practice, and then a little bit more. Work through old exam questions. Find as many 'live' examples of real balance sheets as you can, and work through them.

Secondly, and just as importantly, you have to realize that even when you are capable of working out the various formulae and ratios that you have been taught, you still are not guaranteed to pick up the marks available from the question. This is because the marks are awarded only when you have made the relevant calculation and given an *appropriate* explanation. The word 'appropriate' is very important: it means that you must explain the precise significance of what you have discovered.

Many of the calculations could have diverse meanings in different circumstances. For example, a lengthening of the period of credit taken by a business could mean that the firm was having difficulties and was resorting to the delaying of payments to its creditors. On the other hand, it could mean that the business is in such a strong position that it has been able to persuade its suppliers that it can be trusted with longer periods of credit. Many students would set out both alternatives — this gains no marks. The examiner knows what the alternatives are: what he wants you to do is to tell him which one is correct in the given circumstances.

Finally, note also the words 'relevant calculations' — not all the ratios and so on are relevant to every question: quite the reverse. Only a few will tell you anything important about the health (or otherwise) of the business under review. The examiner does not want you to make a list of every possible calculation that can be made. What he wants you to do is to show him that you have been able to work out which ones are important. These are the ones you should quote in your answer.

Exam technique

So what does all this mean? Is there a simple way of structuring your answer? Perhaps the best advice is to stick to the following procedure (and gear your revision to help you to acomplish this):

1 Read the question carefully. Make sure you understand it and decide which calculations are most likely to be helpful.
2 Look for any 'sore thumbs'. Often the question will include one or two very important clues about what is happening to a business. If you overlook them, the question will be almost impossible to answer properly.
3 Calculate your ratios and so on. Think about which ways each one *could* be pointing. Then think about them all and try to build up a consistent pattern based on the alternatives.
4 Finally, write your answer, referring to the calculations that you have made if they have a *direct bearing* on the view that you have formed of how the firm is faring.

How to approach your revision

First, let's ask ourselves what the objectives of balance sheet analysis are. Really, we are trying to find out just three things about the business:

1 Is it healthy?
2 Can it afford to repay any proposed loans?
3 What if things went wrong?

The first two of these involve looking at the business as a *going concern* which is by far the more important viewpoing — and, unfortunately, the more difficult.

The third is the *gone concern* approach. Every banker likes to know the extent of the risks he is taking and the break-up valuation of the business is the 'bottom line' of that risk if everything went wrong. The risk can be offset by the taking of security and of course (see also Topics 4 and 5).

In general, you may anticipate that exam questions of the type we are considering will not require you to spend any significant time on a break up valuation. The examiner is trying to find out whether you can pick a 'good bet' or not — and that is done on the going concern approach.

That brings us to the question of *techniques*. How do you go about deciding whether a business is a 'good bet' or not. Well, once again we can subdivide things into three main areas. Before doing anything else, jot down a note of the points you would want to consider under the following headings and see if you can set out accurately how you would perform any necessary calculations.

1   *Balance sheet figures*
    Are there any basic facts disclosed by the 'raw' figures in the balance sheet and associated accounts? What particular figures do you think you should be looking at, and what will you be comparing them with?

2   *Ratios*
    To provide easy comparisons with previous years' performance and with other businesses it is very useful to convert the bare figures into standard ratios and percentages. List the important ratios, write down how you would calculate them and explain what they would tell you.

3   *Forecasts*
    Repayment of an advance requires a flow of cash from the borrower back to the lending bank which in turn presupposes that the borrower will have adequate inflows of funds to meet that commitment (as well as all his others). What techniques are available to test this ability to fund repayments?

Balance sheet figures

Net worth

Net work is the measure of whether on balance sheet values there would be a buffer between creditors and the loss of their money if the business were to be liquidated. It represents the amount that — on paper — would be left for the proprietors after assets had been sold and liabilities paid off. It is the amount by which sale values of assets could fall without creditors losing money.

   Often referred to as the 'proprietors' stake' you will probably wish to make this calculation for every business you are asked to look at. There are three stages of working it out:

1   Calculate 'net assets' — deduct from gross assets the amount of all liabilities other than those to proprietors.
2   Deduct fictitious and intangible assets on the basis that they would probably not realize anything.

3 Are there any directors'/proprietors' loans? If these can be postponed to the bank debt, they can also be *added in* to the calculation. An alternative way of making this calculation is to take:

Share capital
plus reserves
plus profit and loss (Profits)
or less profit and loss (losses)
and less intangible assets
plus directors' loans (if postponed).

- Look at the *trend* against previous years — a successful and well run business should show an increasing net worth.
- Look at the adequacy of the amount of the net worth. Do you want to lend more than the proprietors have at stake? Probably not.

Working capital

A business must maintain adequate liquidity to pay its current bills as they fall due.

Work it out by deducting current liabilities from current assets and again look at the trend. What could a declining trend mean?

- Over investment in fixed assets
- Overtrading
- Contraction of scale of business
- Improved utilization of current assets.

Turnover

The total amount of sales during the year, this figure is extracted from the final accounts. It is a guide to whether the business is expanding or contracting.
Look for:

- Decreasing/static turnover — the business may be in a decline.
- Sudden large increases — is an overtrading situation starting to develop?
- Increases not matched by increases in profits.

Accounting ratios

You don't need to calculate all these for every question. However, the first four are usually worthwhile.

Current ratio

Current assets : Current liabilities. Another way of expressing working capital. Look for a steady ratio of between 1½ : 1 to 2 : 1. A low/declining ratio can mean incipient illiquidity, possibly resulting from overtrading. High/increasing ratios can mean unprofitable use of available funds. Check whether turnover is falling. If so business is running down.

Credit taken

Creditors × 52/Purchases. If the purchases figure is not available the annual turnover figure will suffice.

- Is the period lengthening or shortening?
- Is it long or short for the type of business?

Long/lengthening periods can mean:

- Difficulty paying debts
- Healthy company dictating longer periods of credit
- Non-trade creditors included in figure.

Short/shortening periods can mean:

- Creditors pressing for early payment
  (lack of trust or their own problems?)
- Improving cash flow situation.

Credit given

Debtors × 52/Turnover.

- Is the period lengthening or shortening?
- Is it long/short for the type of business?
- Is it consistent with credit given?

Long/lengthening periods can mean:

- Poor credit control
- Irrecoverable debts outstanding.

Short/shortening periods can mean:

- Improved credit control
- Good business refusing to trade with poor payers.
- Cash flow problems resulting in pressure on debtors for early repayment.

Taking longer credit than given can mean:

- Liquidity problems. Debts are called in early but payments are delayed as long as possible.
- Look at the trend. If the position has been static for some years, there is probably no problem.

Stock turnover

Stock × 52/turnover = No. of weeks items kept in stock.

- Is it normal for the type of business?
- Is it rising or falling?

A falling rate of stock turnover is a danger signal

- Unsaleable items may be tying up funds
- Are sales declining? Stock should be reduced in line (if sales can't be restored).

Acid test (liquid) ratio

Liquid assets : Current liabilities. Liquid assets comprise cash, debtors and marketable securities. If you suspect liquidity problems, this will give you a further insight into the developing trend. Usually expect 1 : 1 or better.

Trading ratio

Turnover : Net worth. If there is any question of overtrading, this is a useful check. (Are you sure you know what overtrading is? Make sure before going any further.) Above 10 : 1 = danger of overtrading; above 20 : 1 = almost certainly overtrading.

Gross profit : Turnover

Gross Profit × 100/Turnover = %. Is profitability questionable? Are profits proportionate to volume of business being done? *NB*. The type of business is a vital consideration.

Net profit : Capital employed

Net profit × 100/Net worth = %. Use the *net profit before tax*, as the taxation basis may differ from year to year. This indicates whether business is adequately profitable and whether it would be attractive to further capital investment. If the figure is very low, the proprietors might be better investing their money in something else (if they can get it out).

Net profit : Gross profit

Net profit $\times$ 100/Gross profit = %. If the business does not appear to be generating adequate net profits make this check. If the figure is very low/worsening, the concern's cost control is suspect — running costs are absorbing too much of the income.

Gearing

Loan capital : Equity capital. 'Loan capital' is all long-term borrowing including fixed term loans and mortgages, as well as loan stocks. How would you deal with items such as directors' loans, and 'solid' bank overdrafts? Check it up! 'Equity capital' is net worth.

A highly geared company (where the ratio exceeds 1 : 1) is vulnerable to downturns of profits — interest on the loans has to be paid whether the business is profitable or not. Lenders are also vulnerable in respect of repayment — in a liquidation, the proprietors' stake provides a smaller buffer against loss. Check the gearing ratio if you think the proposition for long-term finance would be better answered by an injection of capital.

Forecasts

There are two principal techniques available to you to check the feasibility of certain advances to businesses.

Cash flow forecast

This is used to assess 'working capital' (overdraft) type finance. Receipts and payments of cash are forecast on a month-by-month basis so as to provide an estimate of how the bank account will fluctuate. Notional funds flows (depreciation, writing-off bad debts, etc.) are excluded. Your own bank will undoubtedly have standard forms for this purpose. Get hold of one and familiarize yourself with the items that are on it and how to complete it.

In some questions your answer will require the construction of a cash flow forecast as an integral part of it from figures supplied in the narrative. Be careful that you include all real receipts and payments, and be sure that you schedule them *in the correct month*. Really, a question that revolves around the drawing up of a cash flow should be looked on as a 'gift' — when you know what to do, producing and completing the schedule is a fairly simple mechanical exercise.

'Rule of thumb' cash flow forecasts are often all that is required if you want to check whether a request for working capital finance will be sufficient to finance a proposed increase in turnover. These can be calculated from the current assets and current liabilities on the balance sheet, as follows:

1 Look at current assets. How much will these have to be increased to permit the increase in turnover? For example,

    Stock   — probably increases in proportion.

    Debtors — may also have to increase proportionally.

    Cash   — possibly no increase required.

The difference between the projected asset levels and the present ones is the amount of finance required.

Where will this come from?

2 Look at the current liabilities. Can any of these be increased?

    Creditors — don't assume credit available from suppliers will increase in proportion.

    Bank   — the difference between the projected need to increase the current assets and the projected increase in current liabilities will have to come from the bank. This is often a vastly bigger increase than the customer expects it to be. Doubling (for example) the turnover could easily require the quadrupling of the bank overdraft!

Forecasts generally

Finally, be aware that many of the questions in the lending section of the POB 2 paper require you to forecast the viability of a proposed project such as the increasing of turnover or the introduction of a new product. Wherever possible you should do this by *forecasting* — projecting quantifiable trends into the future. Say to yourself (for example) 'If last year gross profit on turnover was 10%, turnover next year of $£x$ should produce profits of $£y$'. If the answer proves something about the proposal, write it in your answer and *quote the figures*.

Funds flow forecasts

Funds flows reconcile profits with the cash position; they can be either *forecasts* or *historic*.

Forecasts can be used to indicate the level of funds that will be available in the coming year to meet commitments such as the repayment of a loan account.

1 Calculate funds available by adding

- Retained profits — as forecast for next year.
- Taxation on profits — not payable until following year.
- Depreciation — a notional deduction from profits, not a real outflow.

2 Deduct from the total
- Current taxation — *will* be payable in coming year.
- Interest on proposed loan.

The total represents *disposable funds* available to cover capital repayments and any other additional expenditure which is contemplated.

Historic analysis can be more detailed, showing how a business has been run. The examiner is keen to focus on changes in working capital. This, for our purposes, is simply current *assets* less current *liabilities*. Current assets are debtors, stock, cash, short-term investments. Current liabilities are creditors, bank overdraft. (Do not include tax, directors' loans or HP in current liabilities even if the question shows them there.)

The following diagram sums up the position:

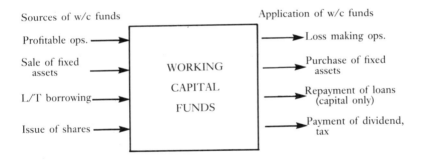

Steps in tackling examination question

1 Calculate the net working capital in each balance sheet and show the amount by which working capital has increased or decreased between the two years.
2 Show the sources of funds as in the diagram above. (Adjustments must be made to the profit figure to allow for items in the profit and loss account that will not at some stage mean a net cash income of the same amount, e.g. depreciation is a cost in P&L A/c, but it does not result in a payment of cash; profit and loss on the sale of a fixed asset — difference between its sale price and net book value at the time of sale.) Total these sources of funds.
3 Show the uses of funds, again as above. Total the items.

4 Difference between **2** and **3** must equal the change in working capital.

Wherever there is an arithmetical calculation that can be made in support of your argument or reasoning, you should make it and include it in your answer. The examiner doesn't want you to deal in broad generalizations; he wants you to decide on specifics — will *this* project succeed in *these* circumstances?

Once you feel confident about your knowledge of this topic, try to answer the 10 multiple choice questions which follow.

Multiple choice questions

1 A high *trading ratio* and a low *current ratio* point to:

   a   poor cost control.
   b   healthy expansion of business.
   c   overtrading.
   d   good stock control.

 c   *answer*

2 A *cash flow forecast* is:

   a   an undertaking of the amount of business that a firm will do in the coming year.
   b   a statement of the amount of business that the firm wishes it could do in the coming year.
   c   an exercise in futility.
   d   an indication of the levels of bank finance that will be required to finance anticipated levels of turnover.

 d   *answer*

3 A shortening period of *credit given* means:

   a   the business has liquidity problems.
   b   the business has improved its credit control procedures.
   c   the business is in a strong position and is able to dictate shorter credit periods to its customers.
   d   possibly all of the above.

 d   *answer*

4 A 'low geared' company is one which has:

   a   a high proportion of loan capital to equity capital.
   b   a high proportion of equity capital to loan capital.
   c   a high level of gross profit to equity capital.
   d   a high proportion of gross profits absorbed by costs.

 b   *answer*

5 In calculating a business's disposable funds available to make loan repayments, depreciation would be:

    a added back to the net profits figure.
    b deducted from the total funds available.
    c ignored, since it is already reflected in the net profits figure.
    d increased to allow for the new assets purchased with the loan monies.

 answer

6 If, looking at a business's balance sheet, the period of credit taken was much longer than the period of credit given, would you:

    a expect liquidation to ensue imminently?
    b expect to see a high credit balance on the current a/c?
    c check the rate of stock turnover?
    d check what the position had been the previous year?

 answer

7 The net worth of a business as disclosed by the balance sheet represents:

    a a realistic assessment of the break-up value of the business.
    b the book value of the assets.
    c the book value of the proprietors' stake in the business.
    d the amount that would go to the creditors in a liquidation.

 answer

8 Working capital represents:

    a the funds invested in a business.
    b the funds available for the day-to-day running of a business.
    c the funds available to pay suppliers.
    d the funds tied up in assets.

 answer

9 Overtrading occurs when:

    a turnover increases beyond the level that can be supported by available capital.

b turnover decreases without a corresponding decrease in assets.

c stock turnover decreases below the level normal for the type of business.

d turnover increases without a corresponding increase in the level of profits.

answer

10 A falling rate of stock turnover may mean that:

a stock levels are too low for an increasing volume of business.

b stock levels are decreasing faster than the level of sales.

c stock levels are inflated by unsaleable items.

d stock levels need to be increased.

answer

 Answers follow on pages 78–81. Score 2 marks for each correct answer.

Answers

1   The correct answer is **c**.

A high trading ratio tells you that the business is doing a lot of trade in comparison with the funds invested in it. A low current ratio tells you that the business might be having liquidity problems. Both are symptoms of overtrading, so the two together would seem to point in that direction.

The question is a good indication of the need to consider how a coherent picture can be built up from all the facts at your disposal. On its own, a low current ratio could also point to good stock control enabling the business to reduce its current assets, and a high trading ratio could (though it is less likely) just be an indicator of healthy expansion of the business.

2   The correct answer is **d**.

A cash flow forecast is no more than an indication of the volumes of business that the customer expects to do, and of all associated payments and receipts — it helps to establish the general levels of finance required, but it can never be exact. For this reason answer **a** is wrong: there can be no undertaking as to the exact amount of business that is to be done.

If the exercise is to have any value, the customer must do his best to make accurate estimates of the volumes of trade he expects. Setting out over-optimistic estimates (answer **b**) would simply confuse the picture, so that too is wrong.

Of course, it is quite possible that the reality will be nowhere near the forecast, with the result that the customer may feel that the whole thing has been an exercise in futility (**c**), but that is not the case. Tell him he wouldn't have got his overdraft without doing one — that should change his mind!

3   The correct answer is **d**.

If you gave any other answer you were not so much wrong as incomplete — you must avoid making up your mind too soon! Most of the accounting ratios can have several possible significances depending on the context. The trick is to consider several ratios together and find the one interpretation that admits of one valid meaning for each of them.

4   The correct answer is **b**.

The gearing of a company is an important consideration, since if the proportion of loan capital to equity capital is too high the business becomes vulnerable to downturns in profit — this condition is known as being 'highly geared' (answer **a**).

Answers **c** and **d** represent useful checks that can be made if you have any doubts about a business's profitability. Gross profit to equity tells you whether the proprietors are getting a reasonable return on their stake in the business. One wonders whether this *can* be too high?

Net profit as a percentage of gross profit tells you whether costs are absorbing too much of the income.

5   The correct answer is **a**.

Depreciation is a *notional* charge against profits — it is not a real outgoing, so although it is reflected in the net profits figure (**c**), it cannot be ignored. It has to be added back to show the actual funds available to the business.

To deduct the depreciation (answer **b**) would only compound the problem — it has already been deducted once when we didn't want it to be, so to do it again would be doubly unwelcome!

Answer **d** states a valid consideration so far as *accounting* practice is concerned, but it tells us nothing more about the amount of disposable funds.

6   The correct answer is **d**.

Such a discrepancy is a worry — it could be a sign of liquidity problems, but only if the position is a new or developing one. Some businesses are able to arrange such fortunate terms of trade, so before you over-react, check back to see what the situation was like in previous years. If you want an example of a business that might take much more credit than it gives, just consider how a grocery supermarket operates . . . ! Certainly in any event, answer **a** is an over-reaction.

Answer **b** is a possibility if the funds collected from debtors are simply held, pending payments of creditors, but a properly run company should be able to find a much more profitable use for the money — if only in a deposit account!

Answer **c** is simply irrelevant, I'm afraid.

7   The correct answer is **c**.

On balance sheet figures, the 'net worth' is what the proprietors could expect to get out of the business if it were to be liquidated at book values. The only adjustment to that figure would be the deduction of fictitious and intangible assets since they would probably not realize anything.

The net worth is the amount that would be available to the proprietors *after* (and only after) the creditors have been paid, so **d** is incorrect. So is **b** — the book values of the assets have of course to be reduced by the sum that would go to satisfy the liabilities.

A *realistic* assessment of the break-up value — answer **a** — would be very useful, of course. If the examiner gives you sufficient information (professional valuations, etc.), you should always calculate an 'adjusted' net worth figure. Don't forget that directors' loans can (if postponed) also be classed as part of the 'proprietors' stake'.

8   The correct answer is **b**.

Answer **c** is part of the 'working capital' of course, but not all of it — some of it is tied up in stock, work in progress, and so on. If working capital is inadequate (that is, if current assets do not exceed current liabilities by an adequate margin), the business may have a perpetual cash crisis (but it depends on the type of trade undertaken).

9   The correct answer is **a**.

Overtrading is a very dangerous situation for a business to get itself into. The inadequacy of the capital backing means that it cannot survive even the smallest setback. The only remedy (if further capital is unavailable) is to cut down on the volume of business being done, but it is extremely difficult to persuade most customers that they must turn away apparently profitable trade.

Answer **b** illustrates another situation that can distort the balance of working capital, but decreasing turnover clearly has nothing to do with overtrading. Neither has decreasing of stock turnover, so **c** must also be wrong.

Increasing turnover without increasing profits *can* happen and it can happen in association with development of an overtrading situation, but neither one is invariably a symptom of the other. A common explanation of the situation in **d** is that the business has reduced its prices too much in search of extra trade.

10   The correct answer is **c**.

It is not the only possible explanation, of course — any reason for more stock being held in relation to turnover would have the same effect — but unsaleable stock is perhaps the most 'dangerous' reason.

Answers **a** and **b** are in fact reversals of the truth — both involve the reduction of stocks in relation to sales, which would mean that remaining stocks would have to be turned over *faster* in order to keep pace.

If there is a reduction of the rate of stock turnover, it means that more stock than before (comparatively) is already being held. Generally, therefore, you would be looking for a reduction, not an increase as in **d** — *that* would only reduce the rate of turnover still further!

Score 2 marks for each correct answer. What was your score? Fill it in on the score grid.

If you scored 12 or less and are still a bit shaky on some points go back and look at the study guide again before proceeding any further.

If you are sure you really understand and are familiar with this topic now, try the 10 further questions which are on pages 227–9. Alternatively you can go on to your next topic and do all the post-tests together at the end.

Topic 4 Business lending 1

Study guide

Introduction

Putting it in context

The section A questions of POB 2, according to the syllabus, will place emphasis on the problems of personal and small company customers. Usually, you would expect to find more of the four questions set to be about business lending than to be about personal lending — so you really need to be able to deal with them effectively.

In topics 4 and 5 we're covering the whole area as concisely as we can. Topic 4 concentrates on the more *technical* aspects of such lending — the types of facility which could be granted, the types of proposition and so on. Topic 5 looks at the specific problems of different *types of business customer*. There is no real need for you to study/revise them in this order. However, we do think that you will find that you do need to study them consecutively, i.e. they form a complete whole which is not realistic to break up into separate units.

Techniques of answering

There is nothing magical about the way to solve an advances problem, whether in the exam or in real life. Most problems repeat themselves with great regularity, varying only as to the details, not the principles. Each type of problem has its own particular range of considerations which must be dealt with; given time (and a bit of experience) you should be able to work out what most of these factors are, but it is much easier to memorize a 'checklist' of questions which has been put together over the years out of the experiences of many bankers!

There is nothing wrong with this technique — it is only sensible to draw on the world's accumulated knowledge — but you do need to be able to *apply* the checklists to the problem you are addressing. Simply knowing the list is not enough!

So what *do* you do? The first step is to read the question and ask yourself what it is about. That will enable you to draw the appropriate list of prompts from up your sleeve (metaphorically!) Thus, if the question is about developing a housing estate, you will select the 'builders' advances' checklist; if it is about buying a shop, you will use the 'advances to retailers', and so on.

Of course, it could be that the question will embrace more than one topic, in which case you will need to consider two (or even more) lists of prompts at the same time! It can also happen that consideration of one list of questions will indicate the need to bring in another which was not apparent at first.

Having selected your list of 'prompts to be considered' about the type of advance that you are faced with, your next step should be to apply these questions to the facts that are at your disposal. Make sure you always bear in mind that it is not enough just to reproduce the checklist; the examiner is looking for you to make reasoned comment on the extent to which the proposal does (or does not) measure up to the principles of good lending. To quote a simple example, there is a world of difference between writing 'to increase turnover will require an increase in working capital' and writing 'this customer does not appear to have made adequate allowance for the increased working capital requirements that will result from the proposed increase in turnover'. Which do you think will gain the higher marks?

Types of propositions

The remainder of the notes in this topic are intended to provide a framework around which you can construct your 'checklists' for the types of proposition that you are likely to encounter. They do not constitute a completely comprehensive list of every 'question that has to be asked', but we have tried to mention the more important points which deserve special consideration. It goes without saying (we hope!) that you will also need to bear in mind the general principles of good lending.

Working capital advances

Overdraft facilities for businesses are one of the commonest types of proposition that you will see. As a 'rule of thumb' it is generally accepted that the proprietor's stake in the business should more or less cover the fixed and intangible assets, with working capital being provided via trade credit and borrowing. The extent to which this is true varies with the type of business conducted. The main point for you to remember is that borrowing for this purpose is normal and does not indicate any problem with the business. In fact, borrowing as and when necessary by way of overdraft allows the business to make much more efficient use of its financial resources than would be the case if it held extra cash to cover all excesses of outgoings over income.

Principal points for you to bear in mind when assessing a proposition include:

Reasons for request

It is important to check *why* a requirement for working capital finance has arisen or increased; some reasons are 'good', some may betoken problems. Don't be too hasty in your judgements, however — make sure that you have pinpointed the underlying cause. For example, borrowing to pay creditors may be 'good' if done in order to obtain discounts, 'bad' if done because they are threatening legal action!

Purchase of capital assets out of current resources may cause 'cash starvation' later. Can the situation be refinanced?

Changes in costs upset the working capital budget. If costs have risen, make sure the business can still be profitable.

Expansion of turnover will usually require more working capital. Questions on this topic are often 'concealed' within questions about the acquisition of capital assets, etc. Make sure you learn (and can apply) a simple rule of thumb to estimate the extent to which a given increase in turnover will increase the overdraft. It goes like this:

1 What increases will be caused in current *assets* — debtors, stock etc.?
2 What increases will be available in *liabilities* (other than bank) — usually just 'trade credit'.
3 Difference will consume any spare cash, and the balance must be borrowed.

Beware of the dangers of *overtrading* (see Topic 3), if expansion is too rapid (if prolonged, an uncontrollable growth of borrowing may ensue).

Amount

Cash flow forecasts are a vital tool for checking the amount of the advance. You will *always* ask the customer for one; if you can prepare one from the information provided in the question (i.e. over and above the 'rule of thumb' mentioned above), it is usually worthwhile doing so. So make sure you are familiar with the format of the forecast.

— Include only movements of *cash* (i.e. exclude notional items such as depreciation).
— Ensure that timings of funds movements are correctly calculated.

 VAT can be an especially complicating issue; there is a good explanation of how it works in Chapter 4 of Marsh & Wild, *Practice of Banking 2*, Pitman.

Management accounts

It's becoming more common for questions to be supported by 'management accounting' information and you need to be able to deal with this. Generally this information will provide you with simple information about the trading *trends* in the business; whether sales are increasing/decreasing, whether stocks are being turned over faster or slower and so on. Make sure you have grasped the concepts — and the associated ones of budgeting and so on — before you move on from this topic. Once again, the section in Marsh & Wild provides a concise analysis. It may 'encourage' you in your studies to know that the examiner has often commented on students 'inability' to get to grips with these techniques!

Purchase of capital assets

The other major type of proposition which you are likely to see concerns the purchase of capital assets. The questions that you need to have in mind are quite straightforward.

Purpose of the advance should be checked first. The main thing for you to check is whether there is any intention to increase output or produce a new product. If so, questions need to be asked about research into demand and the adequacy of working capital (which may have an impact on the overall amount, of course).

Repayment should be accomplished within the useful life of the asset. You should be able to put together simple *profit forecasts* to verify that repayment is feasible. *NB* Many banks now operate 'asset acquisition' schemes that allow for capital repayments to be deferred for some time to allow production to get into full swing.

Appraisal of capital expenditure techniques should be familiar to you — by which we mean you should already be able to *do* them. All the good textbooks show you how. The three methods are:

- *Payback* — calculates number of years taken for gross income to cover costs. It favours projects with early returns. The commonest error is forgetting to 'add back' depreciation when calculating the gross income.
- *Rate of return* — the average annual income as a percentage of the cost. In this case, the profit figure after depreciation (but before tax) *is* used. This highlights the higher yielding projects but takes no account of how long a period has to pass before profits begin to come in.
- *Discounted cash flow* — discounting income in future years deals with the 'timing' problem. If the exam question gives you a table of 'discount factors', it is a clear indication that a discounted cash flow

calculation is required — so make sure you know how to do it! The basis of the calculation again requires you to 'add back' the depreciation.

If you are unsure about doing any of these calculations, it would be a good idea to revise your old 'Accounting' notes, although in fact it is unlikely that you will actually have to complete the calculations in the exam.

Other points that should be considered relate chiefly to the way in which the finance should be obtained. *Bank* finance should be by way of loan account, but don't forget the possibilities of leasing and hire purchase (discussed in detail in Topic 9).

Finally, check the ability of the company to use the new assets (labour, expertise, etc.)!

Building or extending business premises

You can treat any questions on this subject in much the same way as any other question about capital expenditure (as above).

There are a few special points:

Purpose should be checked closely. If the new premises are required to increase turnover or — even more importantly — to introduce a new product line, extra care should be taken to verify that adequate 'market research' has been done and that increased sales are viable.

Amount should be simple to check, consisting mainly of land and building costs. Marks will usually be available for mentioning the need to consider the costs of any removals or relocations (machinery is especially costly to relocate) and to examine any contract with the builder.

Practical points to make include:

- Planning permission
- Need for increased working capital
- Adequacy of labour force/pool.

Financing a specific contract

From time to time you will see questions about financing work under a specific contract, pending payment by the contractor. Your 'checklist' of special considerations should be based around the following points:

- Capacity to complete contract. Is it proportionate to the size of the business?
- Pricings and costings; are they correct?
- Access an adequate pool of skilled labour.

Contract: should be vetted for:

- Terms. When will payments be made? Is the price fixed or should some allowance be made for rises (and falls) in line with changing costs?
- Penalty clauses and onerous conditions.
- Retentions; often 10% of amounts earned will be retained until the whole contract is completed. This can have a major effect on cash flow!

Amount requested must be checked; the bank will normally advance up to 75% of expenditure. A cash flow forecast should be requested (constructed if possible!), reflecting, amongst other things:

- Advance payments
- Retentions
- Possible delays in receipts
- Inflows/outflows in respect of other business.

NB Guarantees, bonds, etc. may increase the extent of the risk.
Security for the advance could include a charge over the contract monies. The ability of the contractor to pay is vital (even if no charge is taken); status reports are required. Borrowing on loan account eases control.

New ventures

Most of the points to be made about new ventures are quite straightforward and should be fairly easy to recall.

Background requires careful investigation since the business has no 'track record' to assess. The customer's character is therefore vital (check: acumen, experience, commitment etc.). It may also be worthwhile to make a similar judgement of any key staff.
Indicators of success can be looked for in:

- Competition. What is the level? (If none, is there a real demand?)
- Location. Does the location of the business matter (i.e. affect trade or costs)? If so, is it a good location?
- Costings and pricings. Have they been calculated properly and accurately? Estimates can be used to produce cash flow forecasts (as always!), operating budgets and cash flows.

Methods of finance: cover the usual range (overdraft, loan, HP, leasing, and so on) as appropriate for the proposal. Don't forget about the impact of:

- Grants

Try to draw up a list of the sources from which grant aid for new businesses is available. If you work in a branch, the information should be to hand — somewhere!

- Small Firms Loans Guarantee Scheme. Learn the basic 'rules' for the Scheme.
  — Loans up to £75,000
  — 2/7 year repayments
  — Possibility for capital repayments to be deferred for up to 2 years
  — Security from business also required if available
  — Guarantee covers 70% of losses.

Management Buy-outs

A very topical subject, but not one that requires much in the way of special consideration; you can treat any proposal in much the same way as you would treat any 'new venture'. If the business is being offered for sale at what is approaching a 'bargain' price don't let this sway your judgement. Your concern should be whether the former managers can make a go of it as proprietors. Consider:

- *Viability*: can the business be run profitably?
  What will change after ownership is transferred?
  Are the managers competent?
- *Amount and repayment*: make the usual moves to establish whether the amount requested is correct (working capital?) and whether income generated will be adequate for repayment to be achieved. This is particularly important as management buy-outs tend to be 'highly geared'.

Once you feel confident about your knowledge of this topic, try to answer the 10 multiple choice questions which follow.

Multiple choice questions

The first five questions are based around the following scenario which is taken from a question set in the POB 2 exam in April 1986. Bearing that date in mind, read the information and then select your responses in the test.

> John James Precision Engineering Limited has maintained a bank account with your branch since it was incorporated ten years ago. The account has worked in credit throughout its history and you have little information on file regarding the company other than that the directors are John James and Mary James.

> Mr James calls to see you today by appointment. He explains that he lives wiith his wife in a house owned by the Local Government Authority. He has just started negotiations with the Local Government Authority to purchase the house for £15,000, a price that represents a 40% discount on the market value. He had intended to approach you shortly to discuss the transaction but a problem has now occurred with his company.

> Apparently, Mr James's largest customers have indicated to him that if he wishes to retain their work he must up-grade his machinery; their orders could then increase from £3,000 to £10,000 per month. The machinery and the associated equipment is available but would cost £25,000. Mr James is uncertain what to do and has approached you today for the first time for your advice. He produces accounts for the past two years to 31 March 1984 and 31 March 1985.

> You have been given the following information regarding the company's account covering the past twelve months:

	£
Present balance	4,100 credit
Debit turnover	126,000
Range	8,700 credit to £1,200 credit
Average balance	4,300 credit

> Set out in detail your response to Mr. James, indicating any further information you may require from him.

JOHN JAMES PRECISION ENGINEERING LIMITED

Balance Sheets as at 31 March

	1984		1985	
	£	£	£	£
Fixed Assets				
Plant & machinery		9,100		8,200
Motor vehicles		4,100		3,100
		13,200		11,300

Cash/bank	6,400	5,600
Debtors	22,900	24,000
Stock/work-in-progress	4,600	4,100
	33,900	33,700
Trade creditors	9,900	8,300
Other creditors	9,400	7,400
Directors' loans	16,600	15,600
	35,900	31,300
Net current assets (liabilities)	(2,000)	2,400
Net tangible assets	£11,200	£13,700
Financed by:—		
Share capital	100	100
Profit and loss	11,100	13,600
	£11,200	£13,700
Sales	109,400	111,600
Gross profit	40,500	39,000
Net profit	2,400	2,500
After directors' remuneration	10,100	8,800
Depreciation	3,100	2,600

1 What do the 'accounts' supplied tell you about the business:

a nothing, since only 2 years' figures are supplied and this is insufficient for a proper analysis?

b since the figures supplied are at least 12 months out of date, it is not worth analysing them until the current year's figures are available?

c it is a small business which appears to be making adequate progress, although not in any way spectacular?

d there is serious cause for concern in the lack of real progress evidenced by the business?

answer

2   If the machinery as proposed is acquired, what effect will it have on the company's requirements for working capital:

   a   none: current levels of working capital are adequate for any increase in turnover?

   b   a working capital advance will be required; a limit of £10,000 should be marked?

   c   an increase in turnover may result, which might require overdraft facilities?

   d   turnover should be maintained at the current level so as to stay within present working capital levels?

 answer

3   If the machinery is acquired and used to increase turnover as suggested, what would be the likely level of annual net funds inflow out of which the costs of the acquisition could be met? Pick the nearest of:

   a   £31,000.
   b   £21,000.
   c   £11,000.
   d   £1,000.

 answer

4   What advice would you give the customer about the possibility of *not* acquiring the machinery:

   a   that he must calculate the result on profits of sales reducing to £80,000 p.a. in order to gauge its effect?

   b   that this course of action is recommended in view of the dangers of placing too much reliance on one customer?

   c   that he should follow this course and increase sales to other customers?

   d   that he should follow this course in order to avoid the increased management burden that increasing the business would bring?

 answer

5   If the decision is taken to acquire the machinery, how would you recommend that the acquisition should be financed:

a   part of the overdraft facility?
b   separate medium-term loan account?
c   factoring?
d   leasing or hire purchase?

answer

The next 5 problems relate to the facts detailed in the following question which was also set in the April 1986 Practice 2 exam. Read the scenario and work out how you would answer the question before making your own choices.

Two years ago, Henry Carr started a new company, Happy Cards Limited, involved in the wholesaling of greetings cards. You knew Mr Carr as a personal account holder and as manager of a local card wholesaler. Apparently, he had been offered a large contract (around £50,000) with a good margin of 30%.

He was able to introduce £15,000 into the new company and you agreed to an overdraft facility of £10,000, secured by a debenture giving a fixed and floating charge and a guarantee by Henry Carr of £10,000. No supporting security for the guarantee was taken, as it was expected that the account would operate in credit after two or three months, but Mr Carr owned a house valued at £40,000, mortgage outstanding £25,000.

In June 1984, two months after the Company started to trade, a credit for over £55,000 was paid into the account, bringing the balance substantially into credit. However, at Mr Carr's request you allowed the overdraft facility to continue.

In July 1985, Mr Carr called to see you bringing with him the audited accounts for the first year's trading, showing a profit of over £10,000. At this time the balance on the bank account was standing at £9,900 debit and on occasions in recent months the overdraft limit had been exceeded by up to £1,000. Mr Carr explained that he had completed a similar order to last year but for half the amount (£25,000); these funds would be received within the next two weeks. This was a busy time of year, stocking for Christmas, and he requested an increase in the limit to £15,000 for five months. You agreed but, as a condition, requested that management figures should be produced monthly. Due to pressure of work the first set of these figures was not produced until the end of November.

The bank account is currently showing small excesses above the £15,000 limit, which you had continued temporarily beyond the end of the year. A meeting has been arranged with Mr Carr for today.

Prepare your notes for that meeting, including any additional information you may require from him.

HAPPY CARDS LIMITED

Balance Sheet as at 31 March 1985

Assets	£	£
Motor vehicles	9,100	
Fixtures and fittings	5,900	
		15,000
Debtors	26,500	
Stock	25,800	
	52,300	
Liabilities		
Trade creditors	24,300	
Other creditors including tax	4,700	
Bank	8,600	
Hire purchase	4,400	
Directors' loan	10,000	
	52,000	
Net current assets		300
Net tangible assets		£15,300
Financed by:		
Share capital		5,000
Profit and loss		10,300
		£15,300
Sales		181,400
Gross profit		48,100
Net profit		10,300
Directors' remuneration		10,400
Depreciation		4,000
Tax		—

Management Figures

| | 1985 | | | 1986 | | |
| | Oct | Nov | Dec | Jan | Feb | Mar |
	£000	£000	£000	£000	£000	£000
Debtors	35.4	34.6	28.8	30.5	31.2	27.8
Stock	26.9	26.3	30.2	27.5	26.5	26.4
	62.3	60.9	59.0	58.0	57.7	54.2
Trade creditors	33.2	31.1	32.7	31.4	31.5	29.2
Preferential creditors	6.1	6.9	6.6	7.4	7.1	7.6
Bank	13.2	13.9	14.5	14.3	14.8	15.3
Hire purchase	2.1	1.7	1.4	1.0	0.6	0.2
	54.6	53.6	55.2	54.1	54.0	52.3

6 What do the accounts for the first year's trading prove to you:

    a the company has had a moderately successful first year and has built up a reasonable capital base?

    b the first year's trading has not been as successful as might have been expected?

    c by the end of the first year there was significant pressure on liquidity?

    d profit margins on sales were too low for successful trading.

answer

7 Are there any specific checks that you would make in view of the fact that around 30% of the first year's sales came from one large order:

    a no; it matters only that the overall level of sales can be maintained?

    b no, since it is clear that similar orders can continue to be obtained?

    c yes; further support requires a 'guarantee' that similar orders can continue to be maintained?

    d yes; at the very least it should be established whether the profitability of larger orders differs.

answer

8 Which of the following is disclosed by the management figures which have been provided for the last 6 months' trading:

    a current liabilities are being maintained at a relatively steady level, which indicates good management?

    b liquidity has deteriorated rapidly, which may indicate trading at a loss?

    c current assets have increased since the previous March, which is a good sign?

    d stocks have been well controlled, remaining at about the same level as at the previous March?

answer

9 The bank's security is a debenture. How would you assess its suitability as cover for the advance:

    a   the principal assets caught are the book debts which are not now providing good cover for the advance?

    b   the principal assets caught are the book debts which provide adequate cover for the advance?

    c   the principal assets caught are the stocks which provide adequate cover for the advance?

    d   the stock and the debtors together provide adequate cover for the advance?

 answer

10 What further information would you request from the customer:

    a   an aged list of debtors?

    b   a cashflow forecast?

    c   proposals as to how profitability can be increased?

    d   all of the above?

 answer

Answers follow on pages 96–105. Score 2 marks for each correct answer.

Answers

1 The correct answer is **c**.

The examiner has provided you with 2 years' figures, so he clearly expects you to make some attempt to gauge the success (or otherwise) of the business. You should appreciate right from the start, however, that you are not expected to produce a *massively detailed* analysis of performance, trends and projections! All that is required is comment on any *indications* that you find in the figures, drawing attention specifically to any particular points that might have a bearing on the proposition to invest in capital equipment.

Answer **a** is therefore quite wrong. The information which we have at our disposal should be enough for us to gain an impression of the business — at least to the extent that we should be able to tell whether the proposition is a 'starter' or not. It *is* true that with only 2 years' figures at hand it will be difficult for us to spot any long-term trends! You could mention that in your answer, but wait until after you have commented on the information that *is* at your disposal. The situation is intended to represent real life, and in real life the customer would expect some initial response from you. It's the same in the exam: the rule is, 'do what you can and *then* ask for any further information'.

Following this rule will also put paid to answer **b**! The underlying principle stated there is quite true; the figures are a year old, and before coming to any final decisions you would surely want to see at least drafts of the last 12 months' figures. But bear in mind that neither the situation nor the question require you to give a final decision yet. Things are at the exploratory stage and Mr James is looking for your initial response only. Part of your response should be to request up-to-date figures — to *confirm* that nothing has happened recently which is inconsistent with the view you have formed of past performance.

Very well; we appear to have come to the conclusion that you should perform some investigation/analysis of the figures provided, but not to do so in excessive depth.

 If you haven't done so yet, now is the time to do the calculations of the 'ratios' and so on before deciding whether the company is healthy or unhealthy — it shouldn't take you long.

If you've finished, the answer that we think you should have come up with is **c**. The company doesn't appear to be about to set the world on fire, but there is nothing really worrying in the figures. In the exam, you could make specific comment on a few points.

- *Profitability*

  Gross profit has reduced slightly from last year despite a small increase in sales. The profit margins have thus been reduced — in fact from 37% to 35%. Nothing too drastic, but the reason should be sought.

  In real terms, the increase in turnover at around 2% has not matched inflation, and this should be raised too. Possibly both factors are linked to the need for new machinery.

  Net profit has been maintained, indicating good control of overheads and other charges. Part of this is the reduction of directors' remuneration which has been made possible by a reduction in directors' loans, but overall there seems to be nothing to worry about.

- *Capital*

  The accounts show a basic 'shareholders' stake' of £13,700. However, it would also be reasonable to consider the directors' loans as 'quasi-capital' which would increase the capital base to £29,300. This appears to be quite adequate for the volume of business being done.

- *Liquidity*

  Liquidity too appears to be adequate. Don't forget that if we treat directors' loans as capital we should take them *out* of any calculations of current liability. Doing so shows the business to have a liquid surplus of £18,000, an increase of £3,400 from the previous year. The adequacy of the working capital is also confirmed by a brief look at credit taken/given; there is no evidence of any pressure there. Finally, the performance of the bank account also confirms our overall impression.

On balance, then, there is no cause for concern in the past performance of this business, and there is no need for you to undertake any more complicated analysis of the financial information.

2 The correct answer is c

The new machinery would permit the company to increase its sales to its major customer by £7,000 per month — some £84,000 per year. If sales to other customers are maintained at their present levels, this means that annual turnover will jump to nearly £200,000, an increase of around 75%. This needs careful consideration!

It would certainly have an effect on the working capital requirements of the business; presumably extra stock/work in progress would have to be financed, and the amounts due from debtors at any one time would also be increased. Some extra funds may be available to the business by way of increased credit from suppliers, but whether this plus the existing levels of cash would be sufficient to cover the increase is hard to say on the information which we have.

It would be unwise to *assume* that existing levels of working capital would suffice — answer **a**. But it would be safe to say that if turnover increases an overdraft requirement *might* result. The customer should be asked to produce a *cashflow forecast* based around his projections for the increase. This would give an indication as to whether an advance would be required, and, if so, to what level. The point is an important one to make in the exam; the customer may well have omitted to consider the working capital requirement or may have no idea of how to work it out.

It would help if we could place some sort of quantification on the possible requirement, just for guidance; and if you wanted to impress the examiner you could do some 'rule of thumb' calculations. If turnover increases by 75%, we could assume that both debtors and stock would have to increase by a similar percentage. This would create a finance requirement of about £20,000. Where could the funds be found? A further £6,000 trade credit might be possible and the company has around £4,000 cash. The remaining £10,000 would have to be borrowed, presumably from the bank. Now £10,000 was the figure mentioned in answer **b**, so why is it wrong? Chiefly because it is too definite. Our calculations must be seen as a 'rough guide' to the possible level; the estimate must be confirmed by a proper forecast before proceeding.

We don't expect that you gave answer **d** as your answer, but had you thought about it at all? The customer is asking for advice, and this is one possibility that he might consider (i.e. shedding other business). He would in fact have to shed *all* his other business to keep turnover at £120,000 p.a. This would be most unwise as it would make the business entirely dependent on the 'health' of the one and only customer. Indeed, one point that you would be expected to raise in the exam is that even if other business *is* maintained there is a heavy dependence on one customer. You should recommend a full investigation of the state of that customer's business to satisfy the bank that there aren't likely to be any problems.

3   The correct answer is **b**.

We hope that you appreciate by now that as part of your answer to this question you will certainly be expected to produce an estimated *budget* to indicate how much extra income the new machinery would produce.

This would be used to indicate how much would be available to fund the exercise. Let's run through the process by which we arrived at our figure of £21,000. We've already established that turnover could rise to £200,000 p.a. Gross profit levels last year were 35% of sales, which projected forward, would generate £70,000. What funds outflows are there to set against this? Let's assume:

General expenses	£33,000	Up by 30%
Directors' fees	£12,000	To avoid withdrawal of loans
Interest	£ 4,000	15% on £25,000

Thus a net inflow of £21,000 or thereabouts should be available to finance the project. (*NB* Everyone accepts that there will be some variation in the estimates different candidates will make, but your answer should have been somewhere in the same general area!) Don't forget that interest on any overdraft would also have to be allowed for.

In terms of *profits*, the above £21,000 would also have to be adjusted to allow for depreciation both on the new machinery and any old machinery that is retained. This is unlikely to come to more than £8,000 so the venture looks profitable. You could do an 'investment appraisal' if you wanted (and had time) but you would not be penalized if you didn't do so.

4   The correct answer is a.

This is an area where many candidates would fall down in the exam. The question set has asked for 'your response' to the proposal. All too often this is interpreted too narrowly, with candidates concentrating on analysis of the accounts and/or discussion of whether the bank should lend. Such an approach would fail to pick up the many marks that are available for general discussion of the background considerations which should be drawn to the customer's attention.

We have already mentioned the problem of placing too much reliance on one customer; 60% of sales would be going to the only one major client if the machinery were to be acquired. This would undoubtedly create an element of vulnerability both to pressure from, and outside pressures on, this customer. Another problem that such a sudden increase in turnover would create would be the extra burden on the management (Mr James!) to control the extra activity. Similarly, there is the question of whether the workforce would be able to cope or extra labour would be required. If the latter, is it available?

None of these problems is, however, justification for simply rejecting the proposals out of hand, as suggested in answers **b** and **d**. If nothing else, he *must* consider the ramifications of refusing the business. In the worst case, the annual turnover might reduce to £80,000, at which level the ability to generate profits would be in some doubt. Can he make any calculations? Can you?

In all probability, the company would not be profitable on annual turnover of £80,000, so unless sales to other customers can be increased — or new markets found — the company appears to have little choice but to respond to the request. However, the operative word in that statement is 'unless'. It may be that sales elsewhere *can* be increased, as suggested in answer **c**. The problem with answer **c** is that it suggests that you *tell* the customer to arrange such an increase. This is not reasonable! The most that you can do at this stage is to ask whether an increase is feasible. If it *is* feasible, and if the customer can satisfy you that efforts in this direction are likely to succeed, then he should be advised to consider which of the two paths he would favour — giving due consideration to the other points we have mentioned of course!

5 The correct answer is **d**.

We hope you appreciate that there is no one right answer to the question of how to finance the acquisition of this machinery. The examiner — and the customer — will be looking for you to undertake some discussion of the alternative methods of finance. That *doesn't* mean that all the suggestions that we gave you are correct, though! Let's get the 'red-herrings' out of the way.

It wouldn't be a good idea to make the funds available as part of the overdraft facility, for two reasons. Firstly, it would confuse matters and make it difficult for you to tell whether any loan element was being properly repaid and/or whether the overdraft element was operating within agreed limits. It would be much better to keep the two requirements separate from each other. Secondly, it is always best to keep working capital and longer term capital items separate from each other. If the bank is to provide finance for the machinery, a longer term facility would be indicated.

If you gave **c** as your answer, you were wide of the mark, and you will need to ensure that you understand the term 'factoring'. In the context of obtaining finance, it would normally imply an arrangement for a factoring company to take over the company's 'book debts', releasing the funds (or a proportion of them) immediately. It is not a way of obtaining finance for a capital asset!

A separate loan account — answer **b** — should certainly be considered as an option, and there would be marks available for discussing it. As a solution, however, it does suffer from some disadvantages. Principally, these are:

- *Amount*. A requirement of some £25,000 on top of a possible overdraft requirement of £10,000 is starting to become disproportionate to the directors' stake in the business.

- *Security*. The value of tangible security to set against the total finance requirement seems to be a little 'thin'.

The alternatives of hire-purchase or leasing seem more reasonable, and the bank's specialist divisions could be called in to assess which of the two would be most beneficial for the customer. This would leave the branch to provide the overdraft. Security available to cover this would be a debenture; the principal asset charged under this would be the book debts which will increase to a level already estimated at £18,000 or thereabouts. In fact, of course, it is principally the increase in debtors that has given rise to the (anticipated) increase in working capital requirement! Directors' guarantees are also indicated in the usual way.

6 The correct answer is **a**.

As in the previous scenario, you have been provided with a certain amount of historic information and your first step should be to consider what conclusions you can *briefly* draw from it. You don't have to wring every last drop of juice from it, though; just make sure you appreciate the overall picture. There isn't a lot to say with just one year's figures, but what can we glean?

Well, the capital base does appear to have been built up quite well. In addition to the share capital of £5,000, there has been £10,300 of profits retained in the business. Furthermore, the directors' loan of £10,000 can probably be classed as 'quasi-capital', so in total the base stands at £25,300, which is quite acceptable for the size of the business.

If we class the directors' loan as a capital item, we will of course have to 'de-classify' it as a current liability. By doing so we can demonstrate that as at the end of the year there was a current surplus of £10,300. If you went on to expres the liquidity position in terms of ratios you should have come up with figures of 0.63 for the 'quick' ratio and 1.25 for the 'current' ratio. Both of those are adequately healthy, and answer **c** is therefore wrong.

Checking into profitability shows that gross profit of £48,100 was generated on sales of £181,400; a return of 26½%. This is not an awe-inspiring rate of return but neither can it be said to be inadequate; it is perhaps slightly on the low side of acceptable (if you see what we mean!) Likewise, a net return of 5⅔% on sales should prove adequate for long-term growth provided that it can be maintained. Answer **d** cannot be accepted, then; it takes too pessimistic a view of profitability. There may be more to be said about profits, but we'll come back to that later.

We hope that you spotted that there wouldn't have been much point checking into *credit periods*. The completion of the one large contract right at the outset has created a situation in which the normal calculations for credit given become meaningless. In fact, that one contract may well have distorted all the figures for the year. Whenever you come across such a situation, bear in mind that it can be rewarding (illuminating!) to work out both the overall situation (e.g. gross profit percentage) and then recalculate the specific figures for both the extraordinary item and for the 'remainder'. Unfortunately, you can't do that with the *credit terms* figures, so it's hardly worth looking at them at all.

On balance, then, we can say that the company made an adequate start during its first year, which is all that can be *reasonably* expected. Perhaps it could have done better, but things weren't so bad as to justify answer **b** being accepted.

7   The correct answer is **d**.

If you have read the answer to question **6** carefully you should already know what we are getting at here. The fact that there is an 'extraordinary' item in the total for sales should alert you to the need to give it special consideration. In fact, it would be a good idea with every question to look for any 'sore thumbs' among the facts. You will often find one, and when you do, you can usually assume that the examiner wants you to do something special with it. It won't always be a sales figure, of course, it could be a large bad debt written off or a realization of a capital asset and so on. It doesn't matter what it is; what matters is that you spot it and ask yourself what difference it makes.

So what difference could this one large order make? There are really only two particular areas for consideration.

1   Is it likely to be repeated in future years on a similar basis? If it *is*, then we can use this year's performance to make simple, general projections into the future. From the facts given, it appears that orders of this size are *not* likely to be available every year; in the last 12 months there was a similar order, but only for £25,000. Answer **b** will therefore have to be rejected, as will **c**.
2   If these orders are not to continue on a regular basis, what effect will this have on profits? This question resolves itself into two components:
    • What level of business is likely to be done without these special items?
    • What level of profits is likely to be generated by the 'general' business?

    Let's look at the latter point first. In the first year of trading, we already know that the overall margin on sales was 26½%; we have also been told that the margin on the special contract was 30%. It follows, therefore, that the margin on general business was *lower* than 26½%. It does, in fact, work out at around 25%. (Can you work out how to calculate this figure? You will have to find out how much profit was generated on the 'general' business). Now, this means that if gross profit is to be maintained at the first year level, the total volume of sales will have to be increased, not just equalled — which is why answer **a** is wrong.

The evidence on the second year is not encouraging. We should be looking for monthly sales *averaging* £15,000; this level has not yet been achieved in the period since October. There could have been a high level of turnover in the first 6 months of the year, of course, but our general expectation should be for reduced profits this year. If profits are to climb in future years, we should be looking for some positive proposals to increase either margins or sales, or both.

8 The correct answer is **b**.

Looking more closely at the management figures, then, we can decide what else they can disclose to us.

It's true that current liabilities have remained at about the same level over the 6-month period, as suggested in answer **a**; but that isn't the end of the story. If we compare March this year with March last year, we find on the face of it a similar figure of £52,000 — but last year's figure includes £10,000 directors' loans which we have now decided to treat as quasi-capital. Adjusting for this means that the current liabilities then were £10,000 lower than now, so answer **a** must be wrong.

Of course, absolute figures in themselves don't tell much of a story. The increase in current liabilities may not matter if it is matched by an increase in current assets. Unfortunately, it isn't; they have increased over the year by only £2,000. Although they *have* increased, the increase isn't enough to be classed as a 'good sign' as suggested in answer **c**. Overall, then, liquidity has decreased quite markedly. A surplus of £10,000 has been reduced to £2,000. If you have calculated the 'quick' and 'current' ratios they will show clearly the deteriorating position.

(If you haven't, you should do it now. Draw up a table to show the changes to current assets and liabilities over the last 6 months.

The £8,000 reduction in working capital must have gone somewhere, of course. In the absence of any capital purchases or reductions of directors' loans, the suspicion is that the company has been trading at a loss.

But what about the stock? As suggested in answer **d**, it is more or less at the same level as at this time last year. Isn't that evidence of good control? Well, not necessarily! Stock levels should be consistent with the volume of business being done, and since turnover appears to have turned down, stock levels should have been reduced. The fact that they haven't done so should have raised some simple questions in your mind. Why haven't they been reduced? Is some of it unsaleable? Has it become obsolete? And so on; there are marks available for making these comparatively simple points which form part of the 'additional information' that you will require from the customer.

9 The correct answer is **a**.

The debenture will, of course, provide the bank with some sort of charge over all the company's assets, but the value of each category differs. In the case of Happy Cards, there are really only three items to consider.

- *Fixed assets* (vehicles and fixtures and fittings). These will probably have a value in the balance sheet of around £11,000 now. They will be subject to some HP debt and would in any case probably not realize their full valuation in a forced sale. They do not represent a major component of the security.
- *Stocks*. Currently valued at £27,800 but, as we have noted, there may be some doubt as to their saleability. It is also possible that there would be difficulties with 'Romalpa clauses', not to mention the preferential creditors of £7,600. The amount that could be realized, therefore, is somewhat doubtful.
- *Debtors*. This is the biggest single figure in the cover, but even that is subject to some doubts as there may be bad debts. Assuming that all the debts could be recovered, the value of the cover is decreasing all the time as the bank advance increases. In March last year debts covered borrowing 3 times; by this year it was down to 1.8 times, which is not really a large enough margin for the bank's comfort. Thus, considering the options available to us, the only one which can be selected is answer **a**.

10 The correct answer is **d**.

We have already noted a number of the points that the examiner would wish you to raise, and this question is intended to tie up the 'loose ends'. The point for you to remember is that the Institute is looking for you to show a *comprehensive* understanding of the difficulties. So make sure you ask all the relevant questions, however obvious they may seem to be. Let's just make sure that you know why all those three pieces of information are required.

An aged list of debtors will help us to check the point that we (briefly) raised in the last question: whether any of the debtors are likely to turn 'bad'. It is certainly the case that if we compare average monthly sale with the amount of debts outstanding, debtors appear to be allowed lengthy periods of credit. Perhaps credit control is poor. The list might enlighten us.

A cashflow forecast is vital if we are to verify the customer's statements as to the support required, especially since his 'estimates' haven't been too accurate in the past. Unlike the previous scenario, there just isn't enough information here for you to try to construct even the most basic forecast yourself, so don't try to do it!

Proposals for increasing profitability have also been touched upon. We mention the need again chiefly to emphasize the conclusion that this business is not trading profitably. If the business is to be saved, some positive actions must be taken. Until satisfactory proposals are received the advance must not be allowed to increase any further.

Score 2 marks for each correct answer. What was your score? Fill it in on the score grid.

If you scored 12 or less and are still a bit shaky on some points go back and look at the study guide again before proceeding any further.

If you are sure you really understand and are familiar with this topic now, try the 10 further questions which are on pages 230–3. Alternatively you can go on to your next topic and do all the post-tests together at the end.

Topic 5   Business lending   2

Study guide

Introduction

Putting it in context

The section A questions of POB 2, according to the syllabus, will place emphasis on the problems of personal and small company customers. Usually, you would expect to find more of the four questions set to be about business lending than to be about personal lending — so you really need to be able to deal with them effectively.

In Topics 4 and 5 we're covering the whole area as concisely as we can. Topic 4 concentrates on the more *technical* aspects of such lending — the types of facility which could be granted, the types of proposition and so on. Topic 5 looks at the specific problems of different *types of business customer*. There is no real need for you to study/revise them in this order. However, we do think that you will find that you do need to study them consecutively, i.e. they form a complete whole which is not realistic to break up into separate units.

Techniques of answering

There is nothing magical about the way to solve an advances problem, whether in the exam or in real life. Most problems repeat themselves with great regularity, varying only as to the details — not the principles. Each type of problem has its own particular range of considerations which must be dealt with; given time (and a bit of experience) you should be able to work out what most of these factors are, but it is much easier to memorize a 'checklist' of questions which has been put together over the years out of the experiences of many bankers!

There is nothing wrong with this technique — it is only sensible to draw on the world's accumulated knowledge — but you do need to be able to *apply* the checklists to the problem you are addressing. Simply knowing the list is not enough!

So what *do* you do? The first step is to read the question and ask yourself what it is about. That will enable you to draw the appropriate list of prompts from up your sleeve (metaphorically!). Thus, if the question is about developing a housing estate, you will select the 'builders' advances' checklist; if it is about buying a shop, you will use the 'advances to retailers', and so on.

Of course, it could be that the question will embrace more than one topic, in which case you will need to consider two (or even more) lists of prompts at the same time! It can also happen that consideration of one list of questions will indicate the need to bring in another which was not apparent at first.

Having selected your list of 'prompts to be considered' about the type of advance that you are faced with, your next step should be to apply these questions to the facts that are at your disposal. Make sure you always bear in mind that it is not enough just to reproduce the checklist; the examiner is looking for you to make reasoned comment on the extent to which the proposal does (or does not) measure up to the principles of good lending. To quote a simple example, there is a world of difference between writing 'to increase turnover will require an increase in working capital' and writing 'this customer does not appear to have made adequate allowance for the increased working capital requirements that will result from the proposed increase in turnover'. Which do you think will gain the higher marks?

Appreciation of the risks

In broad terms, all decisions about advances must be based on an appreciation of the risks involved: whether the prospects for repayment are good enough to allow us to lend. In Topic 5 we are going to consider the specific points — especially the risks — that you need to bear in mind when dealing with some of the commoner types of business customer. We can't cover every single type of customer, however, and it is possible that in the exam you may be confronted with a question about a type of business which you have not looked at before. If this happens, remember this concept of *risk*; before you begin to write, you should use your intelligence and judgement to put together your own 'checklist' of the problems that such a trader is likely to face.

It may give you some comfort to consider that if the examiner sets a question on a less common type of business, he will make allowance for the extra difficulty that will arise. Some years ago, for example, a question was set which dealt with the establishing of an air taxi business. Candidates were not expected to show an encyclopedaeic knowledge of the aviation business. They *were* expected to know about the general problems of setting up a new business and to be able to make some intelligent observations about the most obvious specific problems of a company which operates aeroplanes.

The rest of this Study Guide consists of some very basic checklists for common types of customer. For more detailed information we suggest you look at Perry & Fiddes, 'Lending Guides' — Waterlow.

Types of customer

Companies

This is not a Law or POB 1 paper but you should always bear in mind the basic technicalities of lending to companies. 'Easy' marks can be picked up by making appropriate comments.
Concentrate on:

Borrowing powers

Purpose of advance must conform to 'objects' clause.
Company power to borrow:

- is implied for a trading company
- may be limited by Memorandum.

Directors' power to borrow:

- cannot exceed company's powers.
- will be specified in Articles. Has table A been adopted?
  Make sure you know that:
  — Article 79 (1948 Act) contains a proviso limiting directors' powers to the nominal amount of issued share capital.
  — the 1985 Act contains no such limitation.

Power to give securities for its own borrowing is assumed for a company that can borrow:

- Directors' powers must be given in Articles.
- Directors will be interested if they have given personal security and may be precluded from voting.

Groups of companies

Lending to one company in a group on the strength of group performance can lead to problems unless group security is taken; all the assets may belong to other companies in the group.

Cross guarantees (possibly supported by other security) can resolve the problem, but bear in mind:

- Company power to give guarantees:
  — cannot be assumed
  — must have 'commercial justification', which is straightforward in

parent/subsidiary groups but less so with common directors.
- Borrowing powers of each company (and of directors) must be sufficient to cover the whole of the group borrowing.

Retailers

The specific type of question that you need to prepare for concerns the *buying* of a shop (or hairdressers, or garage, or . . .).

Background

There are some obvious (but well rewarded) basic preliminary questions.

- *Expertise* — how much expertise have the customers in the type of business?
  - How much experience do they need?
  - Are they aware of the level of commitment required and will they give it?
- *Competition* — what is the area like?
  - If setting up a new shop, why does the proprietor think it will find a market?
- *Past record* — how has the shop performed in the past?
  - Do the vendors have a *good* reason to sell?
  - Has any past success depended on the personality of the vendors?
  - Beware of glowing reports from vendor's agents who are paid to *sell* it!
- *Buyer's time* — is this a full-time or part-time venture?
  - 'Second' shops require splitting of management time. Is this feasible?

Amount

Here too you can usually pick up marks for 'touching the bases' with some straightforward observations.

- *Stock* — how is it valued and is it saleable?
- *Equipment* — is the valuation realistic?
- *Premises* — as above! If the property is rented, there should be no figure here — but beware of *rent reviews* when looking at income/expenditure.
- *Goodwill* — the price has nothing to do with the figure on the vendor's balance sheet, but is related to:
  - Annual profits: how many years will it take to recover the cost?
  - Annual turnover.
- *Working capital* — an important point often 'forgotten' by applicants. How much will they need 'in the till' to start up?

— Ask for a cash flow forecast.
— Produce your own estimate of total income/expenditure *excluding* notional charges against profits.
— Remember that the availability of trade credit can reduce the borrowing requirement, but giving credit can increase it!

Repayment
The main area for you to look at.

- *Income/expenditure* — estimate the future levels that the business is likely to have.
  — Use the previous proprietor's figures, but consider whether anything will change (wages/rents/profit levels/etc.).
  — Allow for sufficient drawings, especially if proprietors have other commitments such as a mortgage.
  — Practice! Look at past exam questions and make sure you can do them.
- *Term* should not exceed 5/7 years.

Farmers

You don't really have to know anything about farming to deal with a farmer's advance; they can be dealt with like any other business proposition. But there are a few simple 'pointers' that can make life a lot simpler.

Working capital
Advances work to differing cycles according to type of farming, e.g.

- *Arable farmers* work to an annual cycle, peaking prior to sale of harvested crops.
- *Dairy farmers* have a more regular pattern of income throughout the year.

  Budgets should be prepared for both and should reflect these cycles.

'Stock and crop' farms
'Walking the farm' periodically (at comparable times each year) gives the opportunity to assess the current *market values* of the farm's assets. (Managers of 'farming branches' familiarize themselves with the agricultural magazines.) These values may differ greatly from the balance sheet values for the same assets because they are calculated completely differently. Most banks then go on to construct a 'confidential statement' that gives a *realistic* picture of the capital base.

Repayment

The ability to repay an advance can be roughly assessed by the use of simple formulae.

- *Finance charge per acre* is calculated by adding together *all* finance charges and repayments (from whatever source of finance) and rents payable on the land, if any. Divide the total by the farm's acreage. If the result (currently) exceeds £50, repayment difficulties may be indicated.
- *Finance charges to income* is a more accurate pointer than the above which does not allow for farms producing a high yield per acre. Express the total finance charges (as above) as a percentage of the total income produced by the farm.
  — Below 15% indicates no problem.
  — 20% and above indicates that difficulties may be encountered.

Security

Unsecured loans may well be granted if the customer's stake exceeds the borrowing.

If more than 50% finance is called for, security will be required. Make sure that you know the benefits of taking:

- *Agricultural charges*, available from both tenants and owner occupiers. Similar to debenture from limited companies but doesn't give a charge over book debts.
- *Charge over Milk Marketing Board contract*, overcomes the above deficiency in the case of a dairy farmer.

Note: you will not be required to enter into detailed descriptions of *how to take* these items as security.

Builders

The specific type of proposal that you should especially prepare for concerns *speculative house building* on a plot of land owned/to be bought by the builder.

Preliminary questions

Once again there are a few preliminary questions to learn.

Profit forecast should be an early consideration. As a 'rule of thumb', the profit should equal the cost of the land.

Market for houses at the price in the location?

Mortgage availability should be considered:

— Can NHBFC guarantee be given?
— Does selling agent have finance contacts?

Ability of builder to complete project properly is vital:

— Are costings correct?
— Can he control the project?
— Is size of job consistent with past record?
— Is labour force/sub contracting contacts big enough?
— Are other projects to run concurrently?

Planning permission will be required.

— Has it been obtained?
— Are there any conditions to be observed?
— Will performance guarantees (e.g. Road Bonds) be required from the bank?

Amount

This area is normally the crux of any question set.

Customers Contribution must be adequate.

A simple formula to ensure this is to restrict lending to an amount equal to:

— 1/2 land costs, plus
— 2/3 building costs.

Remember that if the project is completed in stages, the 'costs' must be reduced in line with recoveries through house sales!

A *building programme* to develop the estate in phases will usually be required to restrict the borrowing within satisfactory limits. This is a very important concept both in real life and in the exam. Most questions are presented in a form that assumes all the houses have to be built before any are sold. You are required to restructure things so that building is phased and later houses are built using the proceeds of earlier sales.

One word of warning: don't recommend building the houses one at a time if they are to be semi-detached. It doesn't work too well! Flats, of course, have to be built in whole blocks.

A *cash flow forecast* — will confirm the feasibility of the proposal. The examiner usually will expect you to draft a simplified one. Remember to:

● include any 'upfront' costs in month 1 (e.g. laying sewers, clearing land, etc.).
● make sure the customer's contribution goes 'into the pot' right away.

A *separate loan account* Should be maintained for the project to ensure that the 'lending formula' is not exceeded:

● Funds will be drawn down in stages against architect's certificates that previous stages have been satisfactorily completed.

- Repayments will be made when houses are sold. The amount repaid per house must cover the whole advance for the house *plus* some of the profit so as to ensure total repayment before the last house is sold (preferably when the project is 3/4 complete).
- In following the formula, if the limit is reached before houses are sold, the project must be suspended until a sale is made.

Security
The bank will, of course, require a legal charge over the building land, worded so as to allow it to take over completion of the project if necessary.

Produce and goods

There have been no specific questions on this topic for some years, but advances to importers *could* be asked about in either Section A or Section B. Questions, if asked, should be straightforward and are likely to have a practical bias; but don't expect a simple POB 1 'How would you take the security' question.
Your studies should concentrate on these points:

Procedures

Make out a checklist of the basic steps to be taken. Use your textbook if necessary. Have you noted the following?

Letter of pledge usually supported by constructive delivery of goods via documents of title.
Insurance must be effected on goods at all times.
Trust receipt signed by customer is required when goods are returned to customer for sale:

- Goods taken as trustee for bank — protects in case of bankruptcy.
- Proceeds to be paid into account.

NB This process is open to fraud by the customer.
Separate loan account to be opened for ease of control. Ensure that proceeds of sale are applied to the correct account.
Stock checks are required to ensure adequacy of remaining security. This is easiest if borrowing is on separate loan account(s).

Problems

Much can be written about the problems of this type of advance, so it is a fertile soil for questions.

Value of the Security is most obvious:

- Perishable/fashion goods are not acceptable — nor anything where value fluctuates.
- Forced sales normally require (big) discounts.
- Margin between value/loan depends on circumstances.

Record keeping of stock in/out and amount of loan outstanding must be meticulous.

Fraud can be (fairly) easily perpetrated by unscrupulous customers.

NB There are some good points — advances can be self liquidating and profitable for all concerned *if* . . . !

Discounted bills

While not 'lending' in a strictly technical sense it is worthwhile ensuring at this point that you have dealt with discounted bills in your revision, since the topic is not unrelated to the previous one. While not as 'fashionable' as they once were, discounted bill facilities do still occur and could well turn up in the exam. If they do, any questions are likely to be procedural — relatively simple if you know the procedures — and related to inland bills.

Redraft this basic checklist and add further detail on why actions are taken. Make sure you can reproduce it from memory. What would happen if the bill was dishonoured?

- Check for genuine underlying transactions: 'accommodation bills' not acceptable.
- Two good names on each bill:
  - status enquiry on acceptor(s)
  - can customer pay if acceptor can't/won't?
- Examine each bill for:
  - technical regularity
  - endorsement by customer
  - acceptance.
- Credit customer with face amount — debit 'discounts' account.
- Present bill at maturity.
- Credit proceeds to 'discount' account and debit customer charges at agreed rate of discount.

Note: In the past, examiners have expressed horror at the lack of knowledge about this basic but simple area. A sound understanding could pay excellent dividends!

Franchises

Franchising operations are becoming increasingly popular, offering the chance for the small entrepreneur to set up his own business but with the benefit of a national name and national advertising.

Generally the points for consideration in a proposal for advance will be the same as for any small business — although it should be noted that franchise operations appear to have a better than average chance of success! You may well find that the franchisor will have helped the applicant with a presentation that will answer most of your questions about competition, market research, and so on.

Special points for consideration include:

- Terms of the agreement — usual clauses include an undertaking to buy supplies from franchisor and pay a royalty on sales, but check for unduly onerous terms or penalty clauses.
- Status of the franchisor is vital:
  - Membership of the British Franchise Association is a good indicator.
  - Status reports can be taken, of course.

Once you feel confident about your knowledge of this topic, try to answer the 10 multiple choice questions which follow.

Multiple choice questions

The following scenario is taken from the September 1985 Practice of Banking 2 paper. Study the information and then answer the multiple choice questions.

John and Brian Barrett are brothers, both in their mid-forties; they are directors and only shareholders of your customers J & B Barrett Builders Limited. The company has banked with you since it was incorporated four years ago; the account has operated throughout in credit. At present, the balance is showing £36,000 credit. Additionally, John and Brian Barrett have private accounts with you; recently you opened high-interest accounts for them in which they have each invested £25,000.

They call to see you today by appointment. They explain that the company is involved in high quality private building. There is a small skilled workforce, including themselves, but some specialised services are subcontracted. They are just completing a contract for a private house; a final payment of £15,000 should be made in two weeks.

The company has the opportunity to purchase a plot of land, containing two acres, for £75,000. The land includes detailed planning permission for six houses. The proposed purchaser, a friend of the Barretts, died suddenly whilst negotiating the transaction; the vendors have offered the site to the Barretts subject to their completing the purchase in three weeks' time.

Brian has been able to re-cost the development; he produces the following estimates for you:

	£
Land	75,000
Services/road	10,000
Building costs	37,500 per house
Sundry expenses	10,000
Selling price	65,000 per house

He has discussed the development with a local estate agent, who is known to you. He produces a letter from the agent agreeing the selling price of £65,000 and indicating good demand for houses at that price in the area. The project will take 12 months to complete. The brothers propose to withdrawl £20,000 each from their bank accounts to inject into the company so that the land purchase can be completed on time. They hand you the company's latest balance sheet (see below) and ask you for a maximum overdraft of £250,000 for the building work. They do not expect to use the facility fully.

Set out your reply in detail.

J & B BARRETT BUILDERS LTD

Balance Sheet as at 31 December, 1984

	£	£	£
Plant & machinery		6,000	
Motor vehicle		5,000	11,000
Cash/bank	17,000		
Debtors	3,000		
Stock/work in progress	12,000	32,000	
Creditors	13,000		
Directors	18,000	31,000	
Net current assets			1,000
Net assets			12,000
Financed by:			
Share capital			10,000
Profit & loss			2,000
			12,000
Sales			195,000
Net profit			1,000
After Depreciation			4,000
Directors remuneration			36,000

1   The customers have provided last year's company balance sheet; which of the following statements is correct:

   a the figures must be analysed in great depth in order to establish whether the company is prospering?

   b a brief examination of the figures shows that the company does not appear to have any problems and this will suffice for our purpose?

   c a brief examination of the figures shows that the company appears to be in difficulties, and the advance must be declined?

   d the figures cannot be validily analysed on their own; a series of balance sheets for at least 3 years should be requested?

answer

2   The customers have requested an advance of £250,000. What is your reaction to this figure:

   a the amount has been incorrectly calculated?

   b the amount of the request is correct?

    c   the amount of the request is correct but out of line with the size of the business?

    d   the amount of the request is out of line with the size of the business and the proposition may be considered only if it can be restructured to reduce the borrowing requirement?

answer

3   In what way could the advance be restructured to produce a more acceptable proposition:

    a   the builders could sell vacant plots of land and build houses for the purchasers with the proceeds?

    b   the amount of the borrowing requirement beyond what the bank will lend could be obtained from another lender?

    c   the builders should restrict the construction programme so that proceeds of early sales can be utilized to finance later building?

    d   an injection of further capital into the business is required?

answer

4   The principal item of security for the bank will be a charge over the land to be developed. How would you calculate the maximum amount of advance that should be allowed against it:

    a   the full purchase value of the land?

    b   the full purchase value of the land remaining unsold at any one time?

    c   the full purchase value of the land plus the cost of any building work completed?

    d   a proportion of the purchase value of the land remaining unsold plus a proportion of the cost of any building work completed on such land?

answer

5   How should the advance be made available:

    a   by overdraft on the customers' current account?

    b   debit the maximum amount available to a loan account at the start?

c by drawings from a separate loan as required, repayments to be made to the loan account as each house is sold?

d by drawings from a separate loan account as required; repayment to be made in a lump sum when the project is completed?

answer

The next five questions all relate to the facts set out below, also taken from a question set in the September 1985 Practice 2 examination.

William and Mary King have maintained a satisfactory joint account at your branch in Southtown for a number of years. You know that Mr King is about 40 years old and has been the manager of a newsagent's shop in the Southtown shopping centre for the past five years. Mr King has arranged an interview with you today. Prior to the meeting, you have been advised that the current balances on the accounts — current and deposit — total £2,300 and you are holding various building societies' passbooks showing balances totalling nearly £25,000.

At the meeting, Mr King explains that he was told by his area manager last month that his company had decided to rationalise its retail operation and all of the newsagents' shops, including Southtown, would be sold over the next year. Over the past month he has been discussing with the area manager the possibility of his purchasing the Southtown business. Following these discussions, Mr King has just submitted an offer, subject to contract, of £45,000 for the outlet.

You question Mr King on the proposed transaction and the following points emerge:

(i) the shop is leasehold. A 20 year lease was granted in December 1980 at a rent of £7,500 subject to five-yearly reviews. The landlord is a national insurance company;

(ii) the basis of the consideration was:
Fixtures/Fittings/Equipment	£10,000
Goodwill	£35,000

(iii) stock will have to be purchased at an agreed value; stock levels average three weeks' purchases;

(iv) the company's financial director has submitted figures to him covering the past three years trading (see below). These figures correspond closely to the results he has submitted to the area manager, over the period;

(v) sales for this year are averaging over £6,800 per week, excluding value added tax; Mr King is confident that he can increase sales by 20% this year;

(vi) the funds in the building society accounts represent the money (£20,000) he received from his late mother's estate three years ago;

(vii) he owns his house; similar properties have sold recently for over £30,000 and he has an endowment mortgage of £15,000, taken out when he purchased the property five years ago. Additionally, he owns an estate car, purchased 12 months ago for £5,000.

(viii) currently he earns £10,000 per annum. His wife has not worked for the past year but if they purchased the business, she would assist him in the shop and the cost of wages for other staff would be reduced to £8,000.

He asks for your assistance to purchase the business. How would you respond?

Year to 30 June	1983	1984	1985
	£	£	£
Sales	275,600	300,800	324,900
Gross Profit	49,300	55,200	61,400
Wages (Inc. Manager and National Insurance)	20,700	22,300	23,900
Rent/rates/insurance	10,200	10,600	11,000
General expenses	7,500	8,300	8,700

6 The 'goodwill' of the business is valued at £35,000. What is your opinion of this:

a it is probably about right for the levels of turnover and profits achieved?
b it is overvalued for the level of profits?
c it is overvalued for the level of turnover?
d it is impossible to judge without knowing the norms for the type of business?

answer

7 If the customers buy the business, how much per year might you reasonably expect them to have available to cover drawings, interest and repayment of loans? Make your calculation, then pick the *closest* of the following:

a £41,000.
b £32,000.
c £37,000.
d £18,000.

answer

8   What is the immediate borrowing requirement that would be
    needed to enable the customer to complete the transaction:

    a   £65,000?
    b   £43,500?
    c   £39,000?
    d   £20,000?

answer

9   If the price to be paid for stock is advanced by way of overdraft, a
    cashflow forecast should be requested from the customer to show
    how the balance of the account might be expected to fluctuate.
    Which of the following statements about its construction is correct:

    a   since the shop is fully stocked, no further stock will have to be
        paid for for the first 3 weeks?
    b   stock must be replenished every week and the full cost must be
        shown in the forecast right from the start?
    c   stock must be replenished every week but credit terms may
        enable part of the cost to be deferred?
    d   adequate allowances for depreciation and the writing off of the
        goodwill must be shown?

answer

10   What is your overall view of this proposition:

    a   the amount required is out of proportion with the customer's
        stake?
    b   repayment is not feasible within a reasonable timescale?
    c   security for the proposition is inadequate and it must be
        declined?
    d   on balance, the proposition appears to be an acceptable one?

answer

Answers follow on pages 122–30. Score 2 marks for each
correct answer.

Answers

1 The correct answer is **b**.

In a question of this nature, the examiner is really looking for you to examine the proposition; to see whether it 'stands up', whether it requires restructuring, and so on. He has provided you with a recent balance sheet solely so that you can satisfy yourself that there are no apparent immediate problems with the customers' financial affairs. A brief examination, then, is all that is required (and, indeed, all that you will have time for if you are to do justice to the rest of the question and its answer).

It follows, therefore, that answer **a** must be wrong; you do not need to undertake an 'in-depth' analysis of the figures. All that you need to do at this stage is to establish whether the business has satisfactory levels of capitalization, liquidity and profitability; and it does, as you can tell by the briefest of glances at the balance sheet and the account history. If we count the directors' loans as quasi-capital, there is a capital base of £30,000 which is adequate for the volume of business that has been undertaken in the past. The business is adequately remunerative to the proprietors, and the figures (including the bank balance) show that there is no pressure on liquidity. There is therfore no evidence to support the conclusion given in answer **c** and we hope that you did not give this as your response!

It is true that if we wished to undertake an in-depth analysis of the company's progress we would need a series of balance sheets — answer **d**. But that is not what we want, as we have said! In fact, any sort of historical analysis is unnecessary with this sort of proposition; the latest balance sheet is some 9 months out of date already and we are looking at a project which will extend several months further into the future.

It is much more important to decide whether the company can complete the proposed project than to investigate past history; and to make that decision all we really need from the balance sheet is an idea of whether the size of the project is consistent with the resources and experience of the customer — and we shall be coming to that next, in question **2**!

If we seem to be labouring the point here, it is because it is very important that you learn to recognize the situations in which a detailed analysis of the financial information provided is or is not required. In questions such as this, it clearly isn't required, but you would be surprised (or would you?) how many students spend most of their available time wringing the last possible 'ratio' out of the figures and/or demanding masses of historic information for the previous years. Don't do it; you are just losing valuable time.

2   The correct answer is **d**.

There are three questions that you should have asked yourself about the amount of this (or any other) request.

- How has it been calculated?
- Does the method of calculation reflect the requirement properly?
- Is the amount reasonable in relation to the customers' resources?

How the amount was calculated seems simple enough. The total cost of building the houses (land, services, etc.) comes to some £320,000. The brothers appear to have deducted from this the amounts of cash available to the business (including the £40,000 to be introduced) and asked to borrow the rest — with a bit added on just in case. Now, it would be wrong to say that the amount requested had been 'incorrectly calculated' — as in answer **a** — since that would be too bold a statement. There may, however, be more *appropriate* ways of calculating the requirement since the method used contains some assumptions which may not prove to be correct.

The most important of these assumptions is that all the houses will be built (and therefore all expenditure incurred) before any are sold to generate income. That may be the case, but more probably it will not, since a small building concern like this would not have the manpower to work on all 6 houses at once.

Thus answers **b** and **c** must also be wrong; it would not be fair to say that the amount of the advance *is* correct (although we might have accepted 'maybe'). Answer **c**, however, also contains a proviso which we would accept. A loan of £250,000 (if it was needed) would be much too large for a business of this size to take on, and the proposition would have to be declined unless it could be restructured in some way to reduce the borrowing requirement. And that of course is exactly what answer **d** says.

3   The correct answer is **c**.

The comments which we made about question 2 contain a clue to the solution here. The original request assumed that all the expenditure would be incurred before the project started to produce any income. But that does not need to be the case. If the houses are built one at a time — as they may well have to be — surely they will also be *sold* one at a time, thus generating income that can be used for repaying the borrowing and/or funding future expenditure.

We have already noted that a small firm like this would probably only be capable of building one house at a time. If we assume that the first house would be sold while the second was being built (and so on), that would reduce the borrowing requirement considerably, as we can demonstrate.

Before reading any further, see what calculations you can make in this respect.

Brought to basics, the borrowing requirement for building two houses would be:

		£,000
Expenditure —	Land	75
	Services	10
	House costs (2 houses)	75
	Sundries (say)	5
		165
Less	Existing credit balance	35
	Cash from directors	40
	Total loan	90

From this point on, each further house would require expenditure of £38,750 approximately (including sundries) but would be matched by sales income of £65,000 per house. Provided that sales and building were to keep in step, the borrowing requirement would reduce with each sale and could be extinguished with the fourth to be sold.

This programme keeps the finance requirement to a minimum while allowing the builders to maintain a constant workflow on the site. Only two houses will ever be 'on the go' at any one time — one in the course of construction and one in the process of being sold. Clearly, it would be possible to come up with other programmes (e.g. building two at a time) but these would all require higher levels of finance. It is important, therefore, to establish how much you think you can safely lend the customer, bearing in mind the security and the size of the business, and then put together a programme that would keep the borrowing within the limit. We shall be looking at this in question **4**.

The other suggestions for ways to finance the project are all 'red-herrings' and we trust that you managed to smell them out! Borrowing from elsewhere does nothing to ease the problem of having too high a requirement. Looking for a capital injection is unnecessary if the project can be made self financing.

The idea of selling the plots would probably not work because most buyers would want the house to be built *before* parting with their money; buyers of empty plots might arrange for someone else to do the building!

4   The correct answer is **d**.

Let's deal with each of these in turn.

Answer **a** can't be right except at the beginning. If (when!) houses are sold, the individual plots will be sold off from the original estate and the bank will release each one from its charge when it receives the proceeds of sale. Thus the value of the land remaining covered by the charge will reduce each time.

So why isn't **b** right? Well, as well as reducing the value of the security by sales, the builders will also make increases to its value by adding buildings to the remaining land. These increases can be reflected in our valuation of the security but we would be unwise to 'add on' the whole of the cost of the work done. This is because it is usually more costly to get another building contractor to finish the job off should the customer cease trading. Incidentally, it is worth noting that the power to complete the building works will be conferred on the bank by way of a special 'build-out' clause contained in the legal charge, although if a debenture has been taken from a company this may not be necessary. Other options open to the bank — such as the power of sale — are usually not of much use with the houses uncompleted!

You will have spotted by now that **c** is wrong for *two* reasons (haven't you?), so the correct answer has to be **d**. The bank will wish to limit the advance to a *proportion* of the unrecovered expenditure incurred so far.

The question therefore is, '*what* proportion'? There is no hard and fast answer to this, but most banks work to a formula similar to the following:

Land costs	50%, plus
Building costs	67%

If you apply this formula to the building programme discussed in our answer to question **3** you will see that with two houses completed, the valuation of the security would be some £91,000. Since borrowing had peaked at £90,000, the suggested programme would appear to be about right!

An important point for you to note is that using this method of valuation we can see that once the second house has been completed, there is no leeway for further funds to be advanced until the first proceeds of sale are received. It would be vital to make this clear to the customer (and to yourself!); there is always the temptation to go beyond the limit originally set if sales do not materialize as quickly as was expected. The temptation should be resisted.

After the first house has been sold, the valuation will have to be recalculated to take account of the 'recovered' costs of land and building and further costs of subsequent building. This will be used to monitor the amount outstanding on the advance when the facility is being set up. The customer should be asked to produce a detailed *cash flow forecast* for the agreed building programme; an estimated security valuation can be worked out for it — and compared to it. You will probably not have time to do this in the exam in any detail, but if you are interested (you should be), the examiner's report on this questions shows a detailed forecast.

5 The correct answer is c.

Hopefully, we can dispense with answer **b** straight away. It is quite unnecessary to lend the customer the whole of the amount required at the outset; the bulk of the funds would for some time lie idle on the current account while interest would be accruing on the full loan. Furthermore, it is better banking practice to make the customer spend his own money first before he borrows any of the Bank's. What is needed is a way of letting the customer draw the funds as and when he needs them.

Thus, some sort of overdraft facility is required. However, it is not a good idea to mark the limit on the customer's ordinary current account as suggested in answer **a**. If you were to do this, it would be difficult to tell at any one time how much was being advanced on the project since other transactions on the account would alter the balance. It is important to know how much is outstanding so that it can be compared with the value of the security, so a separate account is needed.

You will already have realized that as between options **c** and **d**, the latter is a 'non-starter'. As each house is sold, the bank will require that at least part of the proceeds should be paid into the separate loan account that will have been set up. At the very least, the repayment should cover the amount advanced for the house (and its land). Preferably it should be more so that the bank does not have to wait for the last house to be sold for the loan to be extinguished.

6 The correct answer is a.

The first step with a proposition of this kind must be to check that the customer is being asked to pay a reasonable price for the business. As suggested in answer **d**, the easiest way would be to look at how such businesses are normally valued — in practice, the advice of a local agent would probably be sought. In the exam, however, the Institute is going to expect you to make an intelligent estimate based on the facts that are available to you. Answer **d** is wrong, then.

The way to check is to compare the profits and the turnover to the asking price for goodwill. (Incidentally, it is also necessary to check whether the fixtures and fittings are worth the asking price; that does not enter the question here, but do bear in mind that you would be expected to mention it.) So let's start with the more important of the two: profits. Last year, the figures given show that the business returned £17,800 to the parent company: a steady increase on previous years. On this basis, the price represents just 2 year's profits. Surely that is not an unreasonable price to pay. Answer **b** must be wrong, therefore.

Turnover has steadily increased to nearly £325,000 last year. The 'goodwill' figure therefore represents some 5½ weeks' sales. If you didn't know, this comparison is a common way of measuring the valuation. In this case, again, it would appear to confirm that the price being asked is reasonable — answer **c** is therefore wrong too, and **a** must be correct.

7   The correct answer is **b**.

Probably *the* most important check that the bank manager can make with this sort of proposition is to work out what he thinks the income from the business will be after the changeover. This involves estimating figures from *all* items of income and expenditure. You can use what has happened in the past as a starting point, but bear in mind that most of them will change and some may be irrelevant. This is how we worked *our* estimates out.

Gross profit	£65,000

Last year, profit was 18.9% of sales of £324,900. This year we have assumed a rate of 17½%, reduced by lack of group discounts from suppliers. Sales of £375,000 have been allowed for, which is a 15% increase on last year rather than the 20% stated by the customer. Without these two adjustments, gross profits would have been estimated as £9,000 higher, thus giving a final total of £41,000 — answer **a**. From gross profit, we must deduce:

Wages	£ 8,000

As you were told it will be!

General expenses	£ 9,600
Rates	£ 3,900

Allow a 10% increase in both to be safe.

Rent	£11,200

A rent review is due in December, so an increase has to be allowed for. We have looked on the black side and put in 50%.

Total outgoings	£32,700
Balance remaining	£32,300

If you hadn't made any changes to the rent, rates and general expenses figures, the answer would have come out closer to £37,000 as shown in **c**.

The examiner expects you to make such a calculation, and show him what you have done. It is unlikely (impossible!) that your figures will match his exactly, but if you consider all the relevant facets your end result should be in the same general area. Ultimately, of course, we shall want to work out whether net income of £32,000 will be enough to cover drawings, repayments and interest, but there are a couple of other steps to be taken first.

Incidentally, answer **d** represents the net total as it would have been using last year's figures — including wages for the manager and so on. We hope you didn't choose that as your answer!

8   The correct answer is **c**.

This is quite a simple question, but an important one. We know that the customers have £25,000 to put in to the project — if you forgot that fact, you probably ended up with answer **a** — so the question to resolve is how much they will be spending. Goodwill is quoted at £35,000 and fixtures and fittings at £10,000, so the only item you have to calculate is the payment for the stock.

Stock levels average enough for 3 weeks' *sales*, so the price will be essentially 3 weeks' *purchases*. We know that sales at the moment are bring in £6,800 per week; 19% of that figure is profit, so the cost of sales must be £5,500 (£6,800 × 81%). Three weeks' purchases will come to £16,500, then. However, VAT will be payable on this amount, so the total expenditure will be £19,000. If you hadn't realized that the sales figure alone could not be used to make your calculation, you probably got answer **b**; the difference of £4,500 is quite significant.

An important point to be made about the stock is that it is always important to ensure that what is taken over is good value for money and does not contain unsaleable items. In this case there is a 'bonus' because the customer already manages the shop; he can use this position over the coming weeks to ensure that good selling lines are stocked up and poor selling ones are run down. If the business was being purchased from a stranger, the reverse would often be found to be the case.

Incidentally, answer **d** did not include the stock at all! £20,000 represents only the cost of the business and fixtures less the customers contribution. It is wrong as the answer to this question, but it may serve as the starting point for another train of thought — how are we going to structure the borrowing? It may be appropriate to lend the £20,000 for the 'capital' items by way of a loan account, and place the £19,000 required for stock on a 'working capital' overdraft facility.

9 The correct answer is c.

The examiner is not going to expect you to put together a detailed cashflow forecast in the exam (thank heavens!), but he can reasonably expect you to make some brief comments on the expected pattern of income and expenditure. It is especially important to note any particular factors that will cause fluctuations in the even flow of cash through the business.

We have already looked at the annual pattern of income and expenditure in question **7** which showed that some £32,000 p.a. is available to meet drawings plus loan repayments and interest; on a monthly basis that comes to around £2,600. Drawings of (say) £700 per month should be adequate to meet the proprietor's needs, thus reducing the amount available to £1,900. Depreciation of assets and goodwill *do not* need to be taken off because they are only a notional charge against profits; they aren't an actual outflow of cash.

Thus, *on average*, exclusive of finance costs there should be a net inflow of cash of £1,900 per month, *but* in some months it will be higher, in others lower. Income will be fairly stable, so fluctuations will centre around the timings of payments out — and the biggest single expense is of course the purchase of stock. Let's think about that.

Stock will begin to be depleted right from the first day of ownership. If adequate levels are to be maintained, therefore, it will have to be replenished right from the start too. Answer **a** is therefore wrong. The important question is as to how it will be paid for. Answer **b** is correct only if the proprietors have to pay cash on delivery for all their purchases; if they can arrange credit terms from their suppliers, however, payment for stock replenishments will be delayed for a while and this will have a significant effect on the forecast. If, for example, it was possible to arrange 1 month's credit for all their orders, the proprietors would not have to make a payment until the second month.

This would increase the net inflow of cash in month 1 by around £29,500! In future months, this amount (for purchases plus VAT) would of course come back into the budget, but always a month in arrears.

NB How have we calculated the £29,500? Can you work it out?

It is, sad to say, unlikely that the 'new' proprietors *could* manage to arrange a full month's credit on all their purchases right from the start.

But credit on half their purchases ought to be possible, and that would increase net inflows in month 1 by at least £14,000 which would reduce the overdraft to £5000 immediately — and there is no good reason why it should fluctuate back upwards thereafter, except of course if the finance costs exceed £1900 per month.

10 The correct answer is **d**.

Let's take the offered reasons for rejection in order. The amount of the initial advance at £39,000 is quite high when compared with the customers' stake, but if our assumptions about credit terms are correct this will almost immediately be reduced to £25,000. This lower figure is the one we should be looking at for the long-term advance. As it is matched exactly by the cash to be put in by the customers it is of quite acceptable proportions.

What about repayment then? We know that there is about £1,900 a month to cover finance payments. Interest at (say) 15% on £25,000 will absorb just over £300 a month, thus leaving over £1,500 to cover repayments. This amount should prove entirely adequate to fund repayment within a reasonable period. If we mark the limit on the overdraft for the first year and ask for repayment of the loan over 3–4 years that should give the customer plenty of leeway.

Security *is* less than inspiring, but with a good proposition such as this we are only seeking cover for the unexpected.

We would require:

- Charge over the lease.
- Second mortgage on the house, equity £15,000.
- Life cover on proprietors.

This should be adequate.

Score 2 marks for each correct answer. What was your score? Fill it in on the score grid.

If you scored 12 or less and are still a bit shaky on some points go back and look at the study guide again before proceeding any further.

If you are sure you really understand and are familiar with this topic now, try the 10 further questions which are on pages 233–6. Alternatively you can go on to your next topic and do all the post-tests together at the end.

Topic 6 Marketing and selling

Study guide

Introduction

Getting it into context

A fairly large chunk of the syllabus is devoted to stating the need for candidates to know about the principles of marketing and selling. While there is no doubt that these are important areas, you shouldn't get them out of proportion. In broad terms, what you need to know about can be split into two major sections:

- The basic principles of marketing and selling, and,
- Market segments and the 'targeting' of services.

Its worth pointing out right at the start that *generalized* questions about these topics haven't been set all that frequently in the past. Among other reasons this is because such questions do not have one right answer; the variety of acceptable answers that can be generated makes it very difficult for the examining team to maintain a satisfactory level of even-handedness in their marking.

Despite this, however, you will see such questions from time to time — and if you're prepared for them you could score very well. Usually these questions will take one of two forms:

- A request for you to suggest a business development programme for a branch of the bank. You'll probably be told the existing 'customer profile' and be allowed to select your own target markets.
- A request for you to suggest ways of promoting at branch level the take-up of a particular service or services. (This is less common than the previous type.)

The examiners (and the revised syllabus) are now placing greater emphasis on the development of an 'integrated' branch marketing plan, so you can expect more of this type of question to start appearing.

Most of Section B will be devoted to specific questions about the recommendation of particular services to customers, of course. In your answers to these specific questions, the examiner will be expecting you to show an understanding of the principles, so you'll still be tested on them!

Finally, bear in mind that all the questions will have a *branch* orientation. You won't be asked to design new products or put together a marketing plan for the whole bank. Questions will concentrate on how to go about selling to your branch's customers (and to potential customers). In order to do this successfully, you'll need to differentiate between the attributes of the service and its benefits — but more of that particular topic later.

Customer perception of needs

There's one useful tip that we can give you at the outset, and that is to try to put yourself in the customer's place. What does the customer perceive as the benefit that he wishes to obtain? This will sometimes require you to take note of the difference between what the customer says he wants and what he really wants. For example, a customer may come in to order a large amount of foreign currency when what she wants is a way of taking her holiday spending money out of the country. There are other systems for doing this which have additional benefits, aren't there?

To take this a little further, we can illustrate the potential problems of responding too directly to the customer's stated needs by looking at the question of late night opening. Late opening facilities were vociferously demanded by the public, but when introduced, the service has been little used! This is because the customers didn't want the late sessions as such; they wanted the potential benefit of the facility.

Try to put into words the real benefit that the customers were seeking by this demand.

Don't assume, though, that it's always wrong to provide the service specifically requested by the customer even if it isn't what is really needed. The fact that he thinks that it is what he needs has to be taken into account. Unless you can demonstrate that a different service offers a better solution to the problem, you may be stuck with providing what was asked for. That is part of the reason why banks continue to provide some late night opening facilities.

Marketing and selling

Try to keep the two items distinct in your mind. *Marketing* is the overall process and consists of several stages:

- Identifying target markets   }   Market
- Assessing the needs of that target   }   Research
- Developing products to meet the needs
- Adapting products to the changing environment

- Bringing these products to the customer.

Selling, on the other hand, is the culmination of the marketing process, of which it is therefore only a part. It is the process by which commitment to a specific service is obtained from a specific customer. The main steps are:

- Identify the need
- Identify the product/product mix
- Arouse the need (if necessary)
- Explain the benefits
- Deal with objections
  — Clarify what they are
  — Show how the product satisfies them, or
  — Rethink the product to be offered
- Close the sale.

Target markets

You'll need to understand the concept of segmenting markets into target groups for which a particular product is appropriate. This process also works in reverse, of course, in so far as understanding the needs of a particular group will enable you to identify the services that they can make use of.

Personal customers

Make sure you know the 'socio-economic groups', since the examiner often uses them to tell you about the customer profile of a branch. There should be a table or list in your textbook. The groupings (A, B, C1, etc.) are not homogeneous in their needs for banking services, however, as each one can be further divided into 'sub-sets' whose specific needs will vary. It is these sub-sets which are the market segments at which your packages of services will be targeted.

The factors which enable you to define more accurately the target markets are those which define the individual's personal circumstances, e.g.

- Age
- Marital status
- Occupation
- Income

NB As the individual's life progresses, these factors will change, and therefore so will the segment.

By and large, those people with similar characteristics will have very similar needs to one another. For practice, define half a dozen 'segments', then jot down the financial needs that you think that they will have — and the bank services that will fulfil them. Here's one group to set you going:

— Early 20s
— Married (no children)
— Buying their house
— Clerical workers/management trainees
— Salary £7,500 p.a. (each)

Business customers

Business customers can be segmented in a very similar way, but using different criteria of course! The principal factors here are:

- Level of turnover. Broad guidelines are:
  — Small   Up to £500,00 p.a.
  — Medium   Up to £5 million p.a.
  — Large   Over £5 million p.a.
- Number of staff
- Sphere of operations:
  — Service
  — Manufacturing
  — Retail

For practice again, jot down 2 or 3 different segments using variations of the above criteria. Then set out the needs such businesses would have, and the bank services that would meet these needs.

Marsh & Wild's *Practice of Banking 2* contains useful tables setting out the needs of different types of businesses (pages 155–157). You can use these to check the work you have just done.

Triggers

The idea of market segmentation can also be used in another way. If a customer comes to you with a request for access to a particular bank service, that request will tell you a lot about the market segment (or segments) that the customer comes from. Knowing what services are useful to those segments enables you to 'cross-sell' other 'products' at the same time. The initial request has thus acted as a trigger which has set off a 'chain-reaction' of selling opportunities.

You may need to find out exactly why the customer needs the initial service before you can proceed, and sometimes the trigger will just be a piece of new information about the customer — but we're sure you understand the technique.

NB This is a very important technique for the exams where the examiners expect you to take every opportunity to 'cross-sell'; indeed some questions are really about nothing else.

Try a few examples:

- Customer moving house asks for a house purchase loan. May also require:
    — Insurance (fire, personal)
    — Loans for furniture (P/L, credit card)
    — Regular bills (Budget A/c, S/O, DD)
    — What else?
- Customer informs you of birth of first child. May also need:
    — Will/executorship service
    — Savings plans for school fees, other costs
    — Investments for funds given to child
    — What else?

Now try a few on your own:

- Business customer starting a new venture may require . . . ?
- Manufacturer expanding production asks for a loan to buy the necessary machines may also require . . . ?

Now set a few scenarios of your own and work out the services that they trigger.

Once again, Wilde & Marsh's *Practice of Banking 2* contains some useful guidance — pages 152 and 158.

Competition

The examiner will expect you to show *some* knowledge of the competition that you face, from other banks and from outside organizations. You won't be expected to display a detailed knowledge of how competing services work, but you should be able to demonstrate an understanding of the range of services available and their principal benefits.

The best source of information on competitors' services — particularly personal ones — is the leaflets that they give away. You could take a tour of the local offices of banks, building societies, the Post Office, and so on, couldn't you? You never know, it might even help you at work. *Do* you know what the bank across the street is offering that might entice your customers away?

It might help you to clarify your ideas if you were to draw up a table showing who competes with the banks in each major field of activity. A possible format would be:

Area	*Bank service*	*Competition from*
Lending	Personal Loans	Finance houses
		Credit cards etc. . . .
	House purchase loan	Building societies
		Insurance Companies?

And so on . . . we aren't going to do all the work for you! Carry on with the other lending services you can think of and then move on to other spheres of activity — Deposit taking, funds transfer and so on.

Don't make your table too detailed at this stage. As we come to look at specific services in later topics you will be able to consider adding notes of ways in which the competition is inferior/superior to bank services.

Local campaigns

As we noted in the introduction, the setting up of a local business development campaign is a 'popular' question — with the examiners — and it is likely that in future there will be more questions on developing an 'integrated plan' for a branch. You need to be familiar with the overall considerations involved in preparing such a campaign.

Bank/economic climate

Not usually part of the question, in reality, the general business development programme for the bank will have an important impact. In its turn, the bank's strategy will reflect the current economic climate.

Local knowledge

Local schemes will adapt bank policy to meet local needs. Local variations from the national norms in the distribution of population and types of business will increase or decrease the importance of certain services. Questions will usually give you an indication of the percentage of local population that falls into each socio-economic group, as well as information about the types of business to be found.

Strengths and weaknesses

Bank customers will rarely represent wholly accurately the local population and business 'mix'. There will be strengths in some areas and weaknesses in others. Once again, the question will usually give you an indication of the current position.

The decision to be made is whether to play to the branch's strengths or to bolster its weaknesses. Both can be valid techniques.

Try to list the advantages (benefits) and disadvantages of pursuing either strategy.

Opportunities and threats

Always look at the data to see whether there are any:

- *Special opportunities* for business development that should be exploited (before someone else beats you to it).
- *Threats* of someone else taking your business — which must be countered, if necessary, at the expense of generating new business.

NB The formula 'Strengths, Weaknesses, Opportunities, Threats' is often referred to as a SWOT analysis.

Objectives

Finally, set specific objectives. Once you have decided who you are selling to and what you are selling, you will have gone a long way towards defining the How, When, and Where questions of the programme. Make sure that you articulate the answers, however. And set a target for how much business you expect to generate.

Marsh & Wild's *Practice of Banking 2* contains a very useful 'flow-chart' on page 167 which sets out the various steps required in putting together a branch marketing plan.

Once you feel confident about your knowledge of this topic, try to answer the 10 multiple choice questions which follow.

Multiple choice questions

1   Which of the following statements best describes the marketing process:

   a   persuading people to buy your products?
   b   designing and producing products to fit the needs of a defined market segment?
   c   selecting products from your existing range to meet the needs of a particular customer?
   d   advertising?

   answer

2   Which of the following is a description of good selling technique:

   a   persuading people that they want a product that they don't need?
   b   persuading people that they need products that they don't want?
   c   showing people that a product will satisfy a need that they have?
   d   never taking no for an answer?

   answer

3   Why do people buy a particular product in preference to another:

   a   because they believe that it will satisfy a perceived need better than the competition?
   b   because the competition is not as good?
   c   they weigh up all the available products and choose the one with the best features?
   d   because they need it?

   answer

4   What is the principal perceived benefit to the customer of borrowing from the bank by personal loan to finance the purchase and installation of fitted kitchen units:

   a   interest rates are lower than for other methods of finance?
   b   arranging the loan is quicker and easier than by other methods?

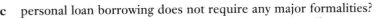

c personal loan borrowing does not require any major formalities?

d it enables the purchase of the kitchen to be completed?

answer

5 In which socio-economic group would you place a foreman in a light engineering workshop:

a B?

b C1?

c D?

d E?

answer

6 Which of the following services might be 'cross-sold' to personal (married) customers who have approached the bank for house purchase loan facilities to finance a house move:

a life assurance?

b revolving credit account?

c advice on drawing up a will?

d all of the above?

answer

7 Which of the following services might be 'cross sold' to a business which is becoming involved in exporting and has approached the bank for advice on the drawing up of documentary collections:

a forward currency contracts?

b foreign currency loans?

c export credit insurance?

d all of the above?

answer

8 In which area of activity do the banks face competition from building societies, finance houses, insurance companies and the Post Office:

a deposit taking?
b lending?
c travel facilities?
d funds transfer?

 _answer_

9 What do the letters SWOT stand for:

a strengths, weaknesses, opportunities, threats?
b sell well or tremble?
c sincerity, welcome, offers, targets?
d sell with offers and threats?

 _answer_

10 What is the best strategy for developing the business of an established branch:

a cross sell to existing customers?
b generate new business in areas where representation is already strong?
c there is no one best strategy?
d generate new business in areas where representation is already weak?

 _answer_

 Answers follow on pages 141–8. Score 2 marks for each correct answer.

Answers

1   The correct answer is **b**.

Marketing is a much misunderstood term, being confused in many people's minds with selling. If you gave **a** as your answer, you are probably one of the people who make this mistake! In fact, selling is just one component part of the wider marketing function which encompasses the whole process of designing, developing, and selling products which fit the needs of a defined market segment.

Advertising — answer **d** — is also only a part of the whole marketing process. In a marketing orientated organization, the advertising 'campaigns' will form an integral part of the overall marketing plan.

In general terms, relating all this to the banking environment, you could say that marketing is strategic and undertaken at Head Office, while selling is the tactical deployment of forces at branch level to achieve the final objective — obtaining customer commitment to use the services.

This is where answer **b** comes in. The bank's marketing department will — we hope! — have equipped the organization with a range of products. Each one of these will have been designed to fit the requirements of a particular type of customer — a 'market segment' to use the jargon. Now, any one customer will 'belong' to a number of market segments in respect of the different facets of his or her life. The job of the branch is to determine what those specific needs are and to select from the available range of services those that will satisfy them. But now we are describing the start of the selling process!

2   The correct answer is **c**.

The most basic factor for you to remember about selling is that customers don't buy services, they buy satisfaction of their needs. They don't purchase the attributes of the service, they purchase its benefits. (You'll be sick of hearing about this by the time you get to the end of the Section B topics!) It therefore follows that good selling technique ultimately revolves around showing the customers how a product will satisfy needs that they have. Now, this concept raises a number of interesting points that merit further discussion.

Firstly, it would be very bad practice to persuade people to want a product that doesn't satisfy a genuine need which they have. Disillusion and dissatsifaction with both your product and your methods will soon ensue. In other words, 'pressure selling' techniques will work — once. Organizations like banks which rely on continued return business really can't afford to use them because they spoil the customer for further approaches. Answer **a** is therefore wholly wrong.

So is answer **b**, if we take it exactly as stated. If you can persuade customers that they need a product (when they don't), they will soon come to want it, but they will just as quickly realize that they have been duped. Their reaction to this realization will be counterproductive in the end. However, you should not take this to mean that customer's needs are necessarily rational, logical, or sensible or that they know what they are! We all have needs for things that an outside observer might feel we could just as well do without — but that doesn't make the need any less real for us. If you want an example of this, think about the type of car you would buy if you had the money, and then ask yourself why you want that particular model. If your reasons are logical and sensible, they are probably just rationalizations and not the real reason at all.

Furthermore, we are all susceptible to having someone arouse in us a latent need that was there in us or in our lifestyle all the time. We just didn't know about it! This arousal can be anywhere on the spectrum from practical (you need to make a will, you know) to psychological (of course, if you want to be the envy of your neighbours ...). There is nothing immoral in the salesman attempting to do this — provided the product will accomplish what he promises.

Answer **d** brings us to the topic of objections. There are those sales people who attempt simply to steamroller over any opposition. Again, this may work in the short term, but it doesn't really pay long-term dividends. It is good selling practice, however, to use customers' objections positively. Find out from them in what way the service doesn't satisfy the customer's needs and then modify your proposals to meet the real situation. If you can't, don't proceed.

3 The correct answer is **a**.

This is probably all becoming 'old-hat' to you by now! The point that we are trying to make is that the customer is buying satisfaction of his needs *as he perceives them*. This is not the same thing as saying that we need — in any absolute sense — the things that we buy. The difference is vital, and you must understand it if you are to become successful at selling (or in the exam). Answer **d** is wrong, then, and we shall not labour this point any further.

Answer **c** is also entirely wrong, but for a different reason. If you believe that people undertake a thorough investigation of the competing products before deciding which one to buy, you credit the human race with too much logic. We just don't do that at all, except on the rarest of occasions. Once we have established that an apparently attractive product really does provide a 'worthwhile' benefit, the most that we will usually do is to undertake a brief comparison with one or two of the more readily available competitors. We certainly don't investigate all the competitors!

Well, you may be thinking, that's all very well, but why is answer **b** wrong? The fact is that it won't always be wrong; but it won't always be right either. If your product is better than that of your competitors, you have a good chance of winning in a 'straight fight'; but you might not get one. Customer inertia, lack of knowledge about alternatives, unwillingness to seek out other suppliers can all conspire against you in the battle for custom. And don't forget that in banking, one organization's services are rarely better in an operational sense than those of its opposition. In fact, it is usually difficult to find any difference between them! Such difference as there is comes from the standard of service (singular): how well the staff seek to meet the needs of the customer by recommending the right services (plural).

4   The correct answer is **d**.

This is the final lesson in our sermon on selling and marketing! By now, you will agree (in your sleep?) that customers buy *benefits* not *attributes*. The benefit of a loan is what you spend the money on (or, to be wholly and painfully accurate, it is the benefit of what you spend the money on!). The benefit is why the customer needs the service; the attributes may be what persuade him to buy your version of the service (but not necessarily so). Answers **a**, **b**, and **c** are all attributes and can be used to explain to the customer why to come to you rather than going to a finance company/money shop/competitor bank/etc. They can't be used to sell the basic idea of the service in the first place.

You might like to sharpen up your selling technique with the following exercise. Select a bank service — any one will do — and then try to specify what benefit it could confer upon a customer. Don't forget that different customers will get different benefits from the same service. Here are a few to get you started.

— The benefit of appointing the bank as my executor is knowing that my family's best interests will be protected after my death.

— The benefit of opening a revolving credit account is not worrying about unexpected bills leaving me 'broke'.

— The benefit of a medium-term savings plan is knowing that I will have money available when my children might want to go to college/university. (*PS* I am middle class!)

— The benefit of a Eurocheque card is . . . ?

5 The correct answer is **b**.

A simple memory test for you this time, useful because the examiner occasionally gives you a branch profile in which the branch's personal customer base is broken down by socio-economic grouping.

For the record, the groups are:

A   Professional (doctors, lawyers, etc.)
    Higher managerial
B   Managerial, Professional (bankers, accountants, etc.)
    Administrators
C1 Supervisors, Clerical, Junior Managerial
C2 Skilled manual workers
D   Semi-skilled and unskilled
E   Unemployed, Pensioners (State)

It is worth pointing out that none of these groupings is homogeneous in their use of bank services. It would, for instance, be quite wrong to assume that the banking needs of all group A people were identical. Even so, there is enough commonality of need for you to know the general band of services that might be appropriate for someone from this group.

6 The correct answer is **d**.

The answer to this question centres around the concept of 'trigger points'. There will be occasions when customers will indicate to you — directly or indirectly — that they have a requirement for a particular bank service. Clearly, when this occurs, you should be prepared to 'sell' the appropriate service to the customer. But, just as importantly, you should be able to seize the opportunity to offer other related services that the customer may not be aware of. The request for the original service will have triggerred the suggestion of the associated services.

Thus — to take a simple example — if a customer requests travel facilities you should start thinking about such related services as travel insurance, credit cards, Eurocheque cards, and so on. Easy, isn't it? Now clearly, every possible service will not be appropriate to each customer. Any inappropriate ones can be deleted after you have thought of them and the remainder can be put forward.

So — for a customer who is wishing to arrange an increased mortgage, what other services suggest themselves?

Life assurance will be required to cover the amount outstanding on the mortgage in any case. But will that be enough to keep the family in comfort if either spouse dies? Most of us are under-insured and the opportunity should be taken to reappraise the position. *NB* The benefit of having adequate life assurance is not having to worry about leaving your family improperly provided for.

Revolving credit accounts enable the customers to budget for the increased HPL repayments *and* allow expenditure on unforseen items. (The benefit of such an account is ... ?)

Wills are a good idea for all but the most impoverished. Houseowners often do not fully appreciate the value of the 'equity' in their houses. In the event of their untimely (or even timely!) death, will the assets be dealt with in conformity with their wishes? The intestacy laws often conflict with what a 'sensible' person would want to happen. (Benefit of a will?)

There are other services that a customer in this situation might need — but we're not going to do all the work for you. Before going on from here, see how many more you can think up.

7 The correct answer is **d**.

This is all becoming too easy for you now, isn't it? The idea of 'trigger points' is well established. Good! But don't go and forget them in the exam; make sure that you always look beyond the obvious confines of the question that has been asked.

In this particular case, you could re-state the question as 'what services are appropriate to a customer who is becoming involved in exporting for the first time?' Certainly, all those mentioned would be highly appropriate, and so would many others. We really aren't going to do the work for you in this case and tell you why — you can work it out for yourself. And while you're about it, work out what other services might be appropriate to these people.

8 The correct answer is **a**.

'Know the competition' is the point of this question. You would be surprised how many bank staff do not know what their competitors — even the other banks — are doing. Or would you? When was the last time *you* went into a branch of another bank (or building society) or the Post Office ...) to check up on the threat they pose to your business? Amazingly, the fools will be quite prepared to tell you. They'll even have leaflets about their services freely displayed and available for you to take away!

These comments may sound facetious, but our intention is serious. What we are saying is that in the exam and (most especially) in real life, you must know where your competition is coming from. In the question which we set you, each of the organizations mentioned competes with the banks in some of these fields. But there's only one in which they all do.

Let's look at each organization in turn.

Building societies will pursue the same customers for:

Lending — some types of facility only (house purchase), but the Building Societies Act is changing all that now.

Deposit taking — direct competitors for all personal deposits (at least).

Travel facilities — most will now offer a full travel service (currency, cheques, insurance, etc.)

Funds transfer — facilities are more limited than bank accounts but have been widening steadily and will do so even more after loosening of legal restrictions.

Now go on to list any other areas where banks and building societies compete.

Finance houses compete for:

Lending — well, of course, in certain areas.

Deposit taking — especially the larger amounts/longer-term funds.

Insurance companies are also in competition with you for:

Deposits — usually not directly, but funds invested in a life policy aren't available for deposit.

Lending — did you know that insurance companies are sources of loans? Well they can be, granting loans against their own policies.

The Post Office has developed a number of competing services, particularly in the areas of:

Deposit taking — Both the National Savings movement and the Girobank use the Post Office as their branches.

Funds transfer — services such as 'Transcash' are available over its counters.

9   The correct answer is **a**.

Well, if you didn't know the answer to this one, you should have been able to work it out. Most of the alternatives that we gave you were pretty silly, weren't they? Really, we just wanted to reinforce this useful business development mnemonic in your mind. Remember the formula:

Strengths. What is there about the branch and its staff that can be used positively to reinforce a business development drive?

Weaknesses. What drawbacks will we have to compensate for? This can be anything from the lack of any staff with corporate lending expertise to a front door that is difficult to open! Correct the faults that you can control; compensate in some other way for the ones that you can't.

Opportunities. Does the existing customer base or the local community offer any specific opportunities that no one else has yet exploited (or which just haven't been exploited to the full)?

Threats. Don't let the drive for new business blind you to the need to hold on to existing custom. Always check whether there are any immediate threats that have to be countered. It may sound a little calculating, but if there are no immediate threats, concentration on existing business can be relaxed a little while searching for new business.

10 The correct answer is **c**.

If there is a 'common' question about business development in general, it is the one in which the examiner sets out a 'branch profile' which tells you what penetration you have into each of the various market segments in your area. You are then asked to devise a business development programme to increase your share of the custom of a segment of your choice. There is no one right answer to these questions. The examiner expects you to be able to:

- Give reasons for selecting the segment that you settle on, and
- Set out a strategy appropriate to that segment, given your existing level of business from it.

In broad terms there are three basic courses that you can take, all of which have their value.

'Cross selling' to existing customers involves the promotion of further services. This has the great advantage of binding those customers closer to you and increasing the level of 'inertia' for them. They become less and less inclined to look elsewhere for financial services. It is an exercise that is simple to undertake: much research into potential 'sales areas' can be undertaken simply by looking through the branch internal files. It has the disadvantage that it does nothing to broaden your customer base.

Generating new business in areas where the branch is already strong is not quite the same thing. It involves looking for new customers from among a segment where penetration is already deep. The branch will — presumably — have built up a reputation among existing customers from this segment and this can be capitalized upon. The major disadvantage of the technique is that it concentrates business into a restricted area and creates vulnerability to 'hiccups' in that market.

Generating new business in weaker areas avoids this danger. In many ways it is the most laudable course of action in that it should bring greater overall stability to the branch's profit base. Unfortunately, it is usually the hardest course to follow — without a 'reputation', an existing core of customers, or simple sources of information, all that you have in your favour is your capacity for hard work! Given these difficulties, it is wise to check the profitability of business from the segment under consideration. Some areas offer only low profits, in which case the result may not be worth the effort!

Score 2 marks for each correct answer. What was your score? Fill it in on the score grid.

If you scored 12 or less and are still a bit shaky on some points go back and look at the study guide again before proceeding any further.

If you are sure you really understand and are familiar with this topic now, try the 10 further questions which are on pages 236–8. Alternatively you can go on to your next topic and do all the post-tests together at the end.

Topic 7 Personal services

Study guide

Introduction

Getting it into context

Questions on personal (as opposed to business) services form an important part of the range available to the examiner. On average you should expect to see at least one in each paper amongst the three which are set in Section B. Don't forget that you have to answer two from the three; a good knowledge of the subject is therefore vital!

The buying process: Keep at the forefront of your mind the idea that selling is really about *buying*: people buy the things that they need or want, and selling revolves around demonstrating to them that they need what you are offering. There are three stages to the process:

- Identify the need
- Identify the service that fills the need
- Convince the customer that your product fills the need.

In the exam you will have to demonstrate that you have covered these three areas properly.

Identifying the need

You'll usually find that a question will present you with the background information about a customer's circumstances. From this information you must decide which bank service or services would be useful. The question itself will sometimes give you a clue as to whether your recommendations should be singular or plural. If it asks you to recommend 'the service', you know you are looking for only one. If it refers to 'services', however, you know that one is not enough! Sadly, though, the examiner is often not so obliging, couching the question in more general terms such as asking for 'advice that you would give this customer'. The best counsel that we can give you with such questions is always to look for a *range* of services that the customer can benefit from.

   This raises two important points. Firstly, your answer shouldn't be confined to comments about a service which the customer appears to think that he (or she) wants. Your task as an adviser is to advise, so do so.

Looking at the circumstances you should tell (inform?) the customer both what is needed and what difficulties you foresee. A typical example of this occurred in the September 1985 paper in which one question really required candidates to question a customer's intention to take early retirement and not just to advise him on what to do afterwards.

That brings us neatly to the second point: don't confine yourself solely to giving advice about financial needs. Bank services cover a much broader area and you should take every opportunity to broaden the discussions with the customers. In the question that we have just mentioned, for instance, candidates who merely wrote about how to deal with the lump sum payment to be received missed an awful lot of marks. They could have gone on to write about pensions, wills, insurance, mortgages, and so on. They could even have discussed how to replace the customer's company car!

Identifying the service

Always remember that different segments of the market have different needs. These needs are met by different products or a different selection of products. Looked at from the opposite perspective, this means that each bank service meets the needs of certain types of customer. It is therefore always worthwhile to ensure that you know which type or types of customer could use the particular service you are studying.

You must know the *attributes* of the bank's personal services in some detail, since the examiner will expect you to give practical advice on how the systems operate. Your own bank's internal publications (procedures manuals, services guides, leaflets, etc.) will provide you with plenty of detail — if you read them! But there are two important warnings to bear in mind:

- *Don't* use your own bank's jargon for describing the operating details. The examiner may not understand what you are getting at — and the customers almost certainly wouldn't!
- *Don't* assume that your own bank's services are exactly the same operationally as those of the other banks, or that other banks can't match your services.

The cost of the service to the customer is an important part of the operating procedure. You should always know the *basis* on which the charge for a particular service is calculated. It would, however, be unreasonable to expect you to memorize the specific rates at which charges are levied, and this is not looked for. Even so, if you can give a general indication of the usual level, you wouldn't go unrewarded.

Convincing the customer

The main thing that you have to be able to do in this connection is explain the *benefit* that will accrue from the service that you are recommending. This is not the same thing as the *attribute*: the one springs from the other. Thus, for example, you could say that a car has a 3 litre, 16 valve engine with fuel injection and turbo boost (attributes), or you could say that it goes very fast (benefit). The customer buys the benefit, because it is the benefit that satisfies his needs. And now we have come full circle!

The examiner will expect you to demonstrate an ability to explain the benefit of a service to the customer, i.e. to what extent the service satisfies the customer's needs as you have identified them. This, of course, is in addition to explaining the method by which the service satisfies the need. A useful technique for expressing the two is use of the phrase: 'which means that . . . ' to link the attribute (first) to the benefit (second).

Have a go at this yourself: try to express our example of the car in this format.

Specific services

The rest of this topic is devoted to giving the basic details of the range of services commonly available to personal customers. We recommend that you use it as a guide to base your studies around, bearing in mind that we can't tell you everything in such a short space. At the risk of repeating ourselves, let us remind you that as you look at each service you should ensure that you know:

- How it operates (attributes)
- What it achieves (benefits)
- Who it is appropriate for (type of customer).

Money transmission services

People at your level shouldn't need much reminding about the various ways in which banks can transfer funds from A to B for customers; cheques, standing orders, direct debits, and so on are probably all too familiar to you in your normal working day. In any case, direct questioning on these topics is rare. Even so, if you are unsure about the workings of a particular service, you should check it up before moving on.

It may be worthwile giving some thought to the more 'modern' innovations in the field, although most of these refer more specifically to business customers.

EFTPOS: Keep abreast of developments in the 'point of sale' use of plastic cards. Not much has been introduced yet, but that doesn't preclude questions.

ATMs: The 'hole in the wall' machines continue to provide a growing range of services. Being in effect computer terminals placed at the disposal of the customers, there is theoretically no limit (except our own restrictions) on the account-related services to which they can give access. Links between the various banks' systems are producing competing networks of machines. Make sure you know the up-to-date position.

Automated credit payments: Several banks now offer an automated system for making payments of varying amounts through BACs to specified beneficiaries. All payment details are held on computer file except the amount, and payment is made when advised by the customer. It's probably not much used by private customers — yet!

Deposits

Facilities for savers can be categorized in several ways, including:

- Ease of access
- Level of interest
- Large or small amount
- Lump sum/regular savings scheme.

For your purposes, what you need to know is:

- Which permutations of the above characteristics are available? (Some aren't, e.g. high interest, small amount, easy access!)
- What are the operating terms of the types of account offered for each available permutation?
- Which type (or types) of customer could validly make use of each of these accounts?

It would be a good idea to construct your own 'table' of the deposit facilities available, listing how they match up under each of these headings. Don't forget to include details of facilities offered by the 'opposition'. Don't confine yourself to banks, either: building societies, finance houses, and local authorities — to name just a few — offer competing savings media, especially for the larger sums.

It is also important for you keep yourself up to date with new developments, which your textbook may not reflect. This is true of all services, of course, but especially so far deposit facilities where the competition with outside organizations has become intense, encouraging rapid development. A typical example of these 'new' services is the interest-bearing current account which has been introduced to attract (retain?) the liquid reserves of the better off. These accounts generally require a minimum balance to be maintained and restrict the 'money transfer' facility to some extent by setting a minimum amount for each transaction and/or restricting the numbe of transactions within a given period.

Advances

You might think, since Section A of the paper is almost wholly devoted to questions about lending, that you can forget about it in Section B. Well, in a sense you're right: you won't be asked to pronounce judgement on a specific lending proposal, and it is unlikely that you will be required specifically to recommend the best method for financing a particular project. Your ability to do these things *will* have been tested in Section A. It is possible, however, that you will have to write about the benefits and attributes of different types of credit facility. This will usually come about in one of two types of question:

- One in which advice on borrowing facilities forms part of the overall financial strategy being proposed for a customer.
- One in which you are required to produce some sort of analysis of the whole range of facilities appropriate to a particular customer (e.g. a talk to a factory's workforce about the benefits of a bank account).

You will have to ensure that you know both the attributes and the benefits of these services (won't you?). It would be a good idea to produce another table — similar to the one you have already drawn up for deposits. You can refer to Topic 2 if you want, where there is some of the basic information that you will require.

Once again, try to make sure that your information is up to date, as these facilities too have been the subject of some changes in recent years. Some particular points to pay attention to include:

- *Revolving credit accounts*: These are rapidly replacing the more old-fashioned budget accounts. Here are a few questions for you.
  — How do the 'rules' of the two types differ?
  — What are the benefits to the customer of the change?
  — Is a revolving credit account in competition with or comp-lementary to the use of a credit card?
- *Credit cards* are an important source of finance for the 'average

man' these days, and various 'gold card' schemes are available to attract the more affluent/higher income earners. Make sure that you know the parameters of these new schemes. Know also the advantages to the retailers of taking credit cards.

- *House purchase loans* are a comparatively recent addition to the banks armories and may not be properly represented in your textbook unless it is an up-to-date one. Bank and building society schemes are very much the same as each other, so the competition is direct. Make sure that you know the differences between endowment mortgages and capital repayment mortgages.

Executor and trustee services

The most important service under this heading is of course the executorship facility.

Draw up a checklist of the benefits of writing a will naming the bank as executor. Does it look something like this?

- *Clarity of wishes*: A will should be drawn up by anyone with any valuable assets, since the rules of intestacy may well not reflect the preferable division of the estates (they almost certainly won't).
- *Professional advice*: When drawing up a will, advice is valuable to ensure that the intentions are properly expressed. Advice on related topics such as insurance can be given at the same time.
- *Tax effective planning* for lifetime gifts will help to reduce the impact of Inheritance Tax on the value of the estate. You should have an idea of the 'tax bands' but the examiner won't expect you to know the actual rates of tax for all bands. See also Topic 2.
- *Continuity*; the bank will (one hopes!) remain in operation as long as it takes to execute the will. Individuals may die (or predecease the testator).
- *Expertise*: at dealing with the complexities and the minutiae of estate distribution.
- *Impartiality*: the bank will be able to advise on the best way to make certain provisions and will then carry them out punctiliously without being influenced by personalities (or those unfortunate family squabbles that so often arise at these times).
- *Investment management*: can be provided if the will creates a trust which requires this.
- *Fees* will be payable for the executorship only when the bank begins to act, although there may be charges for some of the specialist

'setting up' advice. The fee is proportional with the size of the estate, and you ought to know the current general levels of charges.

Trusts (whether created by wills or 'inter vivos' settlements) are usually handled by the same section of the bank and are subject to similar considerations. The usual format is the *discretionary trust* which allows the trustee to exercise great discretion in the management of the assets. The professionalism (etc.) of the bank's staff becomes a major benefit.

Taxation advice

There are two types of taxation with which personal customers most frequently need advice.

- Inheritance tax (already mentioned)
- Income tax (including capital gains tax).

The market is, of course, largely restricted to the 'better off' of our customers. Advice may be given on an ad hoc basis for specific problems or on a long-term basis with the bank having full agency powers from the customer to deal with the taxman on all relevant matters.

Make out your own checklist of the benefits of using the bank's tax advisory service. We aren't going to help you this time! Questions solely on tax advice and tax planning are difficult to set, so you'll usually find that mention of them will be called for in combination with other appropriate services. Why not make a list now of the ones that might go to make up a 'package'?

Investment management

Another service for the 'better off'. Most banks now offer a portfolio management service for those having investments of (usually) £20,000 or more. Usually the arrangement will be to allow the bank's investment managers considerable discretion in the handling of the portfolio.

Benefits of the service include:

- Profession judgement of actions to be taken
- Freedom from administrative details
- Strategy tailored to customer's needs.

Do you know the basis on which the charge for this service will be levied? Find out if you don't!

Don't forget that many banks offer their own Unit Trust service which is useful to all investors — but especially the 'small' ones — in providing a form of investment management at low cost. Banks which don't operate their own Unit Trusts will nevertheless be able to direct a customer's funds into the market when appropriate.

You should already be familiar with the attributes and benefits of Unit Trusts from your Investment studies, but just to be on the safe side, why not make a list of them — now!

Make sure that you understand how 'share exchange schemes' work to allow investors to convert existing holdings of stocks and shares into a Unit Trust investment.

Once you feel confident about your knowledge of this topic, try to answer the 10 multiple choice questions which follow.

Multiple choice questions

1 The following list represents criteria that define the operating conditions of certain types of bank accounts:

   (i)   Ease of access to funds deposited
   (ii)   Level of interest rates on credit balances
   (iii) Rules as to minimum and maximum permitted balances
   (iv)   Lump sum deposits or regular contributions.

   Which combination of them should be considered by a customer looking for a 'home' for savings:

   a   (i), (ii), (iii) and (iv)?
   b   (i), (ii) and (iii)?
   c   (i), (iii) and (iv)?
   d   (ii), (iii) and (iv)?

answer

2 A customer informs you that she has just won a small dividend on the football pools. After paying off her borrowings (car loan), and buying a few luxuries, she will have some £5,000 left, which she wishes to save. She has £750 as a liquid reserve in a Building Society Ordinary Share account which provides an adequate cushion against possible emergencies. What would you recommend that she should do with the £5,000:

   a   deposit it in the existing account with the building society?
   b   place it in a 'high interest deposit account'?
   c   open a 'money fund' account?
   d   purchase stocks and shares?

answer

3 Consider the following list of bank services:

   (i)   Executorship/will advice
   (ii)   Tax planning
   (iii) Pension advice
   (iv)   Insurance advice
   (v)   'Gold cards'

Which of them would you include in a 'portfolio' of services to be recommended to a couple (mid 20s) who have just inherited a considerable sum of money which they are going to use wholly in the purchase of a grocery business:

a (ii), (iii), (iv) and (v)?
b (i), (iii), (iv) and (v)?
c (i), (ii), (iv) and (v)?
d (i), (ii), (iii) and (iv)?

 *answer*

4 Which of the following methods of payment would be most appropriate for the remittance of a customer's annual fire insurance premium on his house:

a standing order?
b direct debit?
c SWIFT?
d CHAPS?

 *answer*

5 In what way does a revolving credit account differ from a budget account:

a the balance of a budget account has to be paid off every month?
b a budget account is funded by a regular monthly credit of an agreed amount?
c a budget account may be used only to meet specified outgoings?
d a budget account may be used to make unexpected payments?

 *answer*

6 Listed below are five benefits of various forms of money transfer services.

(i)   Safety from loss through theft
(ii) Convenience of use
(iii) Disincentive to overspending
(iv) Aid to annual budgeting
(v)   Widespread acceptability

Which of them attach to the use of a credit card:

a (i), (ii), (iii) and (iv)?
b (ii), (iii), (iv) and (v)?
c (i), (ii), (iv) and (v)?
d (i), (iii), (iv) and (v)?

answer

7 When the bank is appointed executor of a customer's will, when do the fees for this particular service first become payable:

a when the will is drawn up?
b when the bank accepts the appointment?
c when the bank begins to act as executor?
d when the estate is fully wound up?

answer

8 Study the following list of investments:

(i) Land
(ii) Commercial property
(iii) Shares in public companies
(iv) 'Gilt-edged' securities
(v) Money market deposits
(vi) Commodity futures

Which of them would be acceptable as part of a portfolio of investments managed by the bank on behalf of a customer:

a (iii), (iv) and (v)?
b (i), (ii) and (iii)?
c (ii), (iii) and (vi)?
d (iv), (v) and (vi)?

answer

9 What is the principal specific benefit of a Unit Trust to the small investor:

a reduced dealing costs?
b Regular 'dividends'?
c units are simple to purchase?

159

d diversified underlying portfolio?

10 What is the current threshold beyond which Inheritance Tax is payable on assets transferred on death:
   a £90,000?
   b £140,000?
   c £220,000?
   d £330,000?

Answers follow on pages 161–6. Score 2 marks for each correct answer.

Answers

1 The correct answer is **a**.

An easy one for you to start with! The four "characteristics" that we have quoted represent the principal variables in the operation of a deposit account. When looking for a safe (and appropriate) home for savings, an individual should consider how important each of these is to him. He can thus construct a 'profile' which will effectively define the account that he wants. Thus the characteristics are all-important.

In practice, of course, there are several profiles that are not available, owing to the interdependence of these criteria. For instance, it is not possible to combine high interest with easy withdrawals in an account with no minimum balance requirement. (If you know differently, please write in and let us know!) The customer must therefore decide which of these characteristics is most important and satisfy *that* requirement before moving on to the next most important, and so on. This is where you come in as the customer's adviser: the customer's wishes and the customer's needs are not necessarily one and the same. It is up to you to point out any unrecognized needs. This is beneficial for the customer and (one hopes) good business for the bank.

As regards deposit facilities, you will usually find that for most customers the two principal determinants of the type of account required are:

- *Ease of access.* It is vital to ensure adequate liquid resources are held before entering into any longer term arrangement.
- *Amount.* If available funds are limited, then the 'large amount' schemes are automatically excluded.

2 The correct answer is **b**.

Here we have a simple practical application of the considerations noted in the previous question. This customer has apparently adequate funds set aside in liquid form to meet any immediate needs and can therefore afford to commit these funds for a somewhat longer period, in order to gain access to a higher rate of return. For this reason (if no other!) we shouldn't be advising her to put the money in a building society account; she can do better than that, so answer **a** is wrong.

We are presuming that the customer would be prepared to trade some liquidity for a higher interest rate on the funds, and, given the amount, this is possible using a 'high interest' deposit account which all the banks operate (under varying names). In general, the operating features of this account are that interest is paid at a somewhat higher rate than 7 day deposit rate, provided that a minimum balance is maintained (usually around £2,000) and greater notice of withdrawal (1 month?) is given. This arrangement would suit her admirably. She could achieve even higher rates of return by surrendering even more liquidity; fixed term deposits or 'moneymarket' types requiring greater notice of withdrawal would be available to her, but they shouldn't be recommended. She cannot afford to take the risk of being unable to release her capital reasonably quickly should she need it, since her liquid reserve is adequate only for 'emergencies'.

Her other banking alternative would be to go for greater liquidity while keeping the rate of return lower. A 'money fund' account (answer **b**) would achieve this, but, given her probable pattern of income/expenditure, she really doesn't need the facility to write 'big cheques' at a moment's notice to draw on these funds. She'll be much better off with the extra interest.

What about the other option given in answer **d** — buying stocks and shares? Well, it's true that some sort of Stock Exchange investment could be considered if the customer felt she could accept the risks. It would offer her some opportunities for more income and capital growth, and the current climate of opinion is very much in favour of the small investor. Even so, we owe it to her to forewarn her of the major dangers of stock market investment and the need to diversify her holdings as much as possible. With only £5,000 at her disposal, she really can't achieve a wide enough spread by direct investment, so the idea should be discouraged. An alternative route would be to buy into a Unit Trust — but you weren't offered that option in the question!

If you want to compare the features and benefits of the various types of accounts for savers which are available through the banks, Marsh & Wilde's *Practice of Banking 2* contains a useful table of comparisons.

3 The correct answer is **d**.

This is a fairly simple question, so we hope you got it right! The point that it is intended to make is that whenever you respond to a customer's request for a particular service, you should always be looking at the total 'package' that you can offer. The question you should be asking yourself is, 'What servic*es* (plural) does this person require in order to satisfy his or her financial and related needs *as a whole*'.

The couple who are just setting up in business present a perfect opportunity for such an integrated approach. Let's look at the areas where the bank can help them.

(1) *Executorship*. There is no doubt that wills should be drawn

up/redrawn following the inheritance. If the business is successful this will become even more important.

(2) *Tax planning.* Ultimately their assets — hopefuly substantial? — will pass to their beneficiaries. Plans should be set in train to reduce the tax burden on such transfers.

(3) *Pensions.* Self-employed customers should enter into pension schemes as soon as possible, both to protect their retirement position and to take advantage of the available tax benefits.

(4) *Insurance.* Similarly, this will be part of the tax/estate planning which we have already mentioned. Furthermore, they will require insurance against loss of earnings through illness etc., as well as commercial insurance of business assets.

And that leaves us with one 'red herring' of gold cards. At this stage, there is no reason to suppose that these customers are appropriate targets for this service which is really aimed at the more well established and well off. Indeed, it could be that access (sorry!) to the extended credit facilities available could be a distraction to them while they are building up their business. In a few years time, if everything goes according to plan and they have established themselves with a good income, then we should look again.

4 The correct answer is **b.**

We thought that we would test your knowledge of some of banking's acronyms as well as your understanding of the services. The *direct debit* is the most appropriate of the systems mentioned since it allows the insurance company to charge the annual premium direct to the customer's account on the due date. This avoids the possibility of him forgetting to do anything about it and leaving himself uninsured. It is a better choice than the standing order quoted in answer **a** since — in its variable amount form — it enables the beneficiary to claim the correct amount, whatever it may be, without the customer having to give any further instructions to the bank. This is very important since the cost is likely to vary (upwards!) every year as insurance rates and property values both rise. Most domestic insurance policies these days incorporate provision for automatic increases in the sums covered, to keep them in line with inflationary trends.

SWIFT — answer **c** — stands for Society for Worldwide Interbank Financial Telecommunications. It is an organization which transmits, via a computer network, messages of various kinds between participating banks throughout the world. A large proportion of these messages concern payment instructions, but it is not used exclusively for this purpose.

*CHAP*s, of course, is a computer based system for making large amount 'same day settlement' payments within the UK. The lower limit for payments is currently £10,000. It is the modern replacement for the traditional 'town clearing' of large cheques (which it will eventually replace). Unless the customer's premiums are extremely high, it is not really appropriate to his needs!

(*NB* If you don't know what CHAPs is short for, go and find out.)

5   The correct answer is **c**.

With a 'traditional' budget account, the customers would add up all their forseeable regular outgoings, divide the total by 12, and contribute the resulting amount each month to a separate account. As payments fell due, they would be made from the account so that (theoretically) by the end of the year, funds out would equal funds in. In fact, some small adjustment is normally called for, since some items such as fuel bills can't be estimated entirely accurately.

The more modern 'revolving credit' account offers greater flexibility. The customer agrees to set aside a stated sum each month, and the account is then marked with a limit equivalent to an advertised multiple of that figure — usually at least 10 times. The account can then be used to make any payment that the customer wishes: either regular payments or unexpected 'one off' items.

You will see, therefore, that answer **b** is wrong because both types of account require regular payments into them. And **d** is wrong because it is the revolving credit account that can be used to make irregular payments! If you gave **a** as your answer, we suspect that you just weren't concentrating. The only thing that we can think of is that you may have been thinking of *charge cards* — but these have nothing to do with budget accounts.

6   The correct answer is **c**.

We hope that you didn't get this one wrong! Our intention was simply to get you to think about the benefits to the customer of holding a credit card. These can be summed up as follows:

Safety: The card is much safer than cash in respect of theft. If the holder reports its loss promptly he will suffer no penalty for its misuse. In any case, the liability is limited to £50.

Convenience: No need to carry bulky cash or cheque books — or multiple cards.

Acceptability The bank operated credit card schemes in the UK operate through thousands of outlets both at home and throughout the world.

Budgeting: Use of a credit card enables the customer to spend when necessary, using the revolving credit limit to spread the burden over the year (or longer).

This isn't an exhaustive list of the benefits. Try to add to it before you go any further.

The facility to borrow without formality does, however, also have its darker side; it can encourage overspending in some users. For this reason, you should always have some regard for the personality of the customer before recommending the service. Certainly there is no way in which a credit card could be classed as a disincentive to overspending as suggested in answer **c**.

7 The correct answer is **c**.

One of the 'selling points' of the bank's executor service is that the fee doesn't become payable until the executorship actually commences. It is taken out of the assets of the estate. This means that the testator doesn't have to find the money 'out of his own pocket' while he is alive. This can be important because the fees are not low — although they are good value for money — and if they had to be paid straight away many potential customers might be deterred.

It is possible that other related fees may be payable earlier in the process. If, for example, the customer has also requested advice on how to draw up the will or how to plan the estate's distribution to minimize tax, there will be a specific charge levied at the outset. Likewise, if the distribution of the estate is spread over a period, there will usually be an administration charge levied for each year that the bank continues to act.

8 The correct answer is **a**.

The bank's investment management service is available to any customer whose portfolio of investments has a value of £20,000 or thereabouts. The normal arrangement is for the bank to have 'discretionary' powers to manage the investments, subject to any overall policy decisions and directions given by the customer. Occasionally, the customer will require that all proposed changes be referred for confirmation, but this is discouraged where possible since it adds to the complexity (and the cost) of the service.

The investment managers are expert in the long-term investment strategies relevant for general investments. These include stocks and shares, 'gilts', cash (deposits), and so on. They will not normally wish to invest in the more specialist or speculative areas. It is for this reason that they wouldn't wish to deal with:

- Land
- Commercial property
- Commodity futures

} Too specialist
and difficult to vary
Too speculative

9   The correct answer is **d**.

In fact, all of the attributes quoted in the question do apply to Unit Trusts. The costs of dealings, which active asset management requires, will of course be 'passed on' to the Unit holders. Nevertheless, the economies of scale available on large deals will result in an effective reduction in costs as compared with those that would be suffered by each individual investor operating independently.

Unit trusts come in all shapes and sizes, and whatever general investment strategy a customer wishes to pursue, it should be possible to find an appropriate trust. The principal decisions that he will have to take are:

- Whether to invest for capital growth or income.
- Whether to reinvest the income ('Accumulation Units') or to withdraw it ('Distribution Units').

If the customer wants regular 'dividends' as in answer **b**, he can have them.

It would be difficult to find a simpler way of investing than the purchase of Units — answer **c**. Nevertheless, the overwhelmingly important advantage that they confer on the small investor is the ability to participate in a properly diversified portfolio. Unless the investment funds are spread over different sections of the economy and different companies within each section, the portfolio will always be vulnerable to fluctuations in the particular area. The costs of this diversification are disproportionate to the returns if the sum available is small.

10   The correct answer is **a**.

The figures quoted represent the first four 'bands' for the levying of tax on the net value of a deceased's estate. The rates are:

£0 – £90,000	0%
£90,001 – £140,000	30%
£140,001 – £220,000	35%
£220,001 – 330,000	40%

The important point that we wish to emphasize (and the reason for including this question) is that the examiner will be favourably impressed if you can show that you know at least the basic threshold below which tax will not be levied. *But*, you must bear in mind that by the time you come to take the exam, the levels may be set quite differently than they were when this book was printed. Keep yourself up to date!

Score 2 marks for each correct answer. What was your score? Fill it in on the score grid.

If you scored 12 or less and are still a bit shaky on some points go back and look at the study guide again before proceeding any further.

If you are sure you really understand and are familiar with this topic now, try the 10 further questions which are on pages 239–41. Alternatively you can go on to your next topic and do all the post-tests together at the end.

Topic 8   Business services: financial

Introduction

This section goes together with Topic 9 to provide a complete review of the services available to business customers. In Topic 9 we look at the administrative services which the banks can provide for their business customers. At the moment, though, we are concerned with the financial services. Please be aware, however, that this division is really an artificial one which has been designed solely to keep each topic unit within manageable proportions. In reality there is no strict or clear dividing line between the two.

Furthermore, you should be aware that a business customer may at any time be utilizing both financial and administrative services. This is especially important in the exam! The examiner will be looking for you to adopt a *comprehensive* approach, which means that you should aim to identify *all* the appropriate services that could be recommended. Far too often, students stop when they have identified *a* service. Don't do this. Always try to look for others, and don't be blinkered in doing so. Just because the customer's most apparent needs are (for instance) financial, that doesn't mean that there are no administrative needs.

Market Segments

Just like personal customers, business customers can be segregated into market segments, the members of each segment having similar needs. The principal deciding factors are:

- *Type of business*: What does the concern do? Customers can be categorized as manufacturers, traders, and services (including the professions). Each category has a different conglomeration of needs.
- *Type of organization*: To a degree, this will reflect the type of business done. Can you differentiate between the needs of companies, partnerships, and sole traders?
- *Size of business*: Once again, this is linked to the previous factor in that companies tend to be bigger than partnerships, and so on — but it isn't a firm rule. Some partnerships are bigger than some companies. Moreover, within any one type there are of course differences of size. There are some very small limited companies and there are some absolutely huge ones.

You could start by making out a chart showing the various permutations that are available using the above factors. Then insert (if you can) an indication of where some customers of your own branch would fit in — this will give you a realistic perspective for your studies. As we (you!) work through the various services, you can cross-reference them to your list, thus creating a grid showing who could use what service. You never know, it might even help you to develop the branch's business!

Financial services

There will be a considerable degree of 'crossover' between the services incorporated under this heading and those that you have studied for the Section A questions. The big difference is that in Section A you'll be asked to pronounce on whether a proposition is viable without giving any great details of the operational aspects. In Section B you'll be concentrating much more on the selection of appropriate services and explaining how they work. Your studies should concentrate, therefore, on how the services work and when they are appropriate. We'll assume that you know by now how the basic lending services work (if you don't, you know what to do, don't you).

Factoring

Make sure that you can distinguish between the three levels of service available:

- *Sales ledger administation*: Taking over the invoicing and collection functions, thus freeing the customer from the need to run his own accounting section.
- *Credit control*: The factor can take over the whole of this function — from checking the credit worthiness of customers and setting limits through to chasing up late payments. Allied to this is the provision of credit insurance, offering the trader protection against bad debts.
  Both of these two functions are *administrative* rather than *financial*, thus showing the close links between the two areas.
- *Factor finance* is available in two forms:
  — *Invoice discounting* is just what its name implies; the factor 'buys' the debts at a discount but retains the right of recourse if they are unpaid. It doesn't involve any administration services.
  — *Full factoring* involves the use of the administrative services too. The factor provides immediate finance for a proportion of each invoice sent out, but also provides credit protection.

Make sure you know how the factor is remunerated for this service and how the customer gets his receipts. Jot down a note of what you think and check it against your own bank's literature.

The benefits of the service include improved cash flow and use of management time. It is an alternative to the overdraft. It is appropriate to all businesses having regular inflows of payments, especially expanding businesses. It is available for export trade as well as inland trade.

How will the use of 'factor finance' affect any overdraft facilities arranged? Would it matter if the bank had a charge over the business's book debts?

Leasing

If factoring is the 'favourite' new service for customers with a cash flow requirement, then leasing is the favourite when it comes to capital purchases. You should be able to differentiate between:

- *Operating leases* where the supplier of the capital item leases it rather than selling it.
- *Finance leases* where the lessor's interest is in providing the finance. The asset required by the lessee is purchased by the lessor but used by the lessee for the whole of its working life.

Your textbook will contain a list of the benefits of finance leasing. Make sure you learn it! It would be a good idea to try to jot down what you think they are before looking them up.

One word of warning; your textbook may indicate that the lessor might have access to tax allowances that wouldn't be available to the lessee if he were to purchase the assets. This used to be true, but changes in taxation rules have altered the position. The lessor now has available only those allowances that would have been available to the lessee. (*NB* This includes regional grants etc.) Do you know what the current tax rules are? You should — find out about them as soon as you can.

Money market services

The various component parts of the London money markets deal in large amount/short-term deposits/loans. The banks deal in them, both on their own account — to balance their books — and, increasingly, on behalf of customers.

Loans via the money market for periods of up to 3 months can be arranged direct in the market. Generally, these will be for £500,000 or more.

Acceptance credits utilize the money markets to discount bills of exchange drawn by a customer on the bank once they have been accepted. Make sure you know how the acceptance facility works and how the bank charges for the service.

Deposits are also available, both directly on the markets for large amounts or at market related rates for smaller (but still large) amounts. The rates will vary according to:

— amount, and
— term (fixed period or notice of withdrawal)

Make sure you know how your own bank's 'money market' deposit schemes work so that you can illustrate your answers with examples. (But beware of thinking that the competition can't do anything different.) Be up to date. Has your bank introduced (for example) 'high interest' current account facilities for professional/well-off personal customers? If so, how do they work and what are the benefits? Is there a special version available for solicitors and other professionals to use as clients accounts?

Merchant banking services

The 'traditional' merchant banking service was the acceptance credit which we have already mentioned, but there are others that you should have some familiarity with — generally concerned with the capital financing of a business.

Raising capital: an advisory service will be available on the best way of covering the need for long-term finance. You won't be required to give the advice, but you should know the differences between (and relative advantages of) equity capital, loan stocks, etc.

A 'popular' topic with the public (and possibly the exam) in recent years has been the methods by which a company can be 'brought to the stock market'. Can you recall from your Investment studies how the various methods work?

Make a brief note of the differences between the following, and when each is appropriate:

- Offer for sale
- Offer for sale by tender
- Introduction
- Placing

You should also know when the USM would be recommended instead of the main market.

Mergers and takeovers: you probably won't need to know much about the 'nuts and bolts' of this area, but don't forget about its existence. Merchant banks (including the banks' specialist sections) will advise on all aspects of mergers with other companies or takeovers of them. (The banks themselves have had first hand experience of these processes!)
Similarly, if the owners of a business wish to sell it, the merchant bank can act as adviser and agent, helping to find a buyer and negotiating a price. Management 'buy-outs' have been 'flavour of the month' recently (see Topic 4), and merchant banks will, of course, advise on these too.

Business advisory services

Finally, you should ensure that you have a good knowledge of the generalized business advisory services that are available. What does your bank offer? Here are some of the main areas for you to structure your studies around.

Business start-ups are quite topical at the moment. Really, questions in this area are intended to get you to bring together all the facilities which are useful to *small* businesses — you don't need to go into the 'bigger' topics such as share flotations and so on.

Make a list — you know what to do by now!

An important part of the advice you can give concerns:

Government schemes and grants: there are so many schemes available these days that the banks have become an important source of introductions to government and local government bodies for grants, loans and other assistance. In addition, the banks themselves operate several government-backed schemes.

You won't have to be an expert on these schemes, but you should have a general idea of how they work. Your branch will probably have an 'information bank' on current facilities. Familiarize yourself with it. If you don't work in a branch, can you arrange to get access to the information?

Problems of small businesses: these are, of course, the difficulties that the above bank services are designed to overcome. More often than not, these tend to resolve themselves into questions of cash flow and credit control. What services are available to deal with them?

The question of expansion is also important. Most banks now have a

172

business expansion plan available. This is again related to a government scheme. Do you know how it works?

Once you feel confident about your knowledge of this topic, try to answer the 10 multiple choice questions which follow.

Multiple choice questions

1 A customer who wishes to set up in business has approached you for advice on how to raise finance beyond the level that can be covered by his own resources. Which of the following media would you *not* recommend:

  a Unlisted Securities Market?
  b Overdraft?
  c Small Firms Loan Guarantee Scheme?
  d Merchant banking services?

 answer

2 A business customer who has an overdraft facility supported by a debenture intends to start using the finance services provided by the bank's factoring company. What effect will this have on the overdraft facility:

  a the overdraft may reduce as funds are released by the factoring finance?
  b funds released by the factoring finance must be used to reduce the overdraft as debenture cover will be reduced?
  c the overdraft can be maintained at the existing level since the debenture cover is unaffected?
  d none: factoring has no real effect on cashflow?

 answer

3 Look at the following list of benefits to the customer:

  (i) Credit management and credit protection
  (ii) Improved cash flow
  (iii) Sales ledger management
  (iv) Release of management time from debt collection
  (v) Beneficial tax treatment

Which of them are available from the use of a factoring service:

  a (i), (ii), (iii) and (iv)?
  b (ii), (iii), (iv) and (v)?
  c (i), (ii), (iii) and (v)?

d (i), (ii), (iv) and (v)?

answer

4 What proportion of debts outstanding will usually be the maximum available as an advance by way of factor finance:

a 100%
b 50%
c 65%
d 80%

answer

5 Finance leasing is a financially viable way of obtaining the use of capital assets because:

a the leasing company has access to 'capital allowances' which might not be available to the lessee?
b the leasing company has access to the same capital allowances as the lessee although not to regional development grants?
c the leasing company has access to the same development grants as the lessee although not to tax allowances?
d the leasing company has access to the same capital allowances and development grants as the lessee?

answer

6 Finance leases differ from operating leases in that:

a under an operating lease, the capital asset never belongs to the lessee.
b under a finance lease, the capital asset never belongs to the lessee.
c under an operating lease, the lessee assumes responsibility for service and repairs of the capital asset.
d under a finance lease, the lessee assumes responsibility for service and repairs of the capital asset.

answer

175

7 A large corporate customer has arranged for the bank to grant a £½ million acceptance facility. How does this work:

    a the bank draws bills of exchange on the company and releases funds to the company as each bill is accepted by the customer?

    b the bank discounts bills which have been drawn on the company by its suppliers, once they have been duly accepted?

    c the bank accepts bills of exchange drawn on it by the company, making them eligible for discount in the discount market?

    d the bank discounts bills of exchange which have been accepted by the company's debtors?

 answer

8 A private company wishes to 'go public' to raise finance for further expansion. The bank's 'merchant banking' arm is advising in the process. Which is the most likely method for arranging the new issue:

    a offer for sale?

    b placing?

    c rights issue?

    d bonus issue?

 answer

9 What types of loan can be raised for a business customer via the London 'money market':

    a only very short-term loans not exceeding 7 days?

    b short-term loans up to 3 months?

    c long-term finance?

    d equity participation?

 answer

10 Where would you recommend that an estate agent should hold large sums of clients funds that he is holding temporarily:

    a clients account?

    b clients deposit account?

    c clients 'high interest' account?

d office account?

answer

Answers follow on pages 178–85. Score 2 marks for each correct answer.

Answers

1 The correct answer is **a**.

We hope that you didn't have too much trouble with this question! The only one of these four facilities that would be inappropriate to a new business is the Unlisted Securities Market. The USM, like the Stock Market generally, is really a vehicle for existing businesses to raise finance. It isn't generally used to float completely new enterprises — and certainly not small business ventures such as this customer appears to be proposing. Of course, the Stock Market have come to have other functions too, but that isn't the subject of our discussions here.

The point of the question really is to emphasize to you the need for a *comprehensive* approach to the subject of finding the services which are appropriate to a customer's needs. It isn't a good idea to stop thinking after you have identified *a* service that would suit. Usually there will be more than one — whether you are dealing with a private customer or a business customer. Just because we are dealing with a business here, you shouldn't forget the concept of 'market segmentation' (discussed in detail in Topic 6). Each customer will be part of a market segment consisting of similar organizations having similar needs. Your task is to identify the bank services that would go to satisfy those needs.

Well then, what sources of finance are there for a customer who is just setting up in business?

Bank facilities are of course available in the usual way. You could/should make a brief list of these if asked a question along these lines in the exam — with a brief note of the attributes and benefits of each one. Your list would certainly include overdrafts and loan account facilities. In addition, you will probably find that your own bank is offering some sort of business 'start up' facility: this will probably be backed by a 'government scheme', which brings us to the second point.

Government schemes: the banks are important sources of advice for small businesses about the maze of government 'support schemes' that are currently available — and the examiner will expect you to be familiar with them. We've already mentioned the 'start up' scheme but there are many others such as the Small Firms Loan Guarantee Scheme — answer **c** — and regional development grants.

Merchant banking services for the raising of longer term finance could also be appropriate, and it would be worthwhile mentioning the more generalized business advisory service that is available either from this source or a separate section of the bank.

Finally, it's worth drawing your attention to the possibility of tabulating your answers. A broad approach to the more generalized questions that are set will produce a lot of points to be made. Tabulation helps the examiner to see what you are getting at, enables you to see if you have omitted anything, and saves you time.

2 The correct answer is **b**.

Factoring finance is an extension of the basic debtor management service provided by the factoring company. A percentage of the amount of each invoice sent out is advanced to the business immediately: interest is charged until the amount is collected from the debtor and the remaining percentage is paid to the customer. Dependent on the arrangement, bad debts may or may not be charged back to the customer. The overall effect of this is to release funds to the customer earlier than would otherwise be the case, and this positive effect on the cash flow should reduce the need for the overdraft. Thus answer **d** is wholly wrong. Similarly, answer **a** is wrong — you would certainly expect the overdraft to reduce, so the word 'may' is what is wrong here.

What effect will this have on the security (the debenture)? Undoubtedly the debenture will be in the bank's standard form and, if taken within the last few years, this will certainly incorporate a fixed equitable charge over the book debts. If the debenture was taken before the *Siebe Gorman Case* demonstrated that such an arrangement was possible, the bank will probably have subsequently taken a supplemental charge over book debts, thus creating a similar position. Even without such a provision, the book debts would be caught under the *floating charge* element of the debenture. None of this will be acceptable to the factoring company who will not be prepared to advance funds without its own (first) charge over the debts. The bank will be required (asked?) to postpone its charge over the debts in favour of the factors. Answer **c** therefore has to be wrong, doesn't it?

The effect on the debenture cover is difficult to estimate without further facts: it will differ from company to company, according to the level of book debts. However, there are two points that can be made. Firstly, it will have some effect since the factors wouldn't be involved if the book debts didn't reach a significant level. Secondly, in many cases (probably most), the book debts are the biggest single item caught under the debenture. It follows then that we can expect the value of the debenture to be reduced; this reduction must be matched by a reduction in the level of the overdraft.

3 The correct answer is **a**.

Another simple question for you — we hope! To get the correct answer (without guessing) you have to know:

1 What the factoring services offer, and
2 What the benefits are.

There are three component parts to the factoring service, and the customer might elect to use all or any combination of them, or they can be used singly.

Debt administration is provided by the factor becoming, in effect, the client's accounting department. Economies of scale allow the factor to offer this service very efficiently and quite possibly more cheaply than the client could achieve. Management time will be released for 'more important' tasks.

Credit control is available as part of the debt administration service: the factor will take the decision on whether to grant credit (and to what extent) to a given customer. Once again, expertise and resources allow an effective and highly efficient service to be offered cheaply. Furthermore, the factoring company will be prepared to back its judgement by 'guaranteeing' the credit which is allowed. The client is thus protected against bad debts.

Factor finance is the ultimate part of the service. The factor will advance a proportion of each outstanding debt at the time that the invoice is raised. As we noted in question 2, interest will be charged until the invoice is settled, whereupon the balance of the funds will be paid over to the client. This, of course, has a beneficial effect on cash flow. In effect, a proportion of all sales will become 'cash' rather than 'credit' items so far as the client is concerned.

The only one of the listed benefits, therefore, that does not apply to factoring is that of beneficial tax treatment. The various factoring services don't in fact, have any effect on the business's tax position. If you thought that this was one of the benefits of factoring, you were probably thinking of leasing, but that's another question entirely — one which we'll be coming to very soon!

4 The correct answer is **d**.

In questions **2** and **3** we mentioned that factors can provide finance by advancing a proportion of each invoice as it is raised. But we were careful not to mention what proportion, just in case you were reading the answer to each question before going on to the next one! Even so, you will have been able to work out that 100% finance is not available, so answer **a** must be wrong.

The actual percentage of outstanding debts that can be advanced may vary according to the agreement between the factor and the client. A number of factors (sorry!) will be taken into account, including the creditworthiness of the client's customers and whether the factor is providing a full management service. Generally, however, the maximum proportion which is available for advance is 80%. It would be unusual for the facility to exceed this level.

5   The correct answer is **d**.

Among other things, this question was designed to test whether your textbook or your knowledge was up to date in so far as leasing is concerned. When finance leases first became popular, part of their attraction was that the leasing company could offset the capital cost against profits as a capital allowance — whether or not the lessee would have been able to claim such allowances. If the lessee did not have adequate profits to make use of the allowances therefore, the lessor would nevertheless be able to do so. The practical effect of this was to make leasing cheaper than buying for such businesses (the banking groups to which the leasing companies belong would always have had adequate profits to make use of the allowances!)

This is no longer the case. Since 1984 restrictions have been placed on the availability of capital allowances to a lessor if the user of the assets would have been unable to claim them if the assets had been purchased directly. Answer **a** is therefore wrong: the leasing company doesn't have access to capital allowances which aren't available to the lessee. You shouldn't however go on to assume that leasing is no longer a useful or competitive service for that reason. It can still be a useful alternative to buying through HP finance or bank loan. All that has happened is that a potential *extra* advantage of cost has been removed. If you think about it, if the cost benefit had been the only advantage of the leasing facility, only clients with no (or inadequate) profits would have used it — and that was never the case.

If the lessor has access to the same tax concessions as the client would have done, it therefore follows that answer **c** must be wrong, doesn't it? So, the only question remaining is whether the lessor would have available any regional development grants that would have gone to the lessee if the asset had been purchased directly. The answer to this is just 'yes'; the lessor does have access to such grants. This is an important point, since if such treatment wasn't available, the leasing company wouldn't be able to offer the client a competitive deal. It would be cheaper to buy — and considerably so. Answer **b** is therefore wrong, and **d** is correct.

6   The correct answer is **c**.

In order to answer this question correctly, there are just two areas of the leasing process that you need to know about: ownership and servicing. Let's consider the question of ownership first.

An operating lease is usually granted where the lessor is the manufacturer or the distributor of the asset that the client wishes to acquire. It is most commonly seen when dealing with items such as office equipment (photocopiers, word processors and so on). To all intents and purposes, the equipment is 'hired' to the user, and it is never envisaged that the true ownership of it would pass to the user.

With a finance lease, matters are somewhat different. The lessor is a separate party from the supplier of the equipment. Technically, the lessor buys the equipment from the supplier and then leases it to the client. We say 'technically', because in reality the lessee will usually write the 'specification' for the equipment, and will liaise with the seller to ensure that what is supplied meets that specification. Even so, the lessee doesn't become the owner. Indeed, the regulations governing leasing preclude there being any intention in the leasing agreement that the lessee should at any time become the owner of the assets. Thus, both answers **a** and **b** consist of statements which are correct; both operating leases and finance leases are the same in this respect, so neither of them can be the answer.

So, let's think about the question of servicing and repairs. With a finance lease, as we hae seen, the lessor is separate from the supplier of the assets. Although the leasing company becomes the true owner of the assets, its real interest is in providing the finance. The leasing agreement will invariably make the lessee responsible for maintaining and repairing the equipment. Answer **d** therefore does represent a correct statement of fact.

An operating lease is quite different. Here the lessor is closely involved with the provision of the assets, either as manufacturer or as distributor. The leasing agreement in this case will leave the responsibility for servicing and repairs with him. Answer **c** is thus incorrect and cannot be the answer to the problem. Thus it is **d** that we're looking for.

7   The correct answer is **c**.

Let's look first at how an acceptance facility does work. In essence, it is very simple, so we hope you got the answer to this one correct! The steps are:

- The customer draws term bills of exchange for agreed amounts on the bank.
- The bank accepts the bills and returns them to the customer.

- The customer can then discount the bills either with a bank or via the money market.
- The acceptance of the bank will enable the customer to obtain a very 'fine' interest rate.
- Before the bill falls due, the customer must provide the bank with adequate funds to meet its obligation. This may be accomplished by the discounting of a further bill!

It is a part of this process that was described in answer **d**, but none of it is reflected in the other answers. What then do they represent?

The procedure set out in answer **c** is a standard 'discounted bill' facility in which commercial bills — accepted by the customer's clients — are discounted by the bank. These bills are not of such high 'class' as those accepted by the bank and therefore do not command such favourable rates of discount. Nevertheless, this can be a reasonably cheap way of raising finance. The bank, before discounting the bills, will be looking for 'two good names' to each one. In other words, it will be looking to see that the acceptor appears to be good for the money. It can be presumed that the drawer/beneficiary of the bill *is* good since this is the bank's customer: the bank wouldn't be entering into the arrangement in the first place if it had any doubts.

The procedure suggested in **b** is not a way of making funds available to the customer (who is the acceptor of the bills and therefore liable on them). When a bill is discounted, the funds released go, of course, to the previous holder of it. Usually this will be the drawer; in this case this is the supplier. It could happen that the bank would discount such a bill for the supplier, but it wouldn't help the customer by doing so (although it wouldn't hurt, either).

The arrangement suggested in **a** is really something of a nonsense. If the bank has granted a loan to its customer, there is no need to draw bills of exchange for the sums due: it wouldn't make the customer any more liable for the money. Even if such bills were drawn and accepted, the *bank* would be the holder. It could discount them if it wished, but this wouldn't make funds available to the customer, would it?

8 The correct answer is **a**.

In recent years, there has been a great deal of interest in the floatation of new issues, so you really ought to have known enough to get this right. There are a number of ways in which a new share issue can be brought to the market. An offer for sale — as suggested in answer **a** — is by far the most common. The principle is simple. A prospectus is issued, backed up by advertising, to tell the public about the new issue. Application forms are attached for those who wish to buy. Prospective

183

purchasers indicate how many shares they wish to subscribe for. Usually the shares are issued at a fixed price, but occasionally an 'offer for sale by tender' is seen. In this case, the subscribers are also asked to specify the maximum price that they are prepared to pay for the shares.

A placing — answer **b** — is a method of bringing a share to the market, but it is much less common. Under this system, the shares are 'placed' with large institutional investors in what amounts to private sales. A proportion of the shares have to be placed with the 'market makers' so as to allow the general public access to the new issue.

Finally, an introduction — not one of our options — occurs when a company's shares are already widely held. The Stock Exchange is simply made available as a medium for their future sale and purchase.

Rights issues — answer **c** — and bonus issues — answer **d** — *aren't* methods of introducing a company to the market for the first time, although they are forms of share issue. A rights issue occurs when an existing company wishes to raise further capital by issuing further shares. It first offers its existing shareholders the 'right' to subscribe for the new shares. A 'bonus' issue is different again and occurs when a company issues new shares free of charge to its existing shareholders. This doesn't generate any new capital and is undertaken chiefly to promote the saleability of the shares by reducing the market value of each one. The overall value of a shareholder's total holding will not be affected.

9 The correct answer is **b**.

The money market, as you should know, is concerned with the placing of comparatively short-term deposits of large amounts of money. Every deposit made by someone is, of course, a loan taken by someone else. If the amount required is large enough, if the borrower is secure enough, and if the period of the loan is short enough, therefore, a large corporate customer can use the money market to raise finance at very attractive rates of interest. The 'corporate treasurers' of the very largest companies may well have direct access to the money markets and be able to trade there as principals. In most cases, however, access to the markets will be via the banks — and this applies whether the customer is raising a loan or placing a deposit.

Well — perhaps we had better define our terms now. What do we mean by 'large amounts' and 'short-term'? As regards the amount, we'd normally expect to be talking about sums of £500,000 at the very least, so we really do mean large!

The terms of such loans generally range from overnight up to a maximum of three months. You'll see that this is short-term, but not quite as short as was envisaged in answer **a**, which is therefore wrong.

Answer **c** is also wrong, of course, since it would be impossible to raise long-term finance through the markets if the maximum term is three months!

That just leaves us with answer **d** — equity participation. We hope you'll have realized by now why this answer has to be wrong. The money markets are concerned solely with deposit/loan funds; not investment capital. Investment funds which are available for equity participation are mobilized through the Stock Market, of course — but that's another story!

10   The correct answer is **c**.

You should know from your studies for POB 1 that certain professional customers are required to maintain separate accounts through which they will process funds which they are handling on behalf of their clients. Such funds are held by them in trust and the accounts are in effect trust accounts — they are usually referred to as 'clients accounts'.

> Different types of professional customer are under different legal obligations in this respect. Can you make a list of *who* has to do *what* with clients' funds?

Such professionals will keep their own funds in a separate 'office' account, thus ensuring that there is a proper segregation between the two types of deposit. Answer **d** is therefore wholly wrong.

Traditionally, banks used to offer such customers (principally in the past just solicitors) two alternatives: a clients current account for the short-term processing of funds, and the clients deposit account on which longer-term funds could be held. The advantage of the deposit account is that interest will be paid on the balance, ensuring that the client doesn't 'lose out' unnecessarily while his funds are involved in whatever transaction is taking place. Clearly, if the amount is significant and is being held for any length of time, it would be wrong to hold it on a simple current account as suggested in answer **a** — so this must be wrong. An interest-bearing account is called for.

In recent years, banks have introduced 'high interest' clients accounts for the longer-term amounts held by professional customers. These accounts are in effect interest-bearing current accounts which have been introduced to attract (retain?) the often substantial amounts of clients' funds that can build up. Their principal benefit — over and above the payment of interest — is that they give direct access to funds transfer facilities (cheques, CHAPS, etc.) without the need to give notice of withdrawal. They are therefore much simpler to operate than an 'old fashioned' deposit account and are the service that you should recommend. Answer **b** is therefore wrong, but only just!

Score 2 marks for each correct answer. What was your score? Fill it in on the score grid.

If you scored 12 or less and are still a bit shaky on some points go back and look at the study guide again before proceeding any further.

If you are sure you really understand and are familiar with this topic now, try the 10 further questions which are on pages 000–000. Alternatively you can go on to your next topic and do all the post-tests together at the end.

Topic 9   Business services: administration

Study guide

Introduction

This section goes together with Topic 8 to provide a complete review of the services available to business customers. In Topic 8 we look at the financial services which the banks can provide for their business customers: at the moment, though, we are concerned with the more administrative services. Please be aware, however, that this division is really an artificial one which has been designed solely to keep each Topic unit within manageable proportions. In reality there is no clear dividing line between the two.

Furthermore, you should be aware that a business customer may at any one time be utilizing both administrative and financial services. This is especially important in the exam! The examiner will be looking for you to adopt a *comprehensive* approach, which means that you should aim to identify all the appropriate services that could be recommended. Far too often, students stop when they have identified *a* service. Don't do this. Always try to look for others, and don't be blinkered in doing so. Just because the customer's most apparent needs are (for instance) administrative, that doesn't mean that there are no financial needs.

Administrative services

The services in this section cover a wide area, and each of then can be a benefit to various different types of customer. If you haven't read Topic 8 yet, it would be a good idea just to flick back now to its introductory section and read what we say there about drawing up a 'chart' on which you cawn cross-reference services with customers. Administrative services can go on the chart in just the same way as financial ones.

Share registration

The bank is able to act as *Registrar* for any company whether it banks with it or elsewhere. Generally (of course?), the service is worthwhile only for public companies (PLCs) which have a broad spread of shareholders. The advantages of using a specialist for this service are:

- Economies of scale/cost savings
- Professional standards
- Release of staff for more productive work.

Memorize these three benefits, because they apply to just about every specialist service that can be 'bought in', from share registration to calculating employees' wages!

To make sure you can list the 'everyday' tasks of a company's Registrars, compile a list now, and then compare it with your textbook (where you'll almost certainly find one). Here's a hint: there's more to it than just keeping a record of who holds the shares, though that's the basis of everything else.

Over and above the question of everyday activities, the Registrars Department can also assist clients with a number of 'one-off' items such as:

- Flotation of new companies
- Bonus issues and rights issues
- Mergers and takeovers
- Employee 'profit sharing' share purchase schemes.

If you're applying the principles of 'cross selling' that we keep trying to emphasize, you'll realize that several of these services could also act as the basis of an introduction to the 'merchant banking' arm of the bank — and vice versa, of course.

Computer bureau

The banks' computer departments, with their large mainframe computers, often have excess computing power over what would be required just to meet their own needs. 'Spare time' can be sold to customers who don't have enough work to justify the purchase of their own mainframes. However, the market for such facilities may well decrease significantly with the advent of smaller, cheaper computers such as the PC (or personal computer) that can take over these services for the smaller customer.

Wages and salaries calculations are the most obvious use that can be sold. Using existing programs, the bureau can process information provided by the customer to calculate wages, taxes, pension contributions, and so on. If wages are paid by BACs, output can be in a format that can be fed directly into the system.

Sales ledger and purchase ledger administration services are also available (jointly or independently) and these also share the 'usual three' advantages that we have already noted. Sales ledger administration isn't necessary if the customers are already taking advantage of a full factoring service.

Jot down a note of how you think these services work and then check against your textbook/bank advertising literature. What is the basis on which charges are levied? You won't need to know the detailed rates, but the principles should be understood.

The benefits of these services include:

- Improved credit control
- Improved cash flow.

Cash management systems are now being introduced by all the major banks to take advantage of modern funds transfer systems to ensure that the customer never leaves funds lying idle — even overnight. Make sure you know how they work.

Funds transfer

You should by now be familiar with the operational details of the various 'traditional' systems for transferring funds on behalf of customers.

Make a list now. Indicate the types of transaction for which each is particularly suitable/unsuitable.

Electronic funds transfer is very much in the news these days — and has been for some years — so it isn't unreasonable to expect questions about it. Some aspects are covered in Topic 7 in so far as it affects personal customers. Specific business considerations include the following points:

BACs: the BACs system is able to process both debits and credits, so it can transmit payments and claims for payment.
Make sure you're familiar with the direct debit system and its operation. What conditions must an 'originator' fulfil before being allowed to start raising debits?

Make a list of the sorts of credits that it can be useful to transmit via BACs (we've already given you some clues!) What are the advantages to the remitter? Pay particular attention to the benefits of paying employees' wages by bank transfer.

CHAPS: the CHAPS system is designed to permit customers to remit same day (cleared) payments of large amounts direct to the accounts of beneficiaries. Currently limited to a minimum payment value of

£10,000, it should ultimately (soon?) replace the old paper based systems such as the Town Clearing or use of Bankers' Payments, etc. Access to the system is via branch banks, or those customers making large numbers of such payments may arrange to have direct access to the computer network via 'gateways' provided by the settlement banks.

> Make a list of the customers who could use the service and the types of payment they might be making.

The chief benefit of CHAPS to both the remitter and beneficiary is improved cash flow control. Payments don't need to be sent off until the due date, and on receipt they are available immediately as cleared funds.

Pensions

Self-employed customers (sole traders, partners, professionals, etc.) who don't participate in a pension scheme through any of their sources of income may set up personal pension plans. Up to certain levels, payments out of income for this purpose can be offset against the individual's tax liability. It would be worthwhile before the exam finding out what the current level of allowance stands at; it would give a favourable impression to the examiner if you could point this out (in the answer to a question where the information is relevant, of course!).

Loanback facilities on such plans can be useful for long-term finance of such projects as buying into a partnership, purchasing a practice, and so on. The main points for you to remember are:

- Loan maximum is limited to the *cash commutable value* of the plan (never 100% of its total value).
- Loans are repaid on retirement (so term can be very long) in one lump sum.
- Payments into plans are offset against tax, so loans are tax effective (benefits are received at lower tax rate after retirement).

Insurance

Finally, in this section, you should consider the provision of insurance advice — especially about *life policies*. In just about every question involving a partnership or a sole proprietorship, there will be an opportunity to recommend some sort of life cover (or related policies) — to be provided through the bank's insurance agency, of course!

You should be familiar with the principal types of policy by now, so all we're going to do here is to help you create a framework for your knowledge. There are two ways in which you can categorize your knowledge: by type of policy and by type of customer.

By type of policy: here's a list of (most of) the principal types of personal policies. Work through it and write down:

- What types of 'cover' each one provides.
- What the 'benefit' of each one is to the proposer.
- What sort of customer should take one out.

List of policies

- Term Assurance
  — level
  — reducing
  — convertible
- Whole life
- Endowment
- Health insurance
- Permanent health policies
- Disability insurance
- Family income benefit

Marsh & Wild include a good chart on page 225 that could be useful as a starting point for you.

By type of customer: now think about it the other way round. Look at the different types of business that bank with you and try to work out what personal insurance requirements they might have. Here's one item to get you started: 'Keyman' insurance is becoming more common than ever. What is it, and who would use it?

General insurance is of course also available to cover the risks of being in business. 'Combined policies' are available for traders that cover several of these risks. You should be able to list the principal types of insurance that are generally commercially available, but it's unlikely that such facilities will form the specific basis of a question in the exam. You might well be able to pick up 'bonus marks' by mention of them when appropriate, though.

Just check on what you do know, make a list of the types of insurance policy that you might recommend to a business customer. You'll probably be able to get most of them without doing any further research at all.

Once you feel confident about your knowledge of this topic, try to answer the 10 multiple choice questions which follow.

Multiple choice questions

1   Which of the following statements about the work of a Registrar's Department is correct:

  a the work is concerned solely with the maintenance of a register of shareholders?

  b the work is concerned solely with the making of dividend payments?

  c the work is concerned with all aspects of share registration?

  d the work is concerned with the maintainance of a register of business opportunities to be passed on to bank customers?

 answer

2   Look at this list of services:

  (i) Payroll calculations
  (ii) Sales ledger administration
  (iii) BACs payment instructions
  (iv) Purchase ledger administration.

Which of them could be provided by the bank via its computer bureau for a medium-sized company:

  a (i), (ii), (iii) and (iv)?

  b (i), (ii), and (iii)?

  c (i), (iii) and (iv)?

  d (ii), (iii) and (iv)?

 answer

3   Which of the following would usually be the principal selling point to the employer of paying wages by means of bank transfer:

  a security from robbery?

  b cost savings from not handling cash?

  c ability to computerize the payroll?

  d improved cash flow?

 answer

4 Which of the following payment services can be accessed by way of the BACs system:

    a wages and salaries?
    b payments to suppliers?
    c collection of payments from debtors?
    d all of the above?

 *answer*

5 What is the chief benefit to the remitter of making payment by way of the CHAPS system:

    a improved cash flow management?
    b access to cleared funds immediately?
    c the reliability of the system?
    d the confidentiality of the system?

 *answer*

6 Which of the following customers are the target market for the CHAPS service:

    a accountants and solicitors?
    b estate agents?
    c any customer making large value payments?
    d major corporations?

 *answer*

7 Who can arrange a 'loanback' facility on a personal pension plan:

    a self-employed people?
    b anyone with no pension provisions under any source of earnings?
    c anyone holding a personal pension plan?
    d any one participating in a pension scheme?

 *answer*

8 What are the benefits of a 'loanback' arrangement:

    a a low rate of interest?
    b low cost owing to the tax advantages?
    c long term of the borrowing?
    d low cost and length of term?

9 Read this list of different types of insurance and assurance policies:

    (i)   Term assurance
    (ii) Endowment assurance
    (iii) Disability cover
    (iv) Family income benefit insurance

Which combination of these would be particularly beneficial to a member of a partnership to cover commitments related to his working life:

    a (i), (ii), (iii) and (iv)?
    b (ii), (iii) and (iv)?
    c (i), (iii) and (iv)?
    d (i), (ii) amd (iii)?

10 What sort of life cover is provided by 'keyman' assurance:

    a whole life assurance?
    b temporary assurance?
    c endowment assurance
    d health insurance?

Answers follow on pages 195–200. Score 2 marks for each correct answer.

Answers

1 The correct answer is **c**.

If you gave answers **a** or **b** as your response to this question, you can be forgiven to some extent because the two factors mentioned do form an important part of the work of a registrar. However, the word 'solely' should have given the game away, so we don't have too much sympathy for you.

Maintainance of the register and payment of the dividends are perhaps the two most time-consuming parts of the routine work undertaken. The benefit to the company is principally that it is released from the need to keep its own staff to do these things. Staff time is thus released for more productive endeavours, or the workforce may be reduced. In either case, it will usually be found that the registrars — because of their expertise and the economies of scale that can be achieved — will be able to do these jobs more cost effectively.

However, the services that are available from the Registrars don't stop there: a number of 'non-repetitive' services are also available. Most important of these is the ability to take over any 'capital adjustments' that the company wishes to make. These include mergers, takeovers, rights issues, and so on. The clerical effort which these require is considerable and would usually be quite beyond the capacity of most customers.

We hope you didn't give **d** as your answer! Certainly, banks do keep a record of such enquiries, but they don't usually entrust the task to the Registrars.

2 The correct answer is **a**.

All of these services are available from the bank's computer bureau. Let's look at each one briefly. Payroll calculations are more and more being made by computer, with the consequent savings of staff time and costs. Smaller businesses may be able to accomplish this by using PCs, but larger firms will need more computing power. Use of the bank's 'mainframe' can be a valuable solution as suggested in (i). An added advantage of using the computer is that output can be recorded on tapes that can be fed directly into the BACs system for payments to be made to employees' accounts. Of course, they have to have bank accounts first!

Really, purchase ledger administration — (iv) — by computer confers very much the same advantages in terms of cost and time saving. *And* payments can be made by BACs. Furthermore, the greater control over the timing of payments should result in their being made at the optimum time — which can have a positive effect on cash flow control.

Sales ledger administration services — (ii) — again can result in a more cost-effective and efficient job being done. And making sure that debts are collected on time should also have a positive effect on the cash flow situation. Of course, if the bank's factoring service is being used, this service becomes unnecessary. The customer will have to balance the higher costs of the factoring facilities against the added benefits which they confer. (Do you know what they are?)

Lastly, we come to the BACs services — (iii) — which in fact we have already mentioned several times! You should be aware, however, that the computer bureau could be used to generate other BACs entries than those we have mentioned. Don't forget that BACs can handle *debit* instructions as well as credits. A business requiring to generate such items will need access to someone's computer power if it doesn't have enough of its own.

3 The correct answer is **b**.

We have already covered this topic to some extent in question **2**, so you should have had some clues. In fact, *all* of these benefits can accrue from the payment of wages via bank transfer, so all you are being asked to do is to rank them in order. The most important clearly is the time (and therefore the cost) saving of not having to handle large amounts of cash on a weekly or monthly basis. You will probably know quite well how time consuming it is in branches to have to make up the large amounts of cash required by businesses still paying this way. Well, just think how much extra work is needed to break it all down into individual wagepackets. And that doesn't count the work involved in working out in the first place just how much cash will be required, and in what denominations.

The next major selling point is the removal of the security risk. Companies that still pay in cash have had to set up costly security arrangements to protect themselves against the danger of robbery. The overwhelming majority employ security couriers to transport the cash from bank to wages office, but that still leaves the wages office vulnerable! With crime apparently becoming increasingly violent, the advantages of doing away with cash become more convincing.

The ability to computerize — answer **c** — is not *conferred* by converting to bank transfer, since the calculation part of a cash-based system can also be computerized. Nevertheless the facility is extended, as the production of BACs input can be added on to the program.

Cash flow will not necessarily be affected, and if it is, it may be improved or it may deteriorate! Often, cash for wages will be withdran the day before payment is made; if payment is made through BACs, the employer's account will not be debited until the date of payment, thus saving a day. However, if funds are remitted through the giro system by paper voucher, the payments must be sent off some days before they are due to appear in the employees' accounts. This will of course have a negative effect on the cashflow.

4   The correct answer is **d**.

Once again, we have covered quite a lot of the answers given here in the previous questions, so we'll be able to deal with this one quickly — very quickly.

The BACs system can transmit both debits and credits, so it can be used both to make payments and to make claims for amounts due. To make payments, all that is required is to know the beneficiary's bank, branch, and account number. Payments for any purpose can be made, although — of course — the costs mean that it isn't suitable for making single payments.

Claims for payment — answer **c** — require greater formality since the debtor's authority to debit the account will be required. This is, of course, the basis of the direct debit system, access to which is restricted to customers who have the support of their banks. An indemnity will be required to cover the possibility of false or erroneous claims being processed.

5   The correct answer is **a**.

The CHAPs system is designed to enable customers to make 'same day settlements' for large amounts (£10,000 plus). For the *remitter*, the great advantage is that the payment doesn't have to be sent off before the day on which it falls due. More traditional systems can result in the payment being debited to the account some days before. This improvement in cash flow control is important, since loss of even one day's interest on such large amounts can come to a considerable sum.

The main benefit to the *recipient* is that the funds received are cleared funds, available for remittance elsewhere (or to be placed on an interest-bearing account). This was the gist of answer **b**, but if you selected this as your response, we suspect that you didn't read the question carefully enough. You were specifically asked to select the chief benefit to the *remitter*.

Options **c** and **d** are both important attributes of the CHAPs system. It does work efficiently and effectively, and the details of each payment are kept secret from parties who aren't involved. If you gave either of these as your answer, you're probably confusing *attribute* with *benefit* (but we've told you about it often enough before). The system has to have these attributes if the customers are to accept it: if it didn't, they would steer clear of it. But they won't use it just because of the attributes: they need a benefit that wouldn't accrue from a more traditional system.

6   The correct answer is **c**.

There is little excuse for you if you got it wrong. The CHAPs system is designed to facilitate the making of large value payments. Therefore it is a suitable service for all customers who have such payments to make. As such, the facility is appropriate to many different types of customer.
Some examples of such customers are:

- Accountants and solicitors making remittances of funds to clients or on clients behalf.
- Estate agents remitting payments (deposits or final settlements) for house purchase.
- Large corporations settling contractual payments or making transfers to the money markets.

You might like to see how many more 'target markets' you can think of.

7   The correct answer is **c**.

A 'loanback' facility involves the raising of a loan against a personal pension plan issued under the *Income and Corporation Tax Act 1970* s.226. The loan is repaid by the *cash commutable value* of the policy on retirement, interest only being covered during the currency of the loan. The CCV will never represent 100% of the value of the plan: only a proportion can be commuted in this way. Anyone who has such a policy can utilize it in this way.

If you gave **a** as your answer, you were on the right lines, but you've been a little too general. These pension plans are aimed at the self-employed, but they don't all take them out — indeed, they may not all be eligible to do so. And without taking one out, it won't be possible to borrow against it!

Answer **b** is in fact the more accurate description of those among the self-employed who are eligible to take out these plans. Anyone who has access to a pension scheme through the source of any part of his or her earnings is ineligible for these plans. But as we have said, we can't assume that everyone who is eligible will have taken one out.

Answer **d** is of course quite wrong. This is a definition of those who are in general employment (people like us, in other words). It won't be possible to raise loans against contributions to such a scheme.

8   The correct answer is **d**.

We've already established that a loan against a personal pension plan is a long-term arrangement, lasting until the retirement of the plan holder. Answer **c** therefore consists of part of the truth. But is it all of the truth? In fact, it isn't; answer **b** also contains a part of the truth. The loan will be repaid out of the CCV of the plan, which in turn represents a proportion of the funds paid into the plan. These contributions are eligible for tax relief, so in effect the funds that are being set aside to repay the loan are subject to tax relief. The cost of repaying the borrowing is thereby reduced.

Answer **d** is just wrong. The interest rate applying on such loans will reflect commercial rates. There is no specific mechanism that would reduce the interest cost to the borrower.

9 The correct answer is **c**.

Let's think about the risks that *specifically* need to be covered for such an individual. That should help us to answer the question more accurately, shouldn't it?

Firstly there is the need for the partnership to cover itself against the death before retirement of any one of the partners. In such an event insurance cover can provide funds to enable the survivors to pay the deceased's estate the value of his share in the business. *Temporary* assurance policies are all that is required to do this: if the partner dies before retirement, the sum assured becomes payable but if he survives, the policy lapses. Usually, such policies will be taken out on a 'cross insurance' basis, i.e. each partner's life is insured for the benefit of the others.

Secondly, the individual partner will need to provide for his family should he die prematurely or should he become unable to work. The former risk can be covered by a *family income benefit* policy, which assures continuation of income rather than paying a capital sum. This type of policy — option(iv) — is especially useful when there is a young family with dependent children.

The disability risk is often overlooked, but it can be very damaging on the level of family income. A *permanent disability* policy really must be taken out — option (iii) — to protect against this risk. Such a policy would protect levels of income even to the extent of providing for pension contributions.

That leaves us just option (ii) — *endowment* policies. An endowment policy becomes payable either on the survival of the life assured to a specified date or on previous death. It is a very useful policy for the provision of a lump sum to meet a specific need such as the repayment of a static loan, or just for investment purposes. Many partners will have such policies, but you shouldn't have included them in your answer because there's no *specific* need for them in this case.

10 The correct answer is **b**.

'Keyman' insurance is taken out by a business to protect itself against the risks of losing — through premature death — the services of a key employee (or director, or partner . . .). Especially in the samller companies, such a loss could be utterly disastrous. Even with insurance, the consequences will be major, but at least there will be some financial recompense that should go some way towards keeping the business afloat until a replacement is found (or a new strategy is adopted).

What, then, is the nature of this risk? Simply, it is the risk that the employee will die before retirement age. This means that insurance cover will be required only up to that date; afterwards, the business has no further interest in the continued survival of the individual — not at least, in a commercial sense! Thus temporary assurance is all that is required.

An endowment policy — answer **c** — could be taken out, maturing at retirement date. This too would provide a lump sum if the person was to die early but it would also provide a lump sum on survival to retirement and this would not be appropriate. In any case, the cost of such a policy would not be justified.

Similarly, whole life assurance — option **a** — isn't appropriate since it will provide a lump sum whenever the life assured dies, whether before or after retirement age.

Health insurance — answer **c** and not to be confused with permanent health insurance — is another thing entirely. This covers the cost (in certain cases) of private medical care. It may be considered worthwhile by a business to assist key employees to cover themselves in this way, but it isn't what is generally understood by the term 'keyman' insurance.

Score 2 marks for each correct answer. What was your score? Fill it in on the score grid.

If you scored 12 or less and are still a bit shaky on some points go back and look at the study guide again before proceeding any further.

If you are sure you really understand and are familiar with this topic now, try the 10 further questions which are on page 244–6. Alternatively you can go on to your next topic and do all the post-tests together at the end.

Topic 10   Foreign business

Study guide

Introduction

Getting it into context

Facilities for importers and exporters form an important part of a commercial bank's business, and the technicalities of the variuos services are quite complex. This is reflected in the fact that — as you will no doubt be fully aware — there is a complete exam on the subject of 'The Finance of International Trade'. There is some good news and some bad news for you in this. On the one hand, you may be relieved to hear that if you still know your stuff from taking FIT, there is really nothing new for you to learn about. And the bad news? Well . . . you still really do need to know *in some detail* the topics that you learned about previously.

   A good strategy for you would be to revise your old notes or textbooks from FIT so as to remind yourself just how much you do (don't) remember. One more piece of good news: you certainly won't have to deal with any questions requiring you to make detailed currency or (especially) forward currency conversions. So if you think you're a little rusty, don't worry. You will, however have to make sure that your general knowledge of these foreign services is up to date: there have been several important changes in recent years.

What to expect in the exam

For such an important topic, foreign business doesn't seem to come up in the exam all that often. This is probably because it is difficult for the examiner to set questions that aren't too specific (i.e. ones that could simply be inserted into the FIT paper).

   As a rule, the questions that you will be most likely to see are fairly general ones which require you to set out the range of facilities that would be appropriate for a trader operating in a specified area of activity. You will have to adopt an *integrated* approach to these questions if you are going to score well. By this we mean that:

— Your suggestions must 'hang together' as a coherent package.

— The services specified must all be appropriate for the customer in question.
— You must give adequate detail of the operational details of each service to convince the examiner that you really do know more about them than just the name!

Generally for these types of questions, your watchword should be 'comprehensiveness'. The examiners are always pointing out that in Section B, students are too easily satisfied with superficial answers; if *a* service has been found, no attempt is made to look for a second one, let alone a third, or . . . ! Nowhere is this more evident than in the area of foreign business.

Lastly, don't forget that there are two specific 'market segments' for whom these services can be provided: importers and exporters. The latter are the more 'important' group in so far as they have available to them a wider range of services, but that doesn't mean you can forget about importers! As you study each service, make sure you are quite clear in your own mind which of the two segments it is directed at — if not both.

Foreign services

As we've said, this is a very wide area, so you'll probably need to break it down into sections. Work through each section in turn and make sure that you have the details committed to memory before you move on to the next one. In this guide, we can't go into detail, so you'll need to 'flesh out' the following broad outline by reference to your textbooks — and your FIT Notes.

Information services

Largely of use to exporters, the banks' information services can be used by customers wishing to obtain general advice about foreign markets or specific assistance with a particular problem. It would be unusual in the exam to see a question concerning just one of these services, but there will often be marks available for mentioning those of them that could form part of an overall 'package' to be put together for a customer.

Make sure that you can distinguish between the two following areas.

- Status enquiries — just like inland enquiries in objective.
- Trade enquiries — not to be confused with status enquiries, these involve 'advertising' for potential customers via the bank's network of correspondents.

Also, you should be aware of:

- Economic research — most banks maintain intelligence sections that can advise on whether a particular project is likely to be economically sound in a specified country or region of the world.
- Documents of foreign trade — general advice on the use/production of documents of foreign trade can be given. Can you recall the most common ones? Make sure you know how they operate. Specific advice on the documentary requirements of particular countries is an important service for exporters, but you won't be asked to give the advice.
- Import/export regulations — closely related to the last point is the question of restrictions or conditions (e.g. exchange controls) imposed by foreign governments on trade with their countries. Banks will advise customers on these topics, but again, this exam won't test you on specifics.

Payments abroad

The introduction of the SWIFT Network has revolutionized the way in which payment instructions are passed between correspondent banks, and the old terms 'air mail transfer' and 'cable transfer' are now largely obsolete. However, these systems will still be used to transmit payment instructions to the (few) countries not covered by the SWIFT network.

To cover all possibilities, the banks today use the terms:

- *International funds transfer*, and
- *Express international funds transfer* which — at extra cost — afford the instructions more expeditious processing.
- *Drafts* — are still of course available if the customer making the payment wishes to send off the remittance himself.
- *Foreign cheques* (and drafts) may well be received by exporters, and these may be collected or negotiated (with recourse).

What conditions are to be met if a cheque is to be negotiated? Try to write them down before looking it up.

Before leaving this topic, it's worthwhile pointing out that the SWIFT network isn't just for processing payment instructions. It can be (and is) used for passing any message between participating banks.

Foreign exchange

As we have already said, you won't need to make any foreign exchange calculations in the exam. You will need to know the basic services available and who they would benefit.

Before going any further, jot down a note of the exchange risks that affect importers and those that affect exporters. What services are available to mitigate these risks?

Currency conversions at spot rate carry risks of loss for both exporters and importers when trade is negotiated in foreign currency.

Forward exchange contracts can remove the risks by setting a rate at which the bank will buy/sell the currency — in advance:

- *Fixed contracts* set all the variables at the outset: amount, rate, and date of completion.
- *Option contracts* allow the customer only the freedom to select the particular date within a period on which the contract will be completed. It is *not* optional whether or not to complete at all.

Currency options are now becoming available, however, and these allow the customer the right to buy/sell currency at a pre-arranged rate *if he wishes*. If he so decides, he may let the option lapse instead.

Does your textbook give details of currency options? If not, you should check your own bank's advertising materials which will give you some basic information on their operation.

Currency accounts are useful to customers who have regular dealings in a particular currency — especially if there are both receipts and payments to be processed. Transfers between the sterling and the currency accounts can be made when the rates are favourable to the customer.

Currency loans to exporters are becoming increasingly popular. If finance is required, the exporter borrows in the currency which he expects to receive and converts the funds to sterling 'at spot'. The loan is repaid out of the currency receipts when the project is completed. In this way, the exchange risk is avoided. An added advantage can be that the rate of interest levied on the loan will be that prevailing in the country of the currency: and that may well be lower than the sterling rate.

This type of loan is not recommended for customers who do not have currency receipts. Can you explain why?

Methods of settlement

Advising customers on how to go about entering the import/export markets is an important part of the bank's business services. Explaining the various methods of settlement is an important part of this, and you will need to be familiar with the principles of each one, and to have some knowledge of the associated documents.

Draw up a checklist of the main ways in which exporters and importers can arrange settlement between themselves. What are the advantages/disadvantages of each, and what are the benefits to each party. When you have finished, compare it to ours, shown below. Ours is just a 'skeleton'; we hope that yours has more detail.

Open account: the importer pays against invoice after receipt of goods. Simple and cheap to operate, it is, however, risky for the exporter. It's only recommended between long-standing trading partners.

Documentary collections use the banks' correspondent networks to deliver documents of title to goods to the importer against payment or acceptance of a bill of exchange. It is a safer system for the exporter since control is retained over the goods until the documents are released. But there are still some risks; can you explain what they are? Are there any risks for the importer?

Documentary credits provide the 'safest' method for both parties, but are also the most costly and complicated. Familiarize yourself with the meanings of the terms:

— issuing bank
— advising bank
— confirming bank
— revocable/irrevocable credits.

The issuing bank is taking a credit risk in that it has to pay out against the credit if the right documents are presented. If the funds cannot be recoverd from its customer, what can it do?

Payment in advance practically removes all risk for the exporter but leaves the importer vulnerable.

Support services

We know we keep 'harping on' about the need for comprehensive answers, but it *is* important — and nowhere more so than in this area. A very familiar type of question requires the candidate to list (and explain!) the services that would be appropriate to a particular customer. It is all too easy to miss marks by restricting your answer to too narrow a range of major facilities. Don't forget that some of the less common 'support services' can also be appropriate. (*NB* The word 'appropriate' is vital. Don't infuriate the examiner by just listing them all without any indication of *why* they are of benefit!)

Credit insurance for exporters is an important topic. Customers trading abroad on open account terms or on a documentary collection (or even documentary credit) basis run some risks of not being paid. So do those undertaking large capital projects.

Jot down a list of those risks. Now compare it with your textbook.

Credit insurance is available via the ECGD, which is not a bank service of course, but one which the bank can direct the customer towards. You need to be familiar with the broad divisions between the schemes.

- Specific guarantees for single large contracts.
- Comprehensive guarantees for ongoing regular trade. Arrangement can be made to cover extended credit periods and foreign currenc debts.

It would be worthwhile to have a clear idea of the extent c cover available for the risks. Marsh & Wilde's *Practice* e *Banking 2* contains a useful table of the percentages (page 248)

Bond support for those exporters undertaking large projects is ofter overlooked. The chief services available are:

- *Tender bonds* to cover the buyer against the risk of the exporte being unable to fulfil his tender if it is accepted.
- *Performance bonds*: once the contract is awarded, the contractor ma require further 'guarantees' of compensation if the work is no completed or is not to an adequate standard.
- *Maintenance guarantees* can also be given when the exporter i required to provide long-term maintenance of the goods/equipmen supplied.

Travel facilities for representatives, site engineers, and so on are s 'obvious' that candidates often omit to mention them. Are you familia with the operation of (and advantages provided by) the following:

— Travel cheques
— Credit cards and charge cards
— Credit opened facilities
— Circular letters of credit (now quite rare)
— Bank accounts abroad

Financing foreign trade

Finally, make sure that you know about the specific ways in which bank can make finance available for customers involved in foreign trade. I

Section B you won't be required to give a decision on whether such finance should be granted, but you should be able to recommend the appropriate media.

Export factoring is directly analogous to inland factoring. The service allows the customer to pass over his sales ledger administration to an expert department. In addition, finance of (usually) up to 80% of the outstanding invoices can be available.

Discounting bills, while not as common as it was once, still can be useful to customers who export on a documentary collection basis. The chief difference from the discounting of inland bills is that the bank may agree to discount the bills prior to acceptance by the importer.

Short-term finance schemes for exporters were introduced by many banks to replace the facilities previously available under ECGD Comprehensive Bank Guarantees. Did you know that the ECGD schemes have been phased out as from October 1986?

Get hold of your own bank's literature on these schemes and make sure you understand them. There will be differences from bank to bank, but in general the provisions will be similar, e.g.

— ECGD (or similar) credit insurance provided.
— 100% finance of the insured value of each shipment.
— Credit terms of 180 days (or longer) can be encompassed.

ECGD specific guarantees for both buyer credit and supplier credit are still available.

Confirming house facilities should also be familiar to you. Jot down a note of how they operate.

Produce advances for importers are also important. They are covered in some detail in Topic 5 — refer back if necessary.

Once you feel confident about your knowledge of this topic, try to answer the 10 multiple choice questions which follow.

Multiple choice questions

1 A dairy farmer who sells all his produce to the Milk Marketing Board has approached you with the request that he be granted a foreign currency loan, the proceeds of which will be used to pay off his sterling overdraft. He makes the request because the interest rate for the currency loan would be 7% p.a. lower than the sterling rate. How would you respond:

    a   agree; it is a good idea that will save him money?

    b   decline; there is a major exchange risk since repayments will be from sterling receipts?

    c   agree, provided that he takes out a forward contract to cover the exchange risk?

    d   refuse; UK exchange control regulations prohibit the 'export' of sterling to repay foreign loans?

answer

2 An importer who anticipated a receipt of US$ 10,000 this month entered into an option forward contract to sell the currency to the bank on receipt. The option expires today and the funds have not yet arrived; he now expects to be paid next month. What will you do:

    a   release him from the contract and buy the currency from him at spot rate when it is received?

    b   insist that he buys US dollars at spot on the open market in order to complete the contract?

    c   extend the agreement by a further month by closing out the existing contract and arranging a new one?

    d   allow him another month on the original contract?

answer

3 Which of the following documents would you invariably expect to see as part of a documentary collection:

    a   bills of exchange?

    b   bills of lading?

    c   commercial invoice?

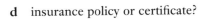

d insurance policy or certificate?

answer

4 When a contract of foreign trade is entered into on a CIF basis, what specific document would you expect to see as part of a resulting documentary collection:

a bills of lading marked 'Freight payable at destination'?
b insurance policy or certificate?
c packing list?
d consular invoice?

answer

5 An importing customer wishes to set up a documentary credit for £50,000 in favour of his suppliers abroad. What would be your main concern in considering this request:

a that the supplier could produce the goods as specified?
b that the goods will be capable of being on-sold at a profit after receipt?
c that the customer is a good credit risk for the amount?
d that the customer has covering funds on deposit with the bank?

answer

6 The exporter in the question above has stipulated that the letter of credit must be 'confirmed'. What does this mean:

a the advising bank must guarantee payment against the specified documents?
b the issuing bank must guarantee payment against the specified documents?
c a copy of the letter of credit must be sent to the exporter?
d the letter of credit may not be cancelled or amended without the consent of the beneficiary?

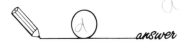

answer

7   One of the documents called for by the letter of credit is a 'clean, on board Bill of Lading'. Which of the following would be acceptable:

   a   a bill of lading specifying 'goods received for shipment'?
   b   a bill of lading specifying goods 'shipped on board' and overtyped 'one case holed'?
   c   an air waybill acknowledging receipt of the goods for shipment?
   d   a bill of lading specifying goods 'received for shipment' and overtyped 'shipped on board' with the date?

answer

8   An exporter who is supplying goods abroad on credit (120 days sight bills of exchange) has asked you to advise on ways of raising finance to cover the working capital requirement that this creates. Which of the following would you recommend:

   a   ECGD (Bills & Notes) Comprehensive Bank Guarantee loan?
   b   ECGD (Open account) Comprehensive Bank Guarantee loan?
   c   discounting bills of exchange?
   d   produce advance against documents of title?

answer

9   The following are some of the risks which can be covered by an ECGD Comprehensive Guarantee:

   (i)   Insolvency of buyer
   (ii) Failure to pay for goods which have been accepted
   (iii) A moratorium on foreign debts by the importing country.

To what extent can losses arise from these risks be recovered under the guarantee:

   a   (i) 90%, (ii) 90%, (iii) 70%?
   b   (i) 75%, (ii) 90%, (iii) 75%?
   c   (i) 80%, (ii) 95%, (iii) 90%?
   d   (i) 90%, (ii) 90%, (iii) 95%?

answer

10 Which of the following facilities could be useful to a sales representative who is about to travel to South America on a 6 month sales expedition:

    a   travel cheques?
    b   credit cards?
    c   credit opened facilities?
    d   all of the above?

answer

Answers follow on pages 212–19. Score 2 marks for each correct answer.

Answers

1   The correct answer is **b**.

It is undeniably true that foreign currency loans — when arranged — are charged at the interest rate appropriate to the currency. Thus, a UK customer borrowing in DM will pay German interest rates, and these may well be lower than UK interest rates. So it does sound quite a good idea to borrow where the cost is lowest. But there must be a problem or everyone would be doing it (wouldn't they?).

The difficulty is that if you borrow a foreign currency, you have to make your repayments (and interest payments too) in that currency. Now, that's all very well if you have receipts in that currency; but if you don't, it'll be necessary to convert sterling receipts into the currency. And that carries an exchange risk: if sterling loses value, the cost of repayments can rise and wipe out any savings or even create a loss. So answer **a** is wrong. It's worth pointing out that if sterling strengthens, the repayments would become cheaper, but it really isn't worth the risk.

Can the exchange risk be covered as suggested in answer **c**. Yes, it can of course, but there is a further problem. Forward currency exchange rates between any two currencies differ from the spot rates. The differential is a direct reflection of the differentials in the interest rates of the two countries. In effect what this means is that the net cost of borrowing (say) in DM and repaying from sterling covered by a fixed contract is *exactly the same* as borrowing in sterling in the first place! The whole thing would therefore be something of an exercise in futility. On balance then, it is a valid exercise to borrow in a foreign currency only if you have receipts in that currency.

By the way, if you gave **d** as your answer, your textbook (or your notes) must be very old — we did warn you about keeping up to date! It is several years now since the UK's exchange control regulations were to all intents and purposes abolished. There are no restrictions on making currency payments to pay off currency loan accounts.

2   The correct answer is **c**.

Let's make the most important point first: the option in an option forward contract concerns only *when*, within a given period, the client will complete the contract. It is not an option whether to complete it or not. If you gave **a** as your answer you probably weren't aware of this simple but basic factor in the equation.

So, the contract has to be completed somehow. Furthermore, it has to be completed within the period of the option. For this reason, answer **d** is wrong. The bank will have to do something much more formal in order to regularize the position.

Theoretically what has to be done first is to 'close out' the original contract: as today is the last day of the option, this must be done immediately. But how can the customer do this when he hasn't yet received the currency? One answer *would be* for him to buy the currency on the open market today at spot rates, but this would present two problems. Firstly, the exchange rate for spot transactions may well mean that he will have to pay more for the funds than he will receive when he sells them back to the bank at the agreed forward rate. Secondly, when the funds do arrive, he will have to sell them at spot — and by then the exchange rates may have changed again! In addition, there will be exchange commissions on all these transactions, so all in all there is every possibility of it being a costly business. Of course, it is possible that the rates will have moved the other way, allowing the customer to make a profit, but this is not to be assumed.

There is a somewhat simpler way of achieving the same objective, however. The bank can extend the contract. In essence this still involves closing out the existing contract and setting up a new one, but the customer doesn't have to organize the whole thing himself. Furthermore, the bank will forgo (some of) the exchange commissions that would be due. Even so, if any loss was to result from a difference between spot rate and the forward rate, this would still fall on the customer.

3 The correct answer is **c**.

All of the documents quoted here might be encountered as part of a documentary collection, but the only one that will always be there is the commercial invoice, since this is in effect a claim for payment. It sets out in detail the terms of the contract between buyer and seller, the quantity and description of the goods, and most importantly the total price to be paid.

You won't, in fact, need to display a comprehensive knowledge of the documents of foreign trade in the POB 2 exam, but the examiner may expect you to show that you are at least familiar with them. The giving of advice to customers who are unused to exporting (or importing) is an important service provided by the banks. So — briefly — what about the other documents?

A bill of exchange — answer **a** — will usually be there as part of the 'set' of documents, particularly if a period of credit is to be granted. The documents can be released against acceptance of the bill. However, if the terms of trade are for payment at sight, there is no real need for a bill, since documents may be delivered simply against payment of the amount due. If the exporter wishes to protest for non-payment, however, there has to be a bill of exchange present.

A bill of lading — answer **b** — will be present only if the goods have gone by sea. There are many other possibilities — air freight, parcel post, container lorry, and so on. Each of these alternatives will produce a different shipping document, so you wouldn't invariably expect to see a bill of lading.

The same is true of the insurance document — answer **c**; it won't always be there. The exporter will incorporate the policy or certificate into the 'set' only if he has arranged the insurance as part of the contract. If the goods have been shipped on C&F or FOB contract terms, for instance, the insurance will be arranged by the buyer.

4 The correct answer is **b**.

If you have read the answer to question **3** carefully, you should have no difficulty in recognizing why this is the right answer! Let's just go over the reasoning to make sure. A CIF contract is one in which the contract price includes the cost of carriage to the importer's country and of insurance on the goods while in transit. The exporter must therefore arrange for these things to be organized. The importer will expect to be presented with a set of documents that shows that this has been done. What does that entail? Chiefly just two things.

Firstly, the freight documentation should show that freight charges have been paid — of course! Answer **c** is therefore wrong on two counts. If freight charges are 'payable at destination', they haven't been paid by the exporter. And anyway, as we have already noted in question **3**, you wouldn't specifically expect to see a bill of lading; the goods may have been sent by other methods than sea freight.

Secondly, you would expect to see an insurance document as evidence that the exporter has made the necessary arrangements. This may be either a policy or a certificate. Exporters who undertake a significant volume of foreign business will usually arrange 'blanket' cover for all their shipments and issue certificates for each cargo on behalf of the insurers.

Answers **c** and **d** are both 'red herrings', as we're sure you spotted. Both of these documents may be required if the importer (or his country's regulations) calls for them. But they don't relate only to CIF contracts. Let's make the 'business development' point again: the bank's International Division will always be able to offer expert advice on the documentation required for exporting to particular markets or countries.

Before you go on from here, jot down a list of the alternatives to CIF as terms of trade — and what each one means! What would the documentation for each one be?

5 The correct answer is **c**.

When it issues a documentary letter of credit, the bank enters into an unconditional promise to pay the specified sum, provided that the beneficiary comes up with the required documents. Thus, the bank is taking on a credit risk. Specifically, it is taking the chance that the customer will be able to pay up when the documents are delivered — as suggested in answer **c**.

In many ways, therefore, the issuing of a letter of credit has to be approached as if it was a proposal for an advance. The bank will wish to satisfy itself that, on balance, the whole proposal is a 'goer'. All of the suggestions made in our other alternative answers are useful points to consider, but aren't our main concern. Let's look at each one in more detail.

If the customer has covering funds on deposit, there is a good indication of the ability to pay! However, one doesn't usually find this happy circumstance. It is much more common to find that the customer will be looking to future income — possibly from sales of the goods concerned — to cover the payment. If you have any reservations about this, you could always look for some 'other' form of security, just as you would for an advance.

If the customer can't demonstrate an ability to pay, the question then becomes one of whether you would be prepared to advance him the required funds. If you are willing to do so, the request does become a straightforward advances proposal. If you aren't willing to lend, the letter of credit request must be turned down.

It may happen (occasionally?) that a customer whom you thought was good for the money turns out not to be. What do you do then? Well, if the bank has paid out under the letter of credit, the correct documents have presumably been presented. Thus, the bank will have control of the goods, which — in extremis — it can sell on its own behalf to recoup at least some of the funds paid away. You might think, therefore, that answers **a** and **b** have some merit; that before issuing a letter of credit the bank should make sure that the goods are saleable. In general terms this is right, but the implications of trying to do so are immense. Just think of all the investigations that you would have to make. No, the bank finds it much more effective simply to satisfy itself that the customer knows his business.

One final point: do remember that when releasing funds under a letter of credit, the bank has no real regard for the goods as such. Payment is made against the *documents*, which must conform exactly to the requirements laid down in the credit. Presumably, if the documents are right, the goods will be right, but that's another story!

6 The correct answer is **a**.

We have already said in question **5** that the bank that issues the letter of credit enters into an unconditional promise to pay out against the supply of certain documents. Thus, all letters of credit — not just those which are 'confirmed' — involve the 'guarantee' mentioned in answer **b**.

Similar considerations apply to answer **c**; once the credit has been issued, it must be transmitted to the exporter so that the documents can be prepared, whether it is confirmed or not. The exporter receives the letter of credit via an 'advising bank' in his own country, and thus has a local point of contact.

In 'advising' the letter of credit, the advising bank does not offer any warranty that the funds will be paid, merely that it is genuine and does emanate from the bank acting for the importer. The exporter is thus relying on the promise to pay of the issuing bank — and he may not know whether this is safe or not. It is quite common, therefore, for the exporter to require that the credit be confirmed by the advising bank which in effect guarantees payment in the (unlikely?) event of the issuing bank not being able to pay.

What about answer **d** then? Well, that covers another point entirely, doesn't it? A letter of credit may be revocable, in which case it can be amended or cancelled without the consent of the beneficiary at any time up until the presentation of documents. On the other hand, it may be irrevocable, in which case the exporter's consent is always required for any changes. You won't be surprised to learn that a revocable credit isn't usually acceptable. The 'safest' type for the importer is thus the confirmed irrevocable credit.

7 The correct answer is **d**.

This is really quite a simple question that tests whether you can recall the meanings of the terms used. 'Clean' means that there must be no indication on the bill of lading that the goods may be damaged or defective in any way. 'On board' means that there must be a clear indication that the goods have actually been put on board a ship (what else?). On this basis, let's look at the alternatives available.

Answer **a** can't be right, because the bill of lading mentions only that the goods have been 'received for shipment'. It could be months before they are actually put on a ship. Answer **d** is OK though, because the fact (and date) of shipment has been added to a 'received' bill. This is a normal practice and is quite acceptable. It is, however, more usual for goods to be shipped before the bill of lading is issued, in which case the document will state right from the start that goods have been 'shipped on board'.

Answer **b** is wrong because it mentions that 'one case holed' appears on the bill of lading. The bill is therefore not 'clean'; the normal terms for a bill like this are 'dirty', 'foul', or 'claused'.

An air waybill — answer **c** — is not a bill of lading at all, so that can't be right. Bills of lading are issued specifically for marine transport. If the letter of credit calls for a bill of lading, it means that the importer requires the goods to be sent by sea, and airfreight will not be acceptable.

8 The correct answer is c.

The discounted bill facility is a long established method of providing finance for exporters as well as those engaged in inland trade. The basic principles of such facilities should be familiar to you by now — if not, you ought to refresh your memory about them before the exam. The only special point that you need to remember about foreign bills is that the bank may agree to discount the bills *before* acceptance, which would be most unusual in respect of inland bills. In effect, the bank buys the bill from the exporter and then collects the proceeds by way of a documentary collection (or whatever) on its own behalf. In case the bill isn't accepted or is dishonoured on presentation for payment, the bank will reserve its right of recourse against the drawer.

If you gave **a** or even **b** as your answer, we can understand if you are feeling puzzled over why you were wrong, since ECGD loan facilities at one time led to a great reduction in the number of discounted bill facilities being granted. The simple answer is that you were wrong because these facilities are no longer available! In 1986, the ECGD announced that it was no longer offering these two types of bank guarantees, and while existing facilities would be allowed to run off, no new ones would be granted. The chances are that your textbook is out of date in this respect, and the lesson to learn is that you must keep your knowledge up to date by reading the financial press — and your own bank's publicity material and so on.

That brings us to an important point. Most of the major banks have introduced special loan schemes for exporters, designed to replace these ECGD short term loans. These are being offered to customers rather than the discounted bill facility mentioned in the question!

 Do you know how these new services work? Make a list of the main provisions, referring to advertising leaflets if necessary.

By the way, an ECGD Open A/c facility wouldn't have been appropriate anyway!

If you gave **d** as your answer, you need to think things out again. A produce loan is granted to the *importer* against the goods (or the documents of title to them) to enable him to pay for them. The exporter has lost control of the goods by this stage, so he couldn't borrow against them, could he?

9 The correct answer is **d**.

There isn't much we can say about this question. You either know the answer or you don't!

ECGD credit guarantees are very valuable and useful to the exporter but they don't cover 100% of the possible losses. The ECGD require the exporters to shoulder some of the loss so as to encourage them to exercise some commercial caution in what they do.

Generally, the maximum cover available is 90% for some risks, and 95% for the rest. Your textbook should have a list of which risks fall into which categories, and it would be a good idea to have a general idea of the split.

There is one special category that you should know about. The ECGD will insure only 80% of losses incurred as a result of the importer failing to take up the goods when they arrive abroad. Furthermore, compensation will be limited to 90% of any claim. This means that in effect cover is limited to 72% of the value of the goods. Work it out for yourself if you don't believe us!

10 The correct answer is **d**.

All three of the specific options given relate to methods of providing the recipient with spending power while abroad, and each has its own advantages.

Travel cheques provide a safe and convenient way of providing for the needs of shorter journeys. They can be obtained in many different currencies and may be given directly in payment for goods or services, or exchanged for cash. They have the advantage of preventing the representative from overspending his limit, but lack flexibility in an emergency.

Credit cards (and also charge cards) are accepted worldwide and can also be used both to settle bills and to obtain cash. The representative has more freedom as to the total amount that he can spend, but the employer is aided in exercising control by the regular statements that will be received from the operating company.

Credit opened facilities enable the withdrawal of cash (within defined limits) at a nominated branch of a bank. It is very useful for people such as 'on-site' engineers, but less so for sales representatives who are likely to be moving around too much to be tied to an encashment point.

In fact, it would be usual for the bank to recommend a mixture of

hese facilities to meet the needs of the particular case. It would be
unusual to use all three, but to limit the choice to one would lead to
nflexibility.

Here's another exercise for you. Make a list of all the other
services that a sales representative could use apart from those
which relate to the making of payments.

Score 2 marks for each correct answer. What was your score?
Fill it in on the score grid.

If you scored 12 or less and are still a bit shaky on some
points go back and look at the study guide again before
proceeding any further.

If you are sure you really understand and are familiar with
this topic now, try the 10 further questions which are on pages
246–9. Alternatively you can go on to your next topic and do
all the post-tests together at the end.

Post-tests

Pages 222–47 contain 10 further multiple choice questions for each topic.

Questions

Topic 1 Principles of lending

1 Why is the source of a customer's contribution to the total amount required important:

    a   it reflects his honesty or dishonest?
    b   it may disclose unexpected facts about his private life?
    c   it may give an indication about his ability to save out of income?
    d   it may disclose borrowing from elsewhere?

 _answer_

2 Which of the following purposes would a bank be cautious about lending for:

    a   holidays?
    b   paying off pressing creditors?
    c   second hand cars?
    d   motor cycles?

 _answer_

3 Which of the following would you consider first in evaluating a loan proposition:

    a   the character of the customer — whether he _will_ repay you?
    b   the customer's resources — whether he _can_ repay you?
    c   the customer's assets — whether he can give you any security?
    d   the customer's calculations — whether he has correctly assessed his requirements?

 _answer_

4 What evidence would you look for from a business to show that a term loan can be repaid:

    a   cash flow forecast?
    b   profit forecasts for future year?
    c   profit levels in previous years?

d   past profits and profit forecasts?

answer

5   What attitude would you take if offered repayment of an advance
from the proceeds of an expected legacy:

a   accept the proposal?
b   accept the proposal only after sight of the will?
c   accept the proposal only if the testator is already deceased?
d   reject the proposal in all but the most exceptional circumstances?

answer

6   When approached with a proposal for a business advance which
offers a high return for the customer but which involves a high level
of risk, how would you respond:

a   decline unless the risks can be minimized?
b   agree if good security can be provided?
c   agree if the customer accepts high rates of interest?
d   agree and levy a large 'arrangement fee'?

answer

7   Which of the following statements is true:

a   all lending should be secured?
b   the bank should never lend more than the customer is putting
in?
c   all lending should be a calculated risk?
d   no lending should involve risk for the bank?

answer

8   Complete the statement 'Credit scoring is . . .':

a   a system which ignores all the principles of lending.
b   a system which assesses personal lending propositions by
concentrating chiefly on the character of the borrower.
c   so accurate that bankers no longer need to know the principles
of lending.

d undertaken to confirm a decision to approve or decline a loan.

9 If a customer has 'connections' with important clients of the bank how will this affect any loan propositions put forward:

a not at all?

b it will be a point in his favour but will not turn a bad risk into a good one?

c it will ensure that the loan is granted unless the risks are very high?

d it will predispose you towards finding fault with the proposals?

10 When should the lending banker look for security:

a for all advances proposals?

b only where the proposal appears to carry a high level of risk?

c only when he is happy that the proposal should be approved, but requires a safeguard against unforeseen events?

d whenever there is security available?

Topic 2   Personal lending

1 The Consumer Credit Act 1974 requires that:

a all bank borrowing must be evidenced by a written agreement form.

b all bank borrowing by persons must be evidenced by a written agreement form.

c all bank borrowing by persons of £15,000 or less must be evidenced by a written agreement form.

d all bank borrowing by persons by way of loan account or structured loan for £15,000 or less must be evidenced by a written agreement form.

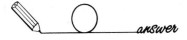

2   As a result of the implementation of the Consumer Credit Act 1974:

   a   land is not acceptable security for borrowing by personal customers.

   b   land is not acceptable security for regulated borrowing by personal customers.

   c   land is acceptable as security for regulated borrowing by personal customers only if related to house purchase or bridging facilities.

   d   land is the only acceptable security for regulated borrowing by personal customers.

answer

3   An agreement for a regulated loan which has been signed on the customer's business premises is:

   a   non-cancellable.

   b   cancellable within 10 days of being signed.

   c   cancellable within 15 days of being signed.

   d   cancellable within 5 days of the borrower receiving his copy.

answer

4   A 'closed' bridging loan:

   a   offers complete security of repayment since the customer's purchaser cannot back out of the transaction.

   b   offers reasonable security of repayment since the customer's purchaser is responsible for any losses and costs if he backs out of the transaction.

   c   offers little security of repayment since the customers purchaser can back out of the transaction at any time before contracts have been exchanged.

   d   offers no security of repayment since the customer has no firm offer of a purchase.

answer

5   What is the position regarding *tax relief* on a bridging advance:

   a   all bridging advances qualify for tax relief?

    b   a bridging advance may qualify for tax relief if taken on a separate account?

    c   all bridging advances qualify for tax relief if taken on a separate account?

    d   bridging loans do not qualify for tax relief?

6   Having granted a bridging loan, a bank will attempt to ensure that the customer's solicitor protects the bank's position, by:

    a   taking a *solicitors undertaking* to do so.

    b   making a status enquiry on the solicitor acting for the customer's purchaser.

    c   insisting on holding the title documents to the property to be sold.

    d   refusing to deal with a solicitor who is not known to the bank.

7   When negotiating with the Inland Revenue on the payment of Inheritance Tax:

    a   personal representatives will be unable to obtain a grant of representation until the amount of tax payable has been agreed.

    b   personal representatives will be unable to obtain a grant of representation until the whole of the tax due has been paid.

    c   personal representatives will be unable to obtain a grant of representation until satisfactory arrangements have been made to pay off the tax due.

    d   personal representatives will be permitted to realize only such assets as are necessary to pay the tax due.

8   A probate advance should be granted:

    a   only if there are sufficient liquid assets to repay the loan.

    b   if there are satisfactory proposals to repay any shortfall once liquid assets have been realized.

    c   if there are sufficient assets in total to repay the loan.

d if the beneficiaries have sufficient assets to repay the loan.

9 When considering an overdraft facility for a personal customer:

a the ability to repay is not important provided that there is adequate security.

b the provisions of the Consumer Credit Act require full documentation.

c security should always be taken where available.

d care should be taken to ensure that expenditure does not regularly exceed income.

10 Revolving budget account facilities are:

a complementary to both loan and overdraft facilities.

b a direct replacement for loan facilities.

c a direct replacement for overdraft facilities.

d a convenient vehicle for offering a customer a *total refinancing* arrangement.

Topic 3   Balance sheet analysis

1 A *cash flow forecast* is useful in assessing:

a applications for working capital finance.

b applications for loans for capital purchases.

c the need for capital restructuring.

d the effectiveness of the firm's credit control.

2 In calculating the *gearing ratio* of a company, what does the 'loan capital' comprise:

a loan stocks and bank advances?
b loan stocks and trade creditors?
c all long-term borrowing?
d all borrowing of any form?

3 A *current ratio* in excess of 5 : 1 may indicate:

a excellent stock control.
b unprofitable use of liquid funds.
c excellent credit control.
d liquidity problems.

4 The *net worth* of the business is:

a the total assets less fictitious and intangible assets.
b the total assets less total liabilities.
c the total assets less total liabilities other than those to proprietors.
d total assets less total liabilities other than those to the proprietors and less fictitious and intangible assets.

5 A *funds flow forecast* is a projection of:

a income from trading less all expenses incurred.
b the time the customers of the business take to pay the company and the time taken by the company to pay its suppliers.
c all sources of capital less all expenses.
d anticipated inflows and outflows of all the firm's funds.

6 *Working capital* is measured by:

a current assets less current liabilities.
b current liabilities plus fixed assets.
c current liabilities less fixed assets.

   d   current assets plus fixed assets.

answer

7   *Turnover* represents:

   a   the total amount of supplies purchased during the year.
   b   the value of stocks retained in the business at the end of the
         year.
   c   the gross profit made by the business during the year.
   d   the total volume of sales during the year.

answer

8   A decrease in *net profits as a percentage of gross profits* indicates that:

   a   gross profits are too low.
   b   gross profits are too high.
   c   costs are being adequately controlled.
   d   costs are absorbing too much of the income.

answer

9   *Net profit as a percentage of capital employed* is a good indicator of:

   a   whether the business is adequately profitable.
   b   the need for further capital.
   c   whether profits are proportionate to the volume of business
         being done.
   d   whether costs are being properly controlled.

answer

10   The *acid test ratio* is calculated by comparing:

   a   current assets : current liabilities.
   b   liquid assets : current liabilities.
   c   debtors : turnover.
   d   creditors : turnover.

answer

Topic 4 Business lending/1

1 A business customer who has a 'working capital' overdraft of
   £10,000 informs you that annual turnover is expected to increase by
   50%. What effect is this likely to have on the overdraft facility:

   a the working capital requirement will rise by 50% and so will
          the overdraft?
   b the working capital requirement will rise by 50% and the
          overdraft will rise by an equivalent monetary amount?
   c the working capital requirement may well rise by 50%; the
          overdraft would have to rise sufficiently to cover the amount of
          the increase which cannot be found from other sources?
   d there will be no effect?

2 A business requests an increase in its overdraft limit to enable it to
   bring forward the payment of trade creditors. To what extent is this
   an acceptable request:

   a it is not acceptable at all?
   b it depends on the underlying reasons for the proposal?
   c it is acceptable only if the amount is fully secured?
   d it is completely acceptable?

3 What does the term 'swinging' mean in relation to an overdraft
   facility and why is it important:

   a it means that the account only rarely goes overdrawn, so the
          bank would be able to call in the advance without undue difficulty?
   b it means that an account only rarely goes overdrawn, enabling
          the bank to verify that the permanent capital is sufficient for the
          volume of business being done?
   c it means that the account periodically returns to credit, enabling
          the bank to verify that the advance could be repaid on demand?
   d it means that the account periodically returns to credit; if it did
          not it would imply that part of the borrowing was being used as
          permanent capital?

4 Which of the following methods of appraising capital expenditure gives the most accurate comparison of the merits of alternative capital investment schemes:

a discounted cash flow?
b pay back?
c rate of return?
d they are all equally useful methods?

answer

5 A business customer wishes to purchase new equipment which will be used to increase turnover. He has produced a cash flow forecast to support his request for increased overdraft facilities; it includes the following items:

(i) Depreciation of the new equipment
(ii) Depreciation of the existing equipment
(iii) VAT payments
(iv) Interest on the proposed overdraft
(v) Retained profits transferred to the capital account.

Which of these should not have been included in the calculations:

a (i) and (ii)?
b (iii) and (iv)?
c (iii) and (v)?
d (i). (ii) and (v)?

answer

6 How would you calculate the 'rate of return' when appraising the benefit of a capital expenditure project:

a gross income before tax and after depreciation and expenses as a percentage of capital cost?
b gross income after tax but before depreciation and expenses as a percentage of capital cost?
c gross income before tax, depreciation and expenses as a percentage of capital cost?
d gross income after tax, depreciation and expenses as a percentage of capital cost?

answer

7   A customer wishes to extend his factory in order to increase production. On which of the following would you require re-assurance:

   a   that there is evidence of demand for the extra production?
   b   that he has access to an adequate workforce to utilize the extra capacity.
   c   that he is able to obtain planning permission for the extension?
   d   all of the above?

 _answer_

8   You have been approached for assistance with the financing of a 'management buy-out' of a local branch of a national light-engineering business. Which is the most important to you in deciding whether to assist:

   a   the market value of the assets to be purchased?
   b   the 'discount' between the market value and the price to be paid?
   c   the anticipated level of profits that can be generated?
   d   the level of profits generated in the past?

 _answer_

9   A customer has approached you for a loan to finance work under a contract which he has obtained for the manufacture of £10,000 worth of widgets per month for the next 6 months. You have asked him to produce a cash flow forecast; what advice would you give him about its construction:

   a   ensure that anticipated receipts have been reduced to allow for any agreed retentions?
   b   ensure that allowance has been made for any possible delays in receipts?
   c   ensure that the figures also reflect any other business that continues to be undertaken?
   d   all of the above?

 _answer_

10 It transpires that the customer in the previous question is to be employed as a sub contractor, supplying widgets to enable the purchaser to complete a large overall contract which has been obtained from the main contractor. You are considering making status enquiries on the following parties:

   (i) The main contractor
  (ii) The contractor
 (iii) The sub contractor.

On which of these would you in fact make enquiries:

a (i) and (iii)?
b (ii) and (iii)?
c (i) and (ii)?
d (i)?

 *answer*

Topic 5 Business lending/2

1 Which of the following statements about directors' borrowing powers is correct:

a directors of a trading company have implied power to borrow?
b directors' borrowing powers are always restricted?
c directors' borrowing powers may not exceed company powers?
d Table A of the 1985 Companies Act restricts directors' borrowing powers to an amount equivalent to the amount of the authorized share capital?

 *answer*

2 Does it matter if a person proposing to take a retail shop has no experience of the particular trade:

a yes, experience has to be acquired first?
b not always; it depends on the individual?
c not always; it depends on the individual and the type of trade to be engaged etc.?
d no, retailing skills are easily acquired?

 *answer*

3   How would you attempt to verify that a proposed loan to buy a shop is capable of being repaid:

   a   examine the profit and loss accounts of the previous proprietors?
   b   estimate the total annual income and expenditure under the new proprietors?
   c   ensure that adequate security is held?
   d   restrict borrowing to an amount equivalent to the customer's stake?

4   A 'Stock and Crop' form is:

   a   intended to give an accurate estimate of the net current market value of a farm.
   b   produced annually as a check on the balance sheet values of the farm's assets and liabilities.
   c   part of an agricultural charge.
   d   best ignored since it is likely to give results which conflict with the balance sheet.

5   A 'rule of thumb' formula to check a farmer's ability to repay his loans is to express his total expenditure on rent and finance charges as a percentage of total income. At which level does the ability to repay become questionable:

   a   10%+
   b   20%+
   c   25%+
   d   35%+

6   What is the normal formula for setting the limit up to which it is safe to lend for estate development:

   a   2/3 land cost plus 1/2 building costs?
   b   2/3 land cost plus 2/3 building costs?
   c   1/2 land cost plus 1/2 building costs?

d 1/2 land cost plus 2/3 building costs?

7 What is the purpose of a 'build-out' clause in the legal charge taken over a plot of development land:

a it enables the bank to complete the development?
b it binds the developer to complete the development?
c it allows the bank to veto any proposals to vary the development plan?
d it gives the bank the power to sell plots on which building has not yet commenced?

8 When discounting bills of exchange, the bank will be concerned to establish that:

a the drawer is financially sound.
b the acceptor is financially sound.
c both drawer and acceptor are financially sound.
d notice of the bank's interest is served on the acceptor.

9 When goods or produce are given as security for bank borrowing, a 'trust receipt' is executed in order to:

a create the charge.
b release the charge.
c preserve the charge over goods held in a warehouse.
d preserve the charge over goods delivered to the customer.

0 When he is satisfied that his business can 'stand on its own feet' can a franchisee sever the links with the franchisor:

a almost certainly not without losing franchise?
b yes provided he continues to obtain supplies from the franchisor?

    c   yes if he has the agreement of the British Franchising Association?

    d   not until after 6 month notice of his intention has been given?

Topic 6   Marketing and selling

1 In which socio-economic group would you place a chartered accountant:

    a   A?
    b   B?
    c   C1?
    d   D?

2 What is a 'market segment':

    a   the personal account holders of a particular branch?
    b   all the potential personal account holders within the catchment area of a particular branch?
    c   a group of customers and potential customers who have similar needs?
    d   a socio-economic group?

3 What is a 'trigger point':

    a   a request for a particular service that should provoke the offering of a range of further services?
    b   the starting point of a branch marketing campaign?
    c   the starting point of a bank marketing campaign?
    d   the point at which the customer's commitment to the service should be sought?

4 What is market research?

    a a waste of time?

    b a method of establishing the needs of a particular market segment?

    c a method of establishing what customers say they want?

    d a method of establishing what customers think they want?

5 Which of the following statements is true:

    a it may be necessary to arouse a customer's latent need for a service before the product can be sold?

    b customers' perceived needs for services are always logical and rational?

    c customers' perceived needs for services are never logical or rational?

    d you can never 'close the sale' unless the customer has a genuine underlying need for the service.

6 Which is the most likely to persuade a customer to select your version of a required service over the version offered by a competitor:

    a the cost of your service?

    b the effectiveness of your service?

    c the benefits of your service?

    d the attributes generally of your service?

7 Which of these is a benefit of a bank 'executorship' service:

    a continuity of service?

    b professional handling of estate?

    c not having to worry about what will happen to your family when you die?

    d fees are not payable until the bank begins to act?

8   Which of these is a benefit of a 'revolving credit' account:

   a   being able to pay unexpected bills if they arise?
   b   the customer decides how much to set aside each month to
       meet outgoings?
   c   the borrowing limit is set at a multiple of the monthly
       contribution?
   d   interest is charged only on the daily debit balance outstanding?

9   Which of these is a benefit of a Eurocheque card:

   a   cheques can be cashed at branch banks throughout Europe?
   b   cheques are made out in the currency of the country being
       visited?
   c   more than one encashment can be made in a day?
   d   the customer is freed from the worry of how to pay bills while
       abroad?

10 Look at the following list of bank services:

       (i)   Travel insurance
       (ii) Cheque card
       (iii) Credit card
       (iv) Regular savings plans.

   Which of these might be cross-sold to an individual who has called
   in to arrange travel facilities for her holidays:

   a   (i), (ii), (iii) and (iv)?
   b   (ii), (iii) and (iv)?
   c   (i), (ii) and (iii)?
   d   (i), (iii) and (iv)?

Topic 7   Personal services

1   How would the maximum available mortgage loan normally be calculated for a married couple both of whom are wage earners? Is the amount equivalent to:

  a joint salaries?
  b joint salaries × 2½?
  c main salary × 2½ plus second salary?
  d main salary × 2½?

 *answer*

2   Customers 'buy' a particular service because of its:

  a attributes.
  b benefits.
  c costs.
  d advertising.

 *answer*

3   In general terms, a bank official's duty when promoting business among personal customers is to:

  a promote as many services as possible.
  b establish the one particular service that the customer *really* needs.
  c put together a package of services that meet the whole of the customer's needs.
  d give the customer what was requested.

 *answer*

4   What is the normal minimum level of investment capital required by a bank's investment management service:

  a £1,000?
  b £5,000?
  c £10,000?
  d £20,000?

 *answer*

5 What is the principal feature of a mortgage protection policy:

   a   the capital amount covered decreases in line with the amount of the outstanding mortgage?

   b   the capital amount is payable on death or on survival to the stated term?

   c   the capital amount is payable on death whenever it occurs?

   d   the capital amount will be increased by a share in the issuing company's profits?

 _answer_

6 What is the special feature of a 'gold card':

   a   it is a credit card with an increased credit limit?

   b   it is a credit card which allows extended repayment terms?

   c   it is a charge card which gives access to unsecured overdrafts at low interest rates?

   d   it is a charge card which offers extended repayment terms?

 _answer_

7 For the average customer what benefits are conferred by a credit card better than by a charge card:

   a   a credit card offers revolving credit and can be used at more outlets?

   b   a credit card offers credit at lower interest rates?

   c   a credit card is simpler to use?

   d   a credit card can be used for 'telephone shopping'?

 _answer_

8 How do the inheritance tax rates levied on lifetime gifts compare with those levied at death:

   a   for each band, they are higher?

   b   for each band, they are lower?

   c   they are the same.

   d   lifetime gifts are not taxed?

 _answer_

9 Which of the following is the average customer likely to consider first when selecting the type of account in which to deposit savings:

   a interest rate and minimum balance?
   b interest rate and ease of withdrawal?
   c ease of withdrawal and maximum balance?
   d ease of withdrawal and minimum balance?

answer

0 Standing orders are particularly useful for:

   a making regular payments where the amount varies.
   b making regular payments where the amount doesn't vary.
   c making irregular payments where the amount varies.
   d making irregular payments where the amount doesn't vary.

answer

Topic 8 Business services: financial

1 Which of the following descriptions of 'factor finance' is correct:

   a it is a service used largely by businesses which are having difficulty raising finance by normal means?
   b it is a simple way of raising finance against invoices outstanding.
   c it is an alternative to an overdraft, used only when an overdraft cannot be arranged?
   d it is inconsistent with an overdraft facility?

answer

2 In a leasing contract, to what extent can the lessee claim capital allowances against tax for the cost of the equipment:

   a the full cost is allowable?
   b the full cost is allowable over a period of years?
   c the allowance will be limited to an amount equivalent to the allowance that would be available to the lessor?

    d   the lessee cannot claim a capital allowances for the cost of the equipment.

3 In an acceptance facility, who is the acceptor:

    a   the customer who has arranged the facility?
    b   the customer's bank?
    c   the party with whom the bill is discounted?
    d   the payee of the bill?

4 Which of the following statements is true about a *placing* of shares:

    a   all the shares are sold direct to the institutional investors?
    b   most of the shares are sold direct to the institutional investors; a proportion must be made available to the public via the market makers?
    c   Stock Exchange dealings are permitted in shares which are already widely held?
    d   it is specific to the Unlisted Securities Market?

5 What is the maximum term that you would usually expect to see for a loan arranged via the money markets:

    a   1 week?
    b   1 month?
    c   2 months?
    d   3 months?

6 Which of the following is always a benefit of factor finance:

    a   improved cash flow?
    b   improved credit control?
    c   invoiced amounts outstanding are collected by the factor?

d saving of time and effort involved in preparation of invoices and maintenance of sales ledger?

 _answer_

7 Which of the following is a benefit of finance leasing:

a the lessee can specify the details of the asset to be acquired?
b the lessor buys the asset in its own name?
c the lessee has full exclusive use of the asset against payment of the agreed rental?
d the lessee's capital is left intact?

 _answer_

8 How does the cost of finance leasing compare with the cost of borrowing in respect of any given asset:

a leasing is lower in cost because of the tax allowances available to the lessor?
b the two methods are comparable in cost?
c leasing is higher in cost because the lessor does not have access to any tax allowances?
d borrowing is higher in cost because of the interest rate charge which does not effect leasing?

 _answer_

9 What is the maximum amount of a loan that can be covered under the Small Firms Loan Guarantee Scheme:

a £25,000?
b £50,000?
c £75,000?
d £100,000?

 _answer_

10 Which size of business is likely to form part of the target market for both term loans and acceptance facilities:

a large?

243

b medium and large?
c small and medium?
d small?

Topic 9 Business services: administration

1 Which of the following might find it appropriate to use the bank's *Registrar's* services:

a a small private limited company?
b large corporations only?
c any public limited company?
d a partnership?

2 Which of the following is a benefit to the recipient of a payment made via the CHAPS system:

a funds are credited direct to the bank account?
b the payment is confidential?
c the amount received will be debited to the remitter's account on the same day?
d the beneficiary has immediate access to cleared funds?

3 Which of the following is a benefit to the employee of having wages paid direct to an account by bank transfer?

a the employee is freed from the risks of loss associated with cash?
b a cheque book will enable him to pay debts without cash?
c standing orders and direct debits will enable him to pay regular bills?
d the employee does not have to bank at the same place as the employer?

4 On whose life should 'keyman' insurance be arranged:

    a any valued employee and/or the proprietor of any business?

    b the directors of a public limited company?

    c the directors of any company?

    d the proprietor of a small business?

answer

5 A company wishing to undertake a 'rights' issue seeks advice from the bank. Which section of the bank could help:

    a registrars?

    b merchant banking?

    c both registrars *and* merchant bank?

    d factoring company?

answer

6 Which is a benefit of using a computer bureau to calculate employees' wages:

    a the employer provides the basic details for each employee?

    b the computer calculates the appropriate amounts for wages, tax, and so on?

    c staff time is released for more valuable work?

    d employees do not need to know the service is being used?

answer

7 What is the minimum amount that can be remitted via the CHAPS system:

    a £5,000?

    b £10,000?

    c £15,000?

    d £20,000?

answer

8   Which is a benefit of 'keyman' insurance:

    a   the policy is taken out on the life of a key employee?
    b   the premiums are paid by the business?
    c   the sum assured is paid in the event of the individual's death?
    d   the business is cushioned against financial loss resulting from the death of the employee?

9   Which is the benefit to a self-employed person of 'permanent disability' cover:

    a   protection against loss of earnings if unable to work?
    b   it is complementary to life assurance?
    c   it is an alternative to life assurance?
    d   medical bills are paid if private medical care is required?

10   Which is the potential benefit of using a computer bureau to run a business's sales ledger:

    a   cash flow can be forecast more easily?
    b   payments to creditors can be more accurately timed?
    c   cash flow may improve?
    d   factor finance is available?

Topic 10   Foreign business

1   Who would a currency loan be useful for:

    a   any customer with a borrowing requirement?
    b   exporters who have currency receipts?
    c   exporters who have sterling receipts?
    d   importers who have to make payments in foreign currency?

2 What is 'optional' for the customer in an 'Option Forward Currency Contract':

    a whether to complete the contract?
    b when to complete the contract?
    c when to complete the contract within a stated period?
    d the amount of currency to be bought or sold?

 *answer*

3 Which of the following methods of settlement is 'safest' for the exporter:

    a documentary collection?
    b open account?
    c irrevocable letter of credit?
    d confirmed irrevocable letter of credit?

 *answer*

4 Which of the following methods of settlement is 'safest' for the importer:

    a payment in advance?
    b documentary collection?
    c open account?
    d confirmed irrevocable letter of credit?

 *answer*

5 How can an exporter protect himself against the terms of a letter of credit being amended without his consent:

    a insist on an irrevocable credit?
    b insist on a confirmed credit?
    c insist on an advised credit?
    d insist on a transferable credit?

 *answer*

6 Which of the following ECGD guarantees will provide appropriate 'credit insurance' for an exporter selling large numbers of small consignments to various importers:

   a comprehensive guarantee?
   b specific guarantee — buyer credit?
   c specific guarantee — supplier credit?
   d comprehensive bank guarantee?

 answer

7 Which of the following risks is *not* covered by an ECGD (Bills & Notes) guarantee:

   a buyer risk?
   b sovereign risk?
   c reserve risk?
   d transport risk?

 answer

8 SWIFT is:

   a a network for transmitting payment instructions between banks.
   b a network for transmitting authenticated messages between banks.
   c a network for transmitting letters of credit from issuing bank to advising bank.
   d a network for transmitting documents of foreign trade between banks.

 answer

9 Which of the following services is likely to be of immediate use to a customer bidding for a large contract to build a hydroelectric power station in a third world country:

   a performance bond?
   b bail bond?
   c maintenance guarantee?
   d tender bond?

 answer

Is a 'factoring' service available to exporters:

a yes, both debt administration and finance facilities are available?
b yes, a debt administration service only is available?
c yes, a factor finance service only is available?
d no, the service is available for domestic trade only?

answer

Answers follow on pages 250–1. Score 2 marks for each correct answer.

Answers

Topic 1   Principles of lending

1c	2b	3a	4d	5d
6a	7c	8b	9d	10c

Topic 2   Personal lending

1d	2c	3d	4b	5b
6a	7c	8b	9d	10a

Topic 3   Balance sheet analysis

1a	2c	3b	4d	5d
6a	7d	8d	9a	10b

Topic 4   Business lending/1

1c	2b	3d	4a	5d
6a	7d	8c	9d	10c

Topic 5   Business lending/2

1c	2c	3b	4a	5b
6d	7a	8c	9d	10a

Topic 6   Marketing and selling

1b	2c	3a	4b	5a
6d	7c	8a	9d	10c

Topic 7   Personal services

1c	2b	3c	4d	5a
6c	7a	8d	9d	10b

Topic 8   Business services: financial

| 1b | 2d | 3b | 4b | 5d |
| 6a | 7d | 8b | 9c | 10b |

Topic 9   Business services: administration

| 1c | 2d | 3a | 4a | 5c |
| 6c | 7b | 8d | 9a | 10c |

Topic 10   Foreign business

| 1b | 2c | 3d | 4c | 5a |
| 6a | 7d | 8b | 9d | 10a |

Score Grid

Topic	Score ?/20	Revision campaign					
		Revision order 1–10	Study guide page no.	MCQs page no.	Score ?/20	Post test page no.	Score ?/20
1							
2							
3							
4							
5							
6							
7							
8							
9							
10							